CHILDHOOD VULNERABILITIES IN SOUTH AFRICA

SOME ETHICAL PERSPECTIVES

EDITED BY

Jan Grobbelaar & Chris Jones

SUN PRESS

Childhood Vulnerabilities in South Africa: Some Ethical Perspectives

Published by African Sun Media under the SUN PReSS imprint

All rights reserved

Copyright © 2020 African Sun Media and the editors

This publication was subjected to an independent double-blind peer evaluation by the publisher.

The editors and the publisher have made every effort to obtain permission for and acknowledge the use of copyrighted material. Refer all enquiries to the publisher.

No part of this book may be reproduced or transmitted in any form or by any electronic, photographic or mechanical means, including photocopying and recording on record, tape or laser disk, on microfilm, via the Internet, by e-mail, or by any other information storage and retrieval system, without prior written permission by the publisher.

Views reflected in this publication are not necessarily those of the publisher.

First edition 2020

ISBN 978-1-928480-94-5
ISBN 978-1-928480-95-2 (e-book)
https://doi.org/10.18820/9781928480952

To reference this title use: Grobbelaar, J. & Jones, C. 2020. *Childhood Vulnerabilities in South Africa: Some Ethical Perspectives*. African Sun Media, Stellenbosch. https://doi.org/10.18820/9781928480952

Set in Iowan Old Style 11/13

Cover design, typesetting and production by African Sun Media

SUN PReSS is an imprint of African Sun Media. Scholarly, professional and reference works are published under this imprint in print and electronic formats.

This publication can be ordered from:
orders@africansunmedia.co.za
Takealot: bit.ly/2monsfl
Google Books: bit.ly/2k1Uilm
africansunmedia.store.it.si *(e-books)*
Amazon Kindle: amzn.to/2ktL.pkL

Visit africansunmedia.co.za for more information.

CONTENTS

Research Justification		IV
List of Abbreviations		V
Preface		VIII
Notes on Contributors		XVI
CHAPTER 1	The plight and vulnerability of children living in South Africa and the calling of the church	1
CHAPTER 2	Seen but not heard? Engaging the mechanisms of faith to end violence against children	33
CHAPTER 3	The contentious issue of corporal punishment in South Africa	65
CHAPTER 4	Reconceiving child theology from a queer theological perspective: for LGBTIQ+ parented families and children	97
CHAPTER 5	The stigmatisation of children living with FASD and their biological mothers	117
CHAPTER 6	Male initiation and circumcision - A South African perspective	137
CHAPTER 7	Recognising and responding to complex dilemmas: Child marriage in South Africa	163
CHAPTER 8	Children and racism	181
CHAPTER 9	Reflections on the effectiveness of child support grants	205
CHAPTER 10	Protecting children in the digital society	229
References		273

RESEARCH JUSTIFICATION

This book addresses different challenges that endanger the lives of children (mainly) in the South African context from an ethical perspective. It provides, in a structured way, analyses and insights of multiple South African scholars from different disciplines and backgrounds. Open and responsible discussions around these different and important contemporary issues that South African children are confronted with, will hopefully lead to ethical guidelines protecting the rights of children where needed. This volume, with its very specific (and carefully selected) grouping of academic fields, wants to assist in alleviating the shortages of academic publications reflecting on these issues. Furthermore, as an open access publication, this book will also assist in countering the prohibitive costs of Western academic publications and directly benefit scholars in Africa. Collating these insights in a single tome provides a sound basis for advancing current knowledge and provides a reasoned foundation for future research in this disciplinary body of knowledge.

— *Jan Grobbelaar & Chris Jones*

LIST OF ABBREVIATIONS APPEARING IN THE TEXT AND NOTES

ACRW	African Charter on the Rights and Welfare of the Child
ACTP	Alternatives to corporal punishment
ARND	Alcohol-Related Neurodevelopmental Disorders
CBS	Contextual Bible Study
CSE	Comprehensive Sexual Education
CEDAW	Convention on the Elimination of All Forms of Discrimination against Women
CTM	Child Theology Movement
CRC	United Nations Convention on the Rights of the Child
CRL RIGHTS COMMISSION	Commission for the Promotion and Protection of the Rights of Cultural, Religious and Linguistic Communities
CSAM	Child Sexual Abuse Material
CSG	Child Support Grant
CPS	Cash Payment Services
EVAC	End Violence Against Children
FARR	Foundation for Alcohol Related Research
FASD	Fetal Alcohol Spectrum Disorder
FAS	Fetal Alcohol Syndrome
FIPPS	Fair Information Practice Principles
FOR SA	Freedom of Religion South Africa

FPL	Food Poverty Line
GDP	Gross Domestic Product
GIN-SSOGIE	Global Interfaith Network for People of all Sexes, Sexual Orientations, Gender identities and Expressions
HMHB©	Healthy Mother Healthy Baby Programme©
ICT	Information and Communication Technology
ICSE	International Child Sexual Exploitation
IOT	Internet of Things
ISPS	Internet Service Providers
JASA	Justice Alliance of South Africa
LCS	Living Conditions Survey
NAD	Native Affairs Department
NIDS	National Income Dynamic Study
JD	Johannesburg Declaration
LBPL	Lower-Bound Poverty Line
LGBTIQ+	Lesbian, Gay, Bisexual, Trans, Intersex, Queer and other
PFAS	Partial Fetal Alcohol Syndrome
P2P	Peer-to-Peer
SACE	South African Council of Educators
SADC	Southern African Development Community
SASSA	South African Social Security Agency
SEME	Search Engine Manipulation Effect
SIDS	Sudden Infant Death Syndrome
SMG	State Maintenance Grants

STATS SA	Statistics South Africa
UBPL	Upper-Bound Poverty Line
UN CRC	United Nations Convention on the rights of the child
UNICEF	United Nations International Children's Emergency Fund
VAC	Violence Against Children
WCC	World Council of Churches
WHO	World Health Organization

PREFACE

In Chapter 1, Jan Grobbelaar discusses the plight and vulnerability of children living in South Africa with the goal to enhance critical academic, theological ethical thinking regarding the daily living contexts of South Africa's vulnerable children, and our moral obligations towards them. The chapter starts with a general analysis of the concepts of 'vulnerable' and 'vulnerability' and draws some lines on how these concepts relate to South Africa's children. Attention is also given to a global and a local perspective on the living realities of South Africa's children, as well as the use of statistics in analysing the vulnerabilities of these children. Throughout this discussion some ethical challenges are indicated. The chapter concludes with a few theological ethical perspectives on the calling of the Church regarding South Africa's vulnerable children.

Selina Palm explores violence against children and the positive role of Christian faith communities in contributing towards ending it in Chapter 2. However, this chapter will also highlight ways in which Christian faith continues to perpetuate practices and beliefs that remain harmful to children and that need urgent challenging. It draws on insights from a 2019 interfaith scoping study that explored the relationship between faith and efforts to end violence against children, to suggest that faith leaders can play important roles across many levels of the child protection system. It will apply these insights to the South African context where child abuse, neglect and violence remain endemic. It will emphasise the ethical dilemma that lies beneath the legal and social status of the child: that children can still be seen to be at the bottom of a hierarchy of human value, or be regarded as the property of their parents. This normalisation of a 'less than' social status can mean that children are likely to be subjected to violence by people they know and care about, such as parents and teachers. Reshaping these patterns to prevent violence requires an ethical reorientation of how adult/child relationships are presented. In this core task, faith communities can play an important role only if they can also critically interrogate harmful theologies within their own traditions and develop a liberating theology for the child.

In Chapter 3, Jan Grobbelaar and Chris Jones focus on the contentious issue of corporal punishment, and how the latter is one of the key drivers of the high levels of violence against children in South Africa. They argue that South Africans, in particular, should concentrate on introducing wide-ranging programmes to support families and teachers in changing attitudes and behaviours that favour and promote harsh and abusive forms of discipline against children. Individual and social norms regarding child discipline should be changed by constantly seeking better ways to discipline children in order to live wisely. In this chapter, the authors focus, among others, on the legal framework and recent developments regarding discipline and corporal punishment in South Africa, the continuing struggle against violence in the lives of children, the role of the Church, and what South Africa, as a pathfinder country, can do in fighting violence against children.

Hanzline Davids reasons in Chapter 4 that The Child Theology Movement (CTM) recently emerged as a global movement with the focus of moving children from the margins to the centre of theological discourse. The focus of CTM is based on the theoretical lenses and methodologies of liberation and feminist theologies. Children are created in the image of the Trinity as full human beings. For this reason, children do theology from their own embodied experiences. Therefore, within a hierarchical system of power, in many cases patriarchy, their theological contribution is often ignored and denied. The embodied theological experiences of Lesbian, Gay, Bisexual, Trans, Intersex, Queer and other (LGBTQI+) people are also often denied within theological discourses. For this reason, in what way does the movement of children to the centre redefine the hierarchal power discourse in a new way? What theological links exist between the disposition of children and LGBTQI+ parents to reconceive Child Theology? Lastly, does the doctrine of the Trinity provide a theological lens for Child Theology? This chapter will engage these questions through employing a Queer Theological Methodology as conceived by Latin-American theologian Marcella Althaus-Reid.

Leana Olivier, Lian-Marie Drostky and Jaco Louw argue in Chapter 5 that community awareness regarding the link between prenatal alcohol use and the children born with Fetal Alcohol Spectrum Disorder (FASD) may lead to the blaming and stigmatisation of biological mothers. The harmful consequences of alcohol exposure in utero can be combated when affected individuals and families seek help as early as possible. Stigma is a major barrier to help-seeking behaviour. The chapter describes the role of self-stigma, structural stigma, stigma by association and public stigma on children living with FASD and their biological mothers. Interviews were conducted with mothers of children with FASD and analysed through the lens of the four manifestations of stigma. Foundation for Alcohol Related Research (FARR) project coordinators also shared their perception of the impact stigma has on intervention programmes. Stigmatisation was closely linked to awareness regarding FASD. Their findings revealed a danger that through confrontational language, policies and even the criminalisation of mothers, public and structural stigma are increasing. Punitive measures to prevent FASD ignore the best practice guidelines on improving health behaviours. Various forms of stigma prevent effective intervention, therefore, they argue that stigmatising language and behaviours must be rejected. Out of a sense of righteous indignation, they may prevent those who need help from seeking it.

In Chapter 6, Chris Jones writes about his interest in male initiation and circumcision, although he is an outsider who did not experience this rite of passage. The chapter starts off with a brief description of how culture and initiation practices are perceived mostly from a South African point of view. It then looks at the current South African situation and how the different challenges regarding male initiation and circumcision can be brought in line with modern times, technology and development. It furthermore focuses on the socialisation of boys and men in African culture, and the importance of rites of passage in different African contexts. It describes what defines being a man in Africa, it looks at different rites of passage, and gives background information of initiation as a rite of passage specifically in South Africa. Intergenerational tensions especially between boys, young men and older men, as well as sexuality and manhood are also looked at. It also connects initiation with ancestors. In conclusion, it deals with the fear of being ostracised if one is not initiated and circumcised, but on the other hand, it also shows that many boys are not destined to become adult men because circumcision costs them their lives or their genitals are damaged severely by this practice.

Lisa le Roux briefly unpacks the nature, drivers and consequences of child marriage, followed by a focus on South African legislation and cultural practices relevant to child marriage in Chapter 7. This is a prelude to an in-depth discussion of three key dilemmas relating to the phenomenon, namely the inadequacy of a legislative response, the clash between the primacy of human rights versus cultural rights, and the reality of transactional intergenerational sex in relationships other than marriages. Recognition of these dilemmas leads to acknowledgement that current responses to child marriage are not merely woefully inadequate, but also fail to grasp the full scale of the problem.

In Chapter 8, Henry Mbaya commences with defining and highlighting racism as a term and a concept; defining its nature and how it is related to identity formation. Then he gives a very brief historical background of the institutionalisation of racism as apartheid in the South African educational system. He further discusses racial consciousness in children by drawing on the wider global context, specifically analysing very briefly, the significance of the so-called Clark doll experiment in the USA. The chapter proceeds to argue that racism is a social construct determined by contextual factors, pointing out that racial diversity, contrary to racism, is a 'natural.' From this perspective, he then discusses responses to efforts of racial integration in schools in post-1994 South Africa. In this context, he argues that schools constitute critical spaces where racist attitudes and practices are formed and inculcated. He highlights the role of literature and media in informing racist tendencies in children. Finally, the critical role that parents and adults play in the socialisation of children's racial attitudes, is emphasised.

Krige Siebrits reasons in Chapter 9 that the child support grant (CSG) programme is one of the cornerstones of South Africa's unusually large social assistance system. The chapter shows that large numbers of children in South Africa are severely affected by poverty and poor living conditions. Against this backdrop, it argues that a credible body of evidence confirms the efficacy of the child support grant programme. The programme provides large amounts of cash to poor households with children and avoids extensive leakage to the affluent; furthermore, caregivers generally use the money to the benefit of children and the programme has not given rise to substantial perverse behavioural responses. Nonetheless, the effectiveness of the programme is undermined by the small size of the grant, the limited skills and knowledge of some caregivers, and the often difficult environments within which recipients and caregivers live. In view of this, he argues for a stronger focus on complementary initiatives to further empower caregivers and improve these environments. The chapter further emphasises that measures to strengthen the education system and to accelerate economic growth and job creation are essential to improve the longer-term prospects of South African children.

Louis Fourie focuses on the protection of children in the digital society in Chapter 10. The pervasiveness of digital technology, and in particular social media and mobile devices, have changed the lives of children forever, as well as created new risks for the emotional, sexual and commercial exploitation of children. The risks can mainly be divided into content (children are receivers of mass produced content), contact (children are active participants in an adult-initiated activity) and conduct (children are perpetrators, actors or creators) risks, and include violence and aggression, sexual abuse, the eroding of values, and the commercial exploitation via data tracking and artificial intelligence algorithms. The complex task of ensuring the safety of children online requires a concerted multi-stakeholder collaborative approach between parents, peers, teachers, children, communities, schools, industry, and law enforcement. In South Africa, it is especially the private sector and government that should take greater responsibility for the digital protection of children. The private sector has a corporate responsibility to promote ethical standards with regard to data, privacy and design. The South African government needs to urgently address the lack of appropriate policy frameworks and national strategies, as well as tend to the limited, fragmented and often-contradictory legislation with regard to the digital rights of children.

With this brief overview of the various chapters in mind, we would like to point out that the focus of this book is not primarily on religion and/or theological ethics in relation to vulnerable children. However, some of the chapters, especially in the first part of the book, contain a definitive reference to the Christian religion and faith communities (1-3), with Chapter 1 setting the scene. This does not mean that it can't be helpful for an audience with a different religious orientation. We consider the discourse in this book valuable enough to inform people from other religious convictions, and even those who do not believe, about the broader social, scientific and ethical lines of thought we deem necessary to support vulnerable children.

These first chapters are followed by a number of chapters (4-7) that focus on certain familial and cultural aspects regarding children, and then in the last part of the book (7-10) the emphasis is directed at larger societal problems that impact children's lives. We, however, decided not to divide these chapters into separate sections with specific section headings, due to the fluent nature of the different themes and approaches.

As already mentioned, this book addresses different challenges that endanger the lives of children (mainly) in the South African context from an ethical perspective. It provides the research of several South African scholars – from different disciplines and backgrounds – systematically and intersectionally, based on scholarly analyses, insights, reasoning and expertise.

The use of multiple data sets in some of the chapters will hopefully position the text as a resource for specialists in ethics and childhood studies, especially those studying the sociocultural contexts of children and families in terms of challenges and opportunities for support. However, not all the chapters rely on statistical data sets, as is so typical of a social science approach, because this was not meant to be the research methodology of the book.

The authors were allowed to follow their own research methodology. They mostly did a literature review of academic resources available. In some cases, the academic literature on the relevant themes are limited and the authors had to use some popular sources. In certain chapters, the authors included findings of earlier empirical research in which they were involved. No empirical study was done specifically for this book. Therefore, it was not necessary to get ethical clearance for any of the research done in this study.

The realisation of such a book is a team effort. We would like to extend a word of thanks to all our co-authors, who enthusiastically agreed to become part of this project. Thank you for your willingness, ideas, time, and academic skills to reflect on this highly relevant and urgent debate within the domain of children and ethics.

For any book to be published, a lot of hard work is done behind the scenes. To all the members of the publishing team – for their kind and professional services – as well as the peer-reviewers for their hard work and valuable input, a word of sincere gratitude.

To my co-editor, Chris Jones, a word of sincere appreciation. It was a blessing to work with you on this project. Thank you for your patience and all your support.

EDITORS

JAN GROBBELAAR
Practical and Missional Theology
Faculty of Theology and Religion
University of the Free State
South Africa
E mail address: jgrobbelaar@petracol.org.za
ORCID: 0000-0002-6442-4465

CHRIS JONES
Unit for Moral Leadership
Faculty of Theology
Stellenbosch University
South Africa
E mail address: chrisjones@sun.ac.za
ORCID: 0000-0002-9483-5337

NOTES ON CONTRIBUTORS

Hanzline R. Davids

Hanzline R. Davids is a former ordained reverend of the Uniting Reformed Church in Southern Africa and queer activist theologian. He holds various degrees in theology. Currently, he is a doctoral candidate at the Faculty of Theology, Stellenbosch University, with research interests in sexuality, gender, religion and reproduction. Davids is employed by Inclusive Affirming Ministries – a lesbian, gay, bisexual, transgender, intersex, queer and other (LGBTIQ+) catalyst organisation that works towards empowering faith communities to welcome and celebrate LGBTIQ+ people in Africa. He is a process coordinator, working specifically with the Anglican Church in Southern Africa and the Uniting Reformed Church in Southern Africa.

Lian-Marie Drotsky

Lian-Marie Drotsky is an experienced occupational therapist with expert knowledge in early childhood development and Fetal Alcohol Spectrum Disorder (FASD). She has worked in various communities in South Africa, the USA and the UK, and has experience in assessing the needs of communities and developing services. She has worked for FARR since 2010 as project manager and offers workshops to educators and therapists on the management of FASD and other learning challenges in class.

NOTES ON CONTRIBUTORS

Louis C.H. Fourie

Louis Fourie is a futurist and technology strategist who consults internationally to governments, industry, organisations and educational institutions. He is the author of a weekly column on Fourth Industrial Revolution Technologies for the Independent Media Group. Until recently, he was the Deputy Vice-Chancellor, Knowledge and Information Technology Services at the Cape Peninsula University of Technology. He is currently a Research Fellow of the Department of Practical and Missional Theology, Faculty of Theology and Religion, University of the Free State, as well as at the Economic and Social Research Foundation, Tanzania. He is an Adjunct Professor of Arkansas University, Little Rock, and an associate of the Inter-University Council of Eastern Africa and the Southern African Regional Universities Alliance. He obtained a doctorate in Theology at the University of Stellenbosch and an MBA (*cum laude*) at the North West University, where he received the Old Mutual Gold Medal for exceptional achievement and the best MBA student.

Jan Grobbelaar

Jan Grobbelaar was a pastor in Komga and Springs for 13 years before joining Petra Institute for Children's Ministry in 1996. He is currently the Facilitator for Research and Academic Development at the Institute. He is a Research Fellow of the Department of Practical and Missional Theology, Faculty of Theology and Religion, University of the Free State. He is also involved with research at other universities. Grobbelaar obtained his DTh in Practical Theology from Stellenbosch University in 2008. His main research interests are the intersection between children/childhood and theology, and intergenerational faith formation. He is the editor and author of a variety of books, chapters in books and articles.

Chris Jones

Chris Jones was a church minister in Ceres for close to 20 years before moving to Stellenbosch with his family at the beginning of 2008 to establish the Unit for Moral Leadership at the Faculty of Theology, Stellenbosch University. He currently heads this unit and is also a Research Fellow within the discipline group Systematic Theology and Ecclesiology. He regularly presents papers at conferences and is the author of a variety of books, chapters in books and articles. He is involved in various community development projects.

Elisabet le Roux

Elisabet le Roux is Research Director of the interdisciplinary Unit for Religion and Development Research at Stellenbosch University, South Africa. Her empirical research is done internationally with and for governments, global faith-based organisations, and development networks and organisations. Over the last ten years she has secured funding and delivered research projects across 21 countries on four continents. The majority of her work is within the Global South and in conflict-affected settings, reflecting on religion, religious leaders and religious communities as role-players within the international development arena. She has a particular interest in religion and various forms of social violence, especially gender-based violence, and her recent interfaith work has included Hindu, Islamic and Christian settings.

NOTES ON CONTRIBUTORS

Jaco Louw

Jaco Louw has been with FARR since 2013 and has overseen comprehensive FASD research, awareness and prevention programmes in the Vredenburg/Saldanha area and in the Witzenberg area. Jaco is involved in managing FASD research projects, overseeing and monitoring the design, implementation and write-up of various studies on FASD. As of 2018, he has been enrolled at Stellenbosch University working on a PhD in psychology.

Henry Mbaya

Henry Mbaya is an Anglican Priest serving in the Anglican Diocese of False Bay since 2012. Prior to that, he served in the Anglican Diocese of Umzimvubu for 27 years. He is currently an Associate Professor in Missiology in the Faculty of Theology at Stellenbosch University. He obtained his PhD in History of Christianity at the University of KwaZulu-Natal in 2005. His research focus is on the interface between African Culture and western Missions in Southern Africa. He is the author of two books, chapters in books and articles. He lives in Kuils River, Western Cape.

Leana Olivier

Leana Olivier is the CEO of the Foundation for Alcohol Related Research (FARR), a national non-governmental organisation (NGO, non-profit) focusing on alcohol-related (especially FASD) research; awareness; prevention; training and community development projects. She also holds the position as a Research Fellow in the Faculty of Medicine and Health Sciences at Stellenbosch University. She regularly consults nationally and internationally on alcohol- related matters that cause harm, such as FASD. Before joining FARR, she was the Provincial Manager and Founder of the Maternal, Child and Woman's Health Directorate in the Department of Health, Western Cape Province. She has vast experience in management, organisational development, community development and research.

Selina Palm

Selina Palm is a senior researcher with the Unit for Religion and Development Research at Stellenbosch University, South Africa. She provides interdisciplinary research on religious violence and human rights for governments and organisations worldwide and is widely published. She is a leadership fellow within the child sector in South Africa and part of a global hub as an academic expert around faith and violence against children. She holds a PhD in Theology and Development from the University of Kwa-Zulu Natal and a Master's degree in Human Rights and in Theology. She has a long track record pioneering new children's and youth rights projects, especially on the African continent.

Krige Siebrits

Krige Siebrits has been a Senior Lecturer in the Department of Economics at Stellenbosch University since 2008. He holds a PhD in Economics from the same University. Before joining Stellenbosch University, he held positions at the Department of Finance (now National Treasury) of the South African Government (1992–1996), the Bureau of Market Research at the University of South Africa (1996) and the Department of Economics at the University of South Africa (1997–2007). He has taught undergraduate and postgraduate courses in public economics, development economics and institutional economics. His main research interests are fiscal policy, public economics and institutional economics. He has published articles in various accredited journals and has contributed chapters to several books on economic policy in South Africa. In addition, he is one of the editors of *Public Economics*, an economics textbook of which the 7th edition from Oxford University Press (SA) will appear in 2020. He is a member of the councils of the Economic Society of South Africa and the Economic History Society of Southern Africa.

CHAPTER 1

THE PLIGHT AND VULNERABILITY OF CHILDREN LIVING IN SOUTH AFRICA AND THE CALLING OF THE CHURCH

Jan Grobbelaar

CHILDHOOD VULNERABILITIES IN SOUTH AFRICA: SOME ETHICAL PERSPECTIVES

INTRODUCTION

It happens so easily, that we do not notice the children around us. The little ones, the poor ones, the suffering ones, the weak ones, the ones without a smile. We are so busy, so selfish, in such a hurry, that we easily look and walk past them. Pass them also in our thoughts and with our actions. In many ways they become 'invisible' to us. We go into lockdown mode. We apply social distancing. We forget them.

This book wants to remind us that our vocation is to remember them; to not forget them. To remember their vulnerabilities and to act morally responsibly, not only to them, but rather with them and for them. To look them in the eyes and walk towards them with determination to share the load of their vulnerabilities with them, to act with them and on their behalf, against their suffering and exploitation, giving them a voice to speak out against the circumstances and powers impacting their lives. This is why the title of this book is: *Childhood vulnerabilities in South Africa – Some ethical perspectives*. The intention is to remind us of the ethical challenges we face with regard to the vulnerable children in our midst and the living realities to which they are exposed. But more so, it also calls us to live and act morally more responsibly with and for the vulnerable children living in South Africa.

This chapter connects with this call and the title of the book by reflecting on the concept of vulnerability in relation to South Africa's children. To do that, we first have to understand who the children of South Africa are. Therefore, it is necessary to start with a demographic overview of the children of South Africa.

THE CHILD SEGMENT OF THE SOUTH AFRICAN POPULATION: A DEMOGRAPHIC OVERVIEW

According to Stats SA (2019:v), South Africa's estimated total population in mid-2019 was 58.78 million people of whom 16.9 million or 28.8% were younger than 15 years. Although reported with a different age interval and estimated a year earlier, it is important to take cognisance of the estimation of the South African Child Gauge 2019 (Hall 2019a:216) that South Africa's total population in mid-2018 was 57.7 million people of whom 19.7 million were children under 18 years. Stats SA (2018a:x) indicates that in 2016 adolescents made up 18,5% of South Africa's population. From these statistics, it seems fair to assume that about a third of the total population of South Africa is children under 18, only in numbers an important segment of the South African population.

The gender division for children is equal (Hall 2019a:216) but it raises the ethical question: Is the position of the girl-child in South African society really equal to the position of the boy-child? It seems that we have to ponder this much more and act accordingly with regard to this situation. In terms of the racial categories used during the apartheid era, 86% of children are African, 8% are Coloured, 4% are White and 2% are Indian (:216). It shows clearly that the child population group in South Africa is not a homogeneous group of people living in the same situations. They are a diverse group of people living in diverse contexts with different real-life experiences. In our reflections about the situation of children in South Africa, we should take this reality into account.

Although the situations of some subgroups and individuals and/or some localities may differ, children are a distinguishable population or social group about whom generalisations may be drawn, as long as it is remembered that these are not true of every child and every context in South Africa. Any generalisation in this chapter, and even in the rest of the book, should, therefore, be academically evaluated with some suspicion because of the many differences present in this population group. The theological ethical challenge is that this population group, and specific subgroups in this totality, as well as the plight of individual children, should more and more become the focus of theological ethical reflection. This is the goal of this chapter and the rest of the book: To contribute to and promote academic theological ethical reflections about the situation of South Africa's vulnerable children and our moral obligations towards them.

As an important part of our reflections, we have the responsibility to critically investigate the concepts and language we often use to describe the factors and situations that influence children's lives, such as 'vulnerable' or 'vulnerability'. In the next section, this concept is discussed. Although this discussion draws some general lines to vulnerability, it is a search to identify how 'vulnerability' relates to children.

THE CONCEPT 'VULNERABLE'

A 'BUZZWORD'[1]

Various terms are used in relation to the plight of people and children in this world. One of these concepts is vulnerability. This concept is used prominently in academic research, in government circles, as well as colloquially, in referring to the situations which endanger many children in the world and in South Africa. The concept is also used in relation to other individuals and population groupings who experience similar marginalisation or social exclusion in one way or another (cf. Brown 2015; Koopman 2013). Many '[p]olicy makers and practitioners are now concerned with addressing vulnerability through an expansive range of interventions' (Brown et al. 2017:1). Vulnerability is used so widely and connected with so many situations and challenges that it seems as if we live in 'a vulnerability zeitgeist or "spirit of the time"' (:1; cf. Brown 2014). The first and important question to ask in this chapter is: What is vulnerability?

---

1   cf. Brown, Ecclestone & Emmel 2017:2.

CHAPTER 1

WHAT IS VULNERABILITY?

A COMPLEX CONCEPT

To answer the question 'what is vulnerability' is easy and straightforward for some people, especially those who experience it every day. For others it is not so easy to get clarity about the meaning of vulnerability. For them it is a very complex concept because of its inherent diversity and the interwovenness of so many factors: of the global and the local, as well as the personal and the systemic aspects. It seems as if the concept of vulnerable inherently contains a simple-complex paradox (eds. Bankoff, Frerks & Hilhorst 2004:1). It is, thus, not so easy to define or understand the nature and meaning of the concept of vulnerability.

The wide range of use and the complexity of the concept has led to a situation where vulnerability as a field of research is burgeoning and the concept is used in many disciplines. Brown (2013:19) declares that in the academic world today, the study of vulnerability is an intellectual field with many disputed and opposing views, reflecting wide divergences of opinion and usage. The result is that vulnerability has no consistent meaning (Herring 2018:12), and that many different definitions of the concept exist (cf. Brown 2015:48). Brown (:32) opines that although vulnerability has already prevailed in research for quite some time, there is still a lot of blurriness around it and that it is used to express a plurality of meaning. Because of its malleability, the concept is clouded with vagueness. Some academics is of the opinion that it is exactly this impreciseness that makes the concept useable: it is broad and can include all forms of hardships or afflictions children experience. For others, this view is problematic. They do not want to use the concept precisely because of the fact that it is so vague and imprecise. This situation is the result of the fact that there exists, in broad terms, two kinds of theoretical approaches to what vulnerability really is: a broader view and a narrower view (cf. Formosa 2014; Levine et al. 2004:46; Walbank & Herring 2014:14).

UNIVERSAL VULNERABILITY

The first, broader approach links the understanding of vulnerability to its Latin origin (Mackenzie, Rogers & Dodds 2014:4). According to Reynolds (2008:135) "the expression 'vulnerable' derives from the Latin word *vulnerare*, meaning to injure or harm. Human beings are open to be wounded. We suffer." The implication is that human embodiment is equally predisposed to be wounded. Thus, vulnerability is an ontological condition of all people, it is "universal and constant, inherent in the human condition" (Fineman 2011:161), it "emerges with life itself" (Butler 2004:31; cf. Käll 2016; MacIntyre 1999; Turner 2006). Nifosi-Sutton (2017:4) confirms this view by stating that "vulnerability is universal in the sense that it unavoidably features in everyone's life or may occur in everyone's life." This is a very broad understanding, to such an extent that children should rather stay in bed, wrapped up in their bedding to escape the possibility of being harmed or wounded than by taking the risk of entering our world (cf. Herring 2018:12)! This approach is known as universal vulnerability or the "vulnerability thesis" (Brown et al. 2017:12).

SITUATIONAL VULNERABILITY

The second, narrower view of vulnerability is used in connection to something specific, to specific factors present in and affecting or influencing people's living situations. It emphasises the specific circumstances or experiences created by people's surroundings which are unfavourable to their welfare and well-being. According to this view, vulnerability is usually connected to something specific, to a person or a thing which endangers the life of another person, a group of people, a community, a whole society or even the globe, or different parts of it. The implication is that it is a situation in which you need protection against this 'something' or 'someone' and the harm it can bring. This view implies that there exists a specific agent(s) that threaten or can harm your interests, even your life, or the interest(s) of a group to which you belong, and against which you need some sort of protection.

In Goodin's (1985:112) view, vulnerability is, in essence, a relational concept that entails dependency: You depend on somebody to provide something you need. According to Goodin,

> references to vulnerability imply two other references. One is *to what* the persons or things are vulnerable. Where do their weaknesses lie? What mechanisms are capable of inflicting harm upon them? The other is *to whom* the persons or things are vulnerable. Who can inflict the harms upon me? Who can protect me against them? One is always vulnerable to particular agents with respect to particular sorts of threats. ... Any briefer description of the situation would be radically incomplete. Like the notions of power and freedom, that of vulnerability is inherently object and agent specific. (p. 112)

In this object-agent relationship of dependency and protection, receiving and delivery plays a huge role. It is this relationship that confronts us with many ethical challenges. It is not so easy to construct these relationships in a way that is ethically responsible to both parties. It will become clearer in the next section that focuses on some challenges for our thinking and actions.

SOME CHALLENGES FOR OUR THINKING AND ACTIONS

Brown (2015:11) recognised that the notion of vulnerability is actually "[a] slippery idea loaded with moral and ethical connotations." The concept of vulnerability is often associated with negative connotations of victimhood and victimisation, of helplessness, neediness and deprivation, of deservingness, transgression and blame, of stereotyping and even pathology. This includes the language we frequently use to express our ideas related to vulnerability, such as 'weakness or to be weak', 'failure', 'to be a problem which should be solved', 'wrong-doing', 'troublesome', 'bad behaviour', 'disadvantaged', 'victims', 'labelling', 'classification', 'stigmatising'. We start to think and talk of the vulnerable as 'them', as different from 'us', emphasising their 'otherness' and see them only as the subjects of our benevolence (MacIntyre 1999:2). It is sometimes accompanied with a strong paternalistic attitude and agenda. We decide who are vulnerable, what their specific vulnerability is and what exactly they need.

Sometimes we struggle with dichotomous representations of people, such as either 'vulnerable victims' or 'dangerous wrong-doers' (Brown 2014:371). As victims, their vulnerability is not of their own doing and, therefore, they have legitimate claims to protection and resources. In such situations, we react easily with merely hand-outs without thinking about what it is doing to the human dignity of the 'victim'. As 'dangerous wrongdoers' they are classified as transgressive to such an extent that they may even be seen as a risk to society. They need attention and sometimes even control because society needs to be protected from them.

According to Luna (2019:86), vulnerability was traditionally used to "describe certain kinds of populations deemed worthy of protection." To this description, Nifosi-Sutton (2017:5) adds that vulnerable and vulnerability are commonly used to "refer to situations involving actual or potential exposure to harm and suffering affecting mainly specific groups of persons." Such groups are sometimes described as vulnerable groups. Labels are sometimes attached to these vulnerable groups: homeless people, poor people, disabled people, and prostitutes.

These labels can help to identify specific protection and/or care for a specific group, but labelling people may become, according to Levine et al. (2004:47), stereotyping when "whole categories of individuals, without distinguishing between individuals in the group who indeed might have special characteristics that need to be taken into account and those who do not." Furthermore, the labelling of groups as vulnerable has burgeoned to the extent that "so many categories of people are now considered vulnerable that virtually all potential human subjects are included" (:46). Mackenzie et al. (2014:6) are of the opinion that "[b]y labelling everyone as (equally) vulnerable, this approach renders the concept of vulnerability potentially vacuous and of limited use ... because it obscures rather than enables the identification of the context-specific needs of particular groups or individuals within populations at risk." In this regard, Levine et al. (2004:46) express the view that "[i]f everyone is vulnerable, then the concept becomes too nebulous to be meaningful." This is true to such an extent that Collins (2014:63) concluded that "the proposition 'everyone is vulnerable' is the beginning of an argument, rather than a conclusion."

The inherent tension between universal vulnerability and situational vulnerability cannot easily be dissolved, although these two streams are not mutually total exclusive. But it is difficult to develop a taxonomy of vulnerability that will include and classify all forms of vulnerability. Luna (2019:87) even rejects "the usefulness of taxonomies to analyze vulnerabilities." Rather than to develop a taxonomy of all possible vulnerabilities, it may be better "to recognise a mutual inherent vulnerability, but also to emphasise ways in which particular individuals in some circumstances have extra vulnerability" (Wallbank & Herring 2014:16). This view on vulnerability is emphasised in Collins' (2014:64) statement that vulnerability should be studied as a real life-concept. With this approach, she moves away from focusing on vulnerability as a theoretical and abstract construct and brought peoples' lived experience to the centre of reflections on vulnerability. She (:64-65) argues that a single description of vulnerability is not necessary because "it would overlook the fact that vulnerability represents all the rich complexity that we might expect of a real-life concept, and we should want this to be reflected in analysis of it."

To guide our thinking about the ethical challenges with which the concept vulnerable, and the real-life realities it expresses, confront us, Brown's (2015:32-49) discernment of five broad themes of meaning present in the academic literature, although difficult to delimit and sometimes overlapping and interwoven, may be helpful. These themes are:

- 'natural' or 'innate' vulnerability, determined by physical and/or personal factors that are often associated with certain points in the life course such as childhood …;

- 'situational' vulnerability, referring to biographical circumstances, situational difficulties or transgressions – this can include the input of a third party or structural force, and can also involve human agency (often to a contested extent);

- vulnerability as related to social disadvantage, the environment and/or geographical spaces;

- universal vulnerability, where vulnerability is seen as a state shared by all citizens, but which is social or political constituted to varying extends;

- vulnerability as a concept closely related to risk. (p. 33)

From the above discussion, it is clear that vulnerability has many faces (cf. Brown et al. 2017). It challenges us to discern very wisely when we deem it necessary to react on any vulnerability we perceive. In such situations, it can come in handy to remember the following pronouncement by Brown (2015):

> Diverse configurations of vulnerability … map onto various notions of citizenship and particular constructions of disadvantage. … When vulnerability is framed as a 'natural' or individual state, it carries very different implications from when it is imagined as socially or politically instituted. The various uses and understanding of vulnerability reveal the profound ethical implications of the concept, and … it becomes evident that any attempt to make sense of vulnerability also brings into focus the nature of the connections between institutions, social practices, individuals and the state. (p. 33)

The above words are also applicable when we relate the concept of vulnerability to children.

THE USE OF THE CONCEPT 'VULNERABLE' IN RELATION TO CHILDREN

Vulnerability related to children essentially means that they are at risk of some form of harm and are not able "to sufficiently protect themself or to be sufficiently protected by others" (Schweiger 2019:289). Brown (2015:48) emphasises this same aspect when she indicates that the concept of vulnerability usually refers to "the particular vulnerabilities of those who are 'in need' or who are likely to come to experience particular dangers or harms." In its most basic form, children need protection and nourishment, especially during the years of their early childhood (MacIntyre 1999:1). It is when children's basic needs for a dignified life are not met that they become vulnerable (Koopman 2013:44).

Children are regularly associated with innate or natural vulnerability. This can be attributed to the fact that innate vulnerability is connected with the specific developmental moments of people during their life course. These moments are dictated by physical, biological or personal factors. "As with other more biologically-inclined accounts, such an approach proceeds from the premise that some people are 'naturally' more vulnerable than others" (Brown, Ecclestone & Emmel 2017:5). This understanding of vulnerability "appears to have particular resonance for children and young people due to dominant developmental ideas, which imagine children as in some way incomplete, not fully developed and dependent on adults" (Brown 2015:47). Nifosi-Sutton (2017:5) is of the opinion that children "are more at risk of harm owing to the fact that they are still developing physically and emotionally and depend on others to satisfy their needs …" In this approach, James (2012) opined, childhood is viewed as a period of inherent vulnerability because of the perceived innocence and lack of competence of children, as a result of which they are thought to require protection. Such thinking is implicit in biological and psychological developmentalism, which implies that, because the child is not yet fully developed, it is vulnerable to any adverse influences that may disrupt the 'normal' completion of the developmental process. (pp. 132-133)

But the view that children are innately vulnerable raises some questions and ethical challenges. Although this view is connected to natural development and is to some extent true, we should take into consideration that our understandings of childhood are social constructs which are constructed differently in different cultures and at different moments in time. There exists an almost universal concept of childhood as a life stage that is different from adulthood, but the way we define what this difference(s) exactly is, leads to different conceptions of childhood (Archard 2004:27-29). Thus, our conceptions of childhood are contextually bound and are very much influenced by social, economic, historic and political circumstances and changes over time. These changes will, in all likelihood, also change "the parameters adults use to define risk, vulnerability and protection" (James 2012:133). The implication is that vulnerability is also a social construct and thus exposed to the same sort of influences and changes as our concept of childhood. If we accept that vulnerable means that there is 'something' present that wants to harm children, how we define that 'something' will influence our understanding of vulnerability and our practical reactions in relation to this vulnerability. This is also true of the link made between 'innate' and 'vulnerability'. If that something is 'innate', how we define and link this innate factor to vulnerability, will define how we shall react.

But it is also true that our view of childhood will always have a huge influence on how we see and define innate vulnerability. Although certain developmental moments and the possible vulnerabilities they exposed children to, is an almost universally generally accepted theory, it is not a static theory but also, among other factors, influenced by our growing biological, psychological and medical knowledge and our cultural situatedness. There also exist many personal exceptions to the generalised accepted developmental moments, which could influence our views of this innate vulnerability. Our views of innate vulnerability are also contextually situated and influenced by, for example, the availability or not of health care facilities. If health care facilities are not available or inaccessible, it may result in children not being regularly vaccinated and becoming prone to various illnesses which can have negative consequences for their 'normal' development. Such a situation indicates that even in innate vulnerability there are systemic factors to be taken into consideration. The systemic factors also come to the fore in state interventions and laws promulgated to protect children from not achieving their developmental outcomes and/or the enhancement of the possibilities to reach these outcomes. Sometimes these measures, although they want to protect children, can lead to or enhance innate vulnerability.

An appropriate question to ask at this point is: What are the views of childhood underlying the construct 'innate vulnerability'? Both Brown (2015:47) and James (2012:132-133), as quoted above, give descriptions of the view(s) of childhood that they identified as lying behind the concept of 'innate vulnerability'. These descriptions include: "in some way incomplete", "not fully developed", "dependent on adults" (Brown), and "perceived innocence", "lack of competence" and "require protection" (James). It seems that the view of childhood underlying innate vulnerability is one-sided, tends to be a negative approach towards children (e.g. incomplete), is very disempowering giving minimal space for their agency and participation as equal human beings with adults, over-emphasising their protection rights, and leaning towards the patronising.

It is true that as children develop, some of them may experience developmental challenges, but it seems that to speak of 'innate vulnerability' confronts us with many challenges as expressed above. Furthermore, is it not perhaps demeaning of children's human dignity to use the concept innate vulnerability as if there is 'something' inside all children that can or even wants to injure, harm, or wound them and let them suffer (cf. Reynolds above)?

Brown (2015:14) indicates that some people criticise the way the supposed 'inherent' vulnerability is sometimes used in the welfare state. In this regard, she referred to the way it "can function as an excuse for failing to tackle overarching structures and systems of marginalisation ... foregrounding personal experience in the difficulties experienced by individuals [children–JG] ... and serving to legitimise justifications for the narrowing of provision."

What makes it difficult to pinpoint children's vulnerability is that their "vulnerabilities are interwoven by the common threads of oppression, poverty, lack of cultural security, family stability, child labor, and the many faces of discrimination" (Johnson et al. 2013:14). Schweiger (2019) describes this interwovenness aptly by stating:

> Inherent and situational vulnerabilities are often intertwined, and situational vulnerabilities are based on, increase and exploit inherent vulnerabilities. A baby's body is highly vulnerable to physical force (inherent vulnerability) but the fact that some babies are at greater risk of being injured by abuse and corporal punishment is driven by social factors (situational vulnerability). (p. 289)

Often their vulnerability is caused by the infringement of their children's rights by these common threads. These infringements, according to Johnson et al. (2013),

> are encapsulated in issues of (1) invisibility due to family secrecy and abuse, ... poor government oversight, etc.; (2) protections that are either poor or nonexistent, ... inadequate or absent laws, policies, supports, ... ; (3) and "undefendedness", the inability or lack of will by adults, communities, or governments to be the advocates ensuring basic needs and the betterment of children's lives. (p. 12)

Vulnerability is not just a predisposition or an exposure to risk but also children's experiences of real hurt and suffering. "In a very special way, their physical, social and even teleological needs are not met" (Koopman 2016:197). Actually, children are "the most extreme form of the vulnerable, the poor and the marginalised ... the epitome of vulnerability" in our world (:197). Wall (2010:Loc. 28-29) even states that "[c]hildren are arguably the most marginalized group in all of history." It also rings true for today and for South Africa's children. What makes children's vulnerability very complex is that it is rarely caused by a single factor. They experience that the issues they face are often "embedded layers of risk. For instance, to address fosterage or mental health as separate experiences is a false discussion of the problem. The problem for children is that they live at the intersection of many of these problems" (Johnson et al. 2013:16).

Mackenzie et al. (2014) remind us to remember that

> [c]hildren are paradigm examples of persons who are vulnerable to harm or exploitation by virtue of the asymmetrical relations of dependency, power, and authority in which they stand to parents or other caregivers. But in the case of children, those to whom they are most vulnerable are not always committed to protecting them from harm or exploitation; indeed, in some cases these very persons might be the ones who, through abuse or neglect, pose the greatest threat to a child's welfare. (p. 14)

Vulnerable children are easily labelled: street children, homeless children, refugee children, disabled children, migrant children, child prostitutes, child soldiers, child criminals. In South Africa, we easily use labels, such as black children, coloured children, white children, Indian children. And when they are labelled, they are stereotyped, and we see them either as victims of other people, social structures or government institutions, or we see them as transgressors who deserve their situation. And it is not only our thoughts about them that are influenced in this way, but also our attitudes and actions towards them, their situations and other role players in their contexts.

As discussed above, it is also important in the case of children to connect the concept vulnerability to their real-life experiences of harm here and now. But we also have to look to the long-term effects of their harms, the "harms to their well-becoming (their future well-being)" because "what happens during childhood has such a crucial influence on the future well-being as an adult," (Schweiger 2019:290). To gain a better understanding of the complex real-life situations and experiences of children living in South Africa and how it connects with the concept of vulnerability, we have to analyse the particularities of their daily living situations. This is exactly wat the authors of the different chapters in this book do: Each one analyses a certain aspect of the diverse living realities to which some children in South Africa are exposed to and that may play a role in their vulnerability: violence, poverty, child support grants, male circumcision, child marriages, corporal punishment, racism, stigmatisation, FASD, LGBTIQ+ children and LGBTIQ+ parented families.

The chapters of this book should be read with cognisance of the influence of two broad perspectives on the living realities of South Africa's children: The global world and their local worlds.

TWO PERSPECTIVES ON THE LIVING REALITIES OF SOUTH AFRICA'S CHILDREN

A GLOBAL PERSPECTIVE

Reflecting in a theological ethical way about children and their living realities in South Africa, we first have to consider the fact that South Africa and its children are part of the bigger globalised village which influences the South African society, the lives of our children, and their everyday living conditions. It is, therefore, necessary to begin this section with a reflection on the impact of the globalisation process on children and their vulnerabilities before we can consider the local

CHAPTER 1

realities. Maybe the 2020 global pandemic caused by the coronavirus (Covid-19) will have a huge influence on the globalisation process and its impact on children, as we know it at the time of writing this chapter. The pendulum may sway to much more emphasis on localisation in world relations than on globalisation. But it is impossible to foresee the future and therefore, this reflection can only be based on what is currently known. For this reason, the reflection starts with perspectives from the important trilogy on the globalised networked and information society by the eminent Spanish born sociologist Manuel Castells (2010a, 2010b, 2010c).

According to Castells (2010c) the globalised network society of the 21st century leads to the exclusion of children in many ways, endangering their lives and making them vulnerable. Castells (2010c:164) even expressed the opinion that although children were abused and victimised through all the ages, they suffer even more in the 21st century because of the exploitive dynamics and influence of the global network society and economy. His observation is that

> there is something different in this beginning of the Information Age: there is a systemic link between the current, unchecked characteristics of informational capitalism and the destruction of lives in a large segment of the world's children. Their suffering has become part of the global system in which they are living. (p. 164)

Castells (2010c) elaborates on this, stating:

> At the roots of children's exploitation are the mechanisms generating poverty and social exclusion throughout the world … With children in poverty, and with entire countries, regions, and neighborhoods excluded from relevant circuits of wealth, power, and information, the crumbling family structures break the last barrier of defense for children. In some countries … misery overwhelms families, in rural areas as in shanty towns, so that children are sold for survival, are sent to streets to help

out, or end up running away from the hell of their homes into the hell of their non-existence. In other societies, the historical crisis of patriarchalism brings down the traditional nuclear family without replacing it, making women and children pay for it. (p. 164-165)

Indeed, the daily living realities of many children are threatening their lives, well-being and healthy development. The marginalisation of children, also South Africa's children, by the globalised network society of the 21st century, confronts us with many theological ethical challenges. Some of them are clearly formulated by Wall (2010):

What assumptions, for example, make invisible the ten million children around the planet who die every year of easily preventable diseases and malnutrition? This number is equivalent to almost two Nazi Holocausts every year, or ten 9/11 terrorist attacks every day. Similarly, what systems of belief permit the worldwide growth in recent decades of children's sex trafficking, sweat shops, and soldiering? Why do children everywhere enjoy narrower human rights than adults? Why, despite greater awareness, does gender discrimination in every society continue to distort children's cultures, educations, and families? What structures of social understanding enable global mass media to manipulate children's lives and thinking in a more invasive way than ever before? (Loc. 33-36).

The above challenges identified by Wall from a Northern America perspective is just as applicable to the situation of the South African society and its many children. South Africa's children are in many ways exposed to these global powers and its negative influences on children's lives. But South Africa's children are not only exposed to global forces. They are also exposed to many challenges originating from the local situation within South Africa. These challenges will become clearer when we look deeper into the local realities to which they are exposed.

CHAPTER 1

A LOCAL PERSPECTIVE

Looking at the local South African context, Smit (2016:3) broadly identified three "social and political contexts" in South Africa in which children experience that they are "not always welcome and welcomed." According to Smit (2016:3-4), these three contexts are:

- inhospitable households which may create feelings of abandonment

- risky and even dangerous communities which may endanger their lives

- violent societies which may threaten their lives.

Growing up in such environments where they are vulnerable, children do not experience just hardships and suffering. They are also robbed of one of the most fundamental requirements for developing into a mature, well-being human: the ability to trust (cf. Smit 2016:1-41). About this trust Kofi Annan (in Johnson et al. 2013) once said:

> There is no trust more sacred than the one the world holds with children. There is no duty more important than ensuring that their rights are respected, that their welfare is protected, that their lives are free from fear and want and that they can grow up in peace. (p. 1)

But we lost this sacred trust (cf. Johnson et al. 2013:1). In this regard, Smit (2016) declares:

> Children and young people read in their communities and their everyday life-contexts all kind of signs and messages warning them to beware. They learn not to trust to survive, in order to protect themselves. They internalise these codes and messages. They socialise in ways that heed these claims and warnings ... They lose hope ... because they experience the worlds in which

they live as not dependable, reliable, trustworthy, reassuring and welcoming. (p. 2)

The message not to trust anything or anyone is conveyed to South African children in many ways. Therefore, it is necessary to uncover the realities which can let them feel that they are unwelcome in our households, our communities and in the South African society at large, and may convey the message to them that nothing is trustworthy. It is these realities that the authors of the different chapters in this book uncovers. These chapters give voice to the children of South Africa to express their struggles and vulnerabilities as a population group and as individuals, to gain a better understanding and insight into the life conditions they are exposed to and the messages these conditions convey to them. To reach this goal, statistics regarding different aspects of children's living realities in South Africa are used. Using statistical data to give voice to children has some challenges of its own.

THE USE OF STATISTICAL DATA

For many a year, children were in general, not used as a unit of statistical observations (cf. Qvortrup 2005). The standard way central statistics bodies functioned in presenting national data were to rather use individuals and households as their statistical unit, leading to the exclusion of children. Although this situation has improved through the publication of child-focused statistical reports by more and more countries, and/or the inclusion of sections about children in current statistical series, as well as growing global reports with a focus on children, there still seems to be a lack of child-centred analysis with regard to all the factors that cause their hardships, and of integrating all these available statistics into an integrated holistic view.

The opinion of the South African Child Gauge 2019 (Shung-King et al. eds. 2019:214) is that, although South Africa is privileged to have a supply of many good reports containing useful data on many issues,

CHAPTER 1

these reports do not focus on children and is not of much use for those who want to improve their understanding of the living realities of children. Despite this situation, the authors of the report add:

> 'Child-centred' data does not only mean the use of data about children specifically. It also means using national population or household data and analysing it at the level of the child. This is important, because the numbers can differ enormously depending on the unit of analysis. For example, national statistics describe the unemployment rate, but only a child-centred analysis can tell how many children live in households where no adult is employed. National statistics show the share of households without adequate sanitation, but when a child-centred analysis is used, the share is significantly higher. (p. 214)

Another challenge is that these reports tend to use different age intervals for their reporting systems and different time frames to report on. For example, Children Count, a project of the Children's Institute at the University of Cape Town, works with a definition of children as all persons aged 0-17 (Hall 2019b:n.p.). The same definition is used by the South African Child Gauge 2019. Statistic South Africa (cf. Stats SA 2019:10) works with a different approach and present their statistical data with the age intervals of 0-4, 5-9, 10-14, 15-19. Certain statistics are also only available for teenagers or adolescents and not for younger children. The result is that some of these statistics are incongruent and thus it is difficult to compare them with each other.

Using **only** statistical information to draw a picture of the situation of children can also be a dangerous act. The numbers can only vaguely express the reality of children's hardships and suffering, and cannot tell the real truth of their daily living conditions, the many threats that endanger their lives, their exploitation, their feelings of abandonment by and mistrust in the world around them, their experiences of being unwelcome and not being welcomed in their households, communities and the South African society. Moreover, numbers can become impersonal. Statistical analyses can objectify children and hide their faces to such an extent that we may become detached from them and the living realities of their suffering. This is one of the ethical challenges we face when we reflect in a theological ethical way on the lives of South Africa's children on an aggregate level: to become immune to the flesh and blood behind the statistics, not to hear their weeping and cries of desolation. Therefore, we have to take serious cognisance of an article written by the Old Testament scholar Brueggemann (1994:383) in connection with Genesis 37:34-35; Jeremiah 31:15 and Matthew 2:18 and his call that adults, like Rachel, should remember the vulnerability, the suffering, the plight of children, and weep about it: "We weep – and remember – perhaps enough to make a difference." To notice children's vulnerabilities, their suffering and plight, their fears and their weeping and to start weeping about their suffering, weeping with them, may be the first step towards living according to a responsible morality towards them.

In light of the above, it is important that we reflect on the question: How can we as Christians, as the church, as local communities and as a society live morally responsibly towards the vulnerable children of South Africa? Can we restore the sacred trust? (cf. above 'A local perspective'). It is impossible to answer the question about our calling in detail within the confinements of this chapter. Therefore, only some broad theological ethical lines, which need further reflection, can be discussed in the next section.

OUR CHRISTIAN CALLING AMIDST THE LIVING REALITIES OF SOUTH AFRICA'S CHILDREN

AN ECCLESIOLOGY OF GROANING AND VULNERABILITY

To weep about and with the children is a deep theological ethical value. It is part of our Christian vocation to remember them and their suffering, their plight and vulnerabilities and to take it to heart. We have to be a "groaning church" (McCarthy 2005:24), lamenting with the Psalms, reflecting our distress over the current conditions as expressed in the many vulnerable children of South Africa and all their vulnerabilities. According to McCarthy (:26) Augustine asserts about the Psalms: "If the psalm prays, you pray; if it groans, you groan." Reading the Psalms, it seems that a dominant voice in the Psalms is inarticulate groaning. "Like the expression of other deep emotions, however, the groaning of the Church resists certain definition: it possesses a quality that Augustine calls *ineffabilis*" (:26). McCarthy (:27) opines that Augustine, through his exegesis of the Psalms, "actively appropriates for the Church the groans which resound throughout the psalter and indicates that, by lamenting with the Psalmist and reflecting deeply and continually on that affect, the Church comes to learn what it is, comes to be what it is." Living a life of weeping and groaning before God, and in the world, about the children's vulnerabilities, their suffering and plight, is part of being who we are as children of God.

This same emphasis on groaning comes to the fore in Paul's letter to the Romans. In Romans 8 we read:

> [22] For we know that the whole creation has been groaning together in the pains of childbirth until now. [23] And not only the creation, but we ourselves, who have the first-fruits of the Spirit, groan inwardly as we wait eagerly for adoption as sons, the redemption of our bodies.

> [26] Likewise the Spirit helps us in our weakness. For we do not know what to pray for as we ought, but the Spirit himself intercedes for us with groanings too deep for words. [27] And he who searches hearts knows what is the mind of the Spirit, because the Spirit intercedes for the saints according to the will of God. (English Standard Version – ESV)

Paul states it clearly: All creation is groaning. All the vulnerable children living in South Africa are groaning. Groaning for things to change in their lives. Are they groaning with hope? Or did they perhaps, with the loss of sacred trust, lose all their hope? Paul explains the relation between groaning and hope with a striking picture. Wright (2004) explains Paul's words in a gripping way:

> At the centre of this remarkable passage is one of his most vivid images of hope: that of birth-pangs. The whole creation is in labour, longing for God's new world to be born. The church is called to share that pain and that hope. The church is not to be apart from the pain of the world; it is to be in prayer at precisely the place where the world is in pain. That is part of our calling, our high but strange role within God's purposes for new creation. (n.p.)

The church in South Africa cannot stand apart from the pain and suffering of the many children in South Africa. Our calling is to be present with them. In our prayers, in our groaning, in our groaning with them, a groaning which cannot be expressed in words. And this groaning is not a mechanism to escape the living realities of the children around us. We cannot groan if we have not stepped into their everyday living realities. We have to sit down with them, listen to their stories, see their realities, experience their hurt and pain, sharing their vulnerabilities, becoming vulnerable ourselves.

This is the place where we can meet each other: in our vulnerabilities. It is not so easy, because we struggle to admit our own vulnerabilities. Even to ourselves. Many of us do not want to be seen as vulnerable. But we cannot escape it. According to the universal view of vulnerability discussed above, all people are vulnerable. In this regard, Brown (2015:Loc. 257) made a profound statement: "Vulnerability is not winning or losing; it's having the courage to show up and be seen when we have no control over the outcome. Vulnerability is not weakness; it's our greatest measure of courage." It takes courage, the courage of the Holy Spirit to become powerless and vulnerable and to go into the world of vulnerable children, knowing that it will make yourself vulnerable. For me it sounds like the Gospel, as expressed in Philippians 2:

³ Do nothing from selfish ambition or conceit, but in humility count others more significant than yourselves. ⁴ Let each of you look not only to his own interests, but also to the interests of others. ⁵ Have this mind among yourselves, which is yours in Christ Jesus, ⁶ who, though he was in the form of God, did not count equality with God a thing to be grasped, ⁷ but emptied himself, by taking the form of a servant, being born in the likeness of men. ⁸ And being found in human form, he humbled himself by becoming obedient to the point of death, even death on a cross. (ESV)

Our salvation became only possible through Christ Jesus who made himself vulnerable by stepping out into the world and empting himself to the point of his death on the cross as an expression of the love of the vulnerable God (cf. Placher 1994) for this world. Part of our calling today, is to follow in the footsteps of the vulnerable Jesus into the world of the vulnerable children in South Africa. In solidarity with the vulnerable children, we have to express "the style, mode, and attitude of brokenness, empathy, softness, and humbleness" (Koopman 2008:241).

Does the Church have the ability to take up the values of groaning and vulnerability, and act morally correct towards the vulnerable children of South Africa? Are congregations able to admit their own vulnerabilities, implement groaning for the vulnerable children of South Africa in their liturgies, in their small group meetings, even in their church council meetings, and all other aspects of their life together? Are they able to welcome the vulnerable children into their midst as Jesus did it (Mt 18:1-5; 19:13-15), and let the vulnerable children experience and feel that they are welcome in our churches, our houses, our communities, in our world? Do the members of the local churches in South Africa have the ability to move into the world of the vulnerable children in the townships, in the informal settings, in their homes, not in the first place to distribute handouts, but to be with them and learn from them and encourage their own agency amidst all the vulnerabilities they are exposed to, or are carrying already? Is it possible for local congregations to develop a culture and ethics of groaning and vulnerability? Or do we experience moral vulnerability to such a degree that we cannot groan and be vulnerable in our daily living situations for the sake of the vulnerable children of South Africa?

Deep theological ethical reflection on the above challenges is important in the church as an institute, in congregations, in our homes, and in our own individual minds. The challenge before us is to develop an "ecclesial ethic of care for all children" (Jensen 2005:xii). On institutional (synodical) level, some churches in South Africa are already in numerous ways involved in 'ecclesial care' for the vulnerable children in our midst. But much more can be done to broaden it to local churches and to our communities. It is important to remember that this care should always be "dignifying care – care that is nonpaternalistic and that respects and supports another's self-determined agency" (Mackenzie et al. 2014:13).

To enhance such efforts, it may be a good starting point to revisit our Anthropology which is so much affected by rationality, autonomy, and independence (Koopman 2008:244). In this regard Koopman declared:

> True humanity is not defined by independence and rationality, but by the willingness to enter into relationships with others. In this relationship with the other, you do not discover a replica of yourself, as Aristotle taught. In the interaction with the other - in the communion, in the relationship - I find my essence and being. I receive my being from the other. We receive our existence out of the hands of the other, and my existence is meaningful because there are others who want to share their existence with me. (p. 245)

In the process, we also have to revisit our Theologies of Childhood. As indicated above, our views of childhood have a huge influence on our understanding of vulnerability in relation to children. Theologies of Childhood is a growing field of study that should get more attention in South Africa. Churches should do research on their members' views of children, which usually have different conceptions of childhood influenced mostly by cultural factors, how it influences the ministry in the congregations, and if and how it should be changed to a more theological sound view.

As mentioned above, the vulnerability of children is not only innate vulnerability. It is also situational or social vulnerability. Sometimes these vulnerabilities are systemic and will not change unless the systems creating it, change. Where it exploits children, the church should acknowledge the unjustness towards children. These situations call unto churches and congregations to take up their public responsibility and address these systems. Sometimes such actions are called advocacy: To speak out on behalf of exploited and marginalised people who do not have a voice, such as the children, to promote justice for them. This is an action that we do not undertake just for practical reasons. There is a clear theological rationale for advocacy on behalf of the marginalised throughout the Bible (cf. Sloane 2012). "It is, perhaps, most obvious in the great prophets of the Eighth Century BC, who were commissioned by God to voice God's revulsion at and rejection of Israel's and Judah's sin and injustice. They, clearly, were authorised advocates of God's concern for the poor" (Sloane 2012:184), which surely included the poor children. We have a God-given responsibility to "use our voice in line with God's purposes – especially God's commitment to justice" (:184; cf. 186).

But sometimes the situation causes so much harm, pain, suffering and hopelessness, breaking down the human dignity of children to such an extent that churches have to pay special attention to them. Reading the chapters of this book, it crosses my mind: Is it not perhaps such a time, a time that the churches in South Africa have to pay special attention to all the vulnerable children and stand alongside them in the public square and speak out against the powers of injustice that enhance their vulnerability?

GOD IS IN A SPECIAL WAY THE GOD OF THE VULNERABLE CHILDREN

It happened in the past that churches in South Africa stood up for the vulnerable people in our country. One such an example is the Belhar Confession. In 1982, the then Dutch Reformed Missional Church, now part of the Uniting Reformed Church in southern Africa, drafted the Belhar Confession amidst all the vulnerabilities and suffering they experienced under the apartheid system. Originally written in Afrikaans, the Office of Theology and Worship of the Presbyterian Church (USA) (n.d.) translated it into English. As part of this important document they confessed:

1. **We believe** in the triune God, Father, Son and Holy Spirit, who gathers, protects and cares for the church through Word and Spirit. This, God has done since the beginning of the world and will do to the end.

2. **We believe**

    - that God has revealed himself as the one who wishes to bring about justice and true peace among people;

    - that God, in a world full of injustice and enmity, is in a special way the God of the destitute, the poor and the wronged;

    - that God calls the church to follow him in this; for God brings justice to the oppressed and gives bread to the hungry;

    - that God frees the prisoner and restores sight to the blind;

    - that God supports the downtrodden, protects the stranger, helps orphans and widows and locks the path of the ungodly;

- that for God pure and undefiled religion is to visit the orphans and the widows in their suffering;

- that God wishes to teach the church to do what is good and to seek the right;

- that the church must therefore stand by people in any form of suffering and need, which implies, among other things, that the church must witness against and strive against any form of injustice, so that justice may roll down like waters, and righteousness like an ever-flowing stream;

- that the church as the possession of God must stand where the Lord stands, namely against injustice and with the wronged; that in following Christ the church must witness against all the powerful and privileged who selfishly seek their own interests and thus control and harm others.

Therefore, we reject any ideology

- which would legitimate forms of injustice and any doctrine which is unwilling to resist such an ideology in the name of the gospel.

Can the Confession of Belhar be applied to the situation of vulnerable children in South Africa in 2020? Some people may immediately reject such a possibility. It was, after all, written as a rejection of the ideology of apartheid based on inhumane and unjust convictions more than 30 years ago. But when you look more closely at this confession, there are a few principles imbedded in it which have a wider relevance than just for the context in which it was written, and are also still relevant today to address the exploitation of children by the forces of globalisation and the unjust global system, as well as the new post-apartheid local system that struggles to address their needs. One of the important principles is the strong emphasis on the human dignity of all people. If you read the chapters in this book, it becomes clear that the human dignity of children is not acknowledged in all spheres of the South African society. Therefore, the Belhar Confession can be seen as an urgent call for the restoration of the human dignity of all children living in South Africa.

Although there is in the confession a special emphasis on the poor, it does not necessarily mean that children are excluded. In his study on the poor in the Gospel of Luke, Bosch (2011:137) observed that when Luke "gives a list of people who suffer, [he] either puts the poor at the head of the list (cf 4:18; 6:20; 14:13; 14:21) or at the end, as a climax" (as in 7:22). He draws the conclusion that "[a]ll who experience misery are, in some very real sense, the poor" (:137-138). Koopman (2016) commented on this view as follows:

> The poor, therefore, seems to be an all-embracing category for those who are in various ways the victims of society - for those who lack every active or even passive participation in society. This marginality comprises all spheres of life, and it makes people feel helpless. The poor, therefore, refers in the first instance to the materially poor, but also to other forms of misery. (p. 250)

Therefore, when the Belhar Confession uses the word 'poor' it can be interpreted in the same way. The implication is that 'poor' may include the vulnerable and suffering children of South Africa.

Right from the beginning, the Belhar Confession was severely criticised by some people for the inclusion of the formulation "that God, in a world full of injustice and enmity, is in a special way the God of the destitute, the poor and the wronged" (cf. Belhar Confession above). Smit (1984) convincingly argued that this belief has a firmly Biblical base. Koopman (2008) confirms this view by stating:

> It would not be an exaggeration to say that the theme of God's special identification with suffering people runs like a golden thread through scripture. This theme is not being referred to coincidentally. It cannot be ignored. Neither can it be countered with other evidence from scripture. This vast biblical evidence

shows that this theme has to do with the heart of the Christian faith. (p. 248)

It seems that in the light of the above discussion it can be confessed that God, in a world full of injustice and enmity, is in a special way the God of the vulnerable, exploited, harmed and wronged children. God's identification with the vulnerable children comes also to the fore in Jesus' teaching to his disciples in Matthew 18:5: "Whoever receives one such child in my name receives me." According to Placher (2010:Loc. 2697), "[t]he distinctive thing about children was their lack of any rights." They had no status in the first century Mediterranean world. They also had no legal protection (:2837). "In the Aramaic that Jesus was presumably speaking, the same word (*talya*) can mean either 'child' or 'servant'" (:Loc. 2699-2700). Children were equal to slaves. The implication was that when you welcome a child, you are actually welcoming the most vulnerable person in the society. It was with this lowest, the most vulnerable in the society that Jesus identified himself with. This is also true for our world: Jesus meets us in the vulnerable children around us. If we do not welcome the vulnerable children into our lives, we are also not welcoming Jesus into our lives.

Furthermore, the Belhar Confession (see above) states explicitly: "God helps ... orphans" and "that for God pure and undefiled religion is to visit the orphans ... in their suffering." It is clear that the Belhar Confession is very relevant for the plight of the vulnerable and exploited children living in South Africa today.

There cannot be any misunderstanding: The Belhar Confession calls on us to act in the interest of the vulnerable children around us. In this regard, Grobbelaar (2012) stated:

> Although it can be argued that the church is not harming children by giving theological justification to an unjust system, as some churches did in the days of apartheid in South Africa, it may be true that the church is contributing to the exploitation of children by not standing enough on the side of the wronged and suffering children of this world and by not witnessing enough against all

the powerful and privileged who selfishly seek their own interests and thus control and harm many children. (p. 65)

Perhaps it is time that the Churches in South should accept a 'Belhar Confession' that states clearly that we stand with God on the side of the vulnerable children of South Africa. Possibly, a part of the Belhar Confession can be reformulated as follows (cf. Grobbelaar 2012:66):

We believe

- that God, in a world full of injustice, exploitation, and wrongdoing regarding children, is in a special way the God of the vulnerable children;

- that the church must stand by children in any form of suffering and need, which implies, among other things, that the church must witness against and strive against any form of injustice done to children, so that justice may roll down like waters, and righteousness like an ever-flowing stream;

- that the church as the possession of God must stand where the Lord stands, namely against injustice and with the wronged children; that in following Christ the church must witness against all the powerful and privileged who selfishly seek their own interests and thus control and harm children.

Do we believe it?

CHAPTER 2

SEEN BUT NOT HEARD? ENGAGING THE MECHANISMS OF FAITH TO END VIOLENCE AGAINST CHILDREN

Selina Palm

INTRODUCTION

In South Africa today, many children face high levels of physical, sexual, verbal and emotional abuse, as well as sustained neglect and exploitation. Families and homes, despite their protective possibilities, often remain the most vulnerable place for young children. Violence against children, either silenced or hidden from public sight, can become a normalised pattern for both adults and children with concerning long-term consequences. In the last few decades, this issue has received more sustained attention. Increasingly, evidence shows that it is imperative that both children and adults understand that children have full rights to bodily integrity and to grow, survive, thrive, participate and make their voices heard.

This chapter will explore the role of Christian faith communities[1] in ending violence against children in South Africa today, in the light of recent strategies identified by experts as effective in preventing violence. It will draw on key insights from global child protection experts in a 2018 scoping study (Palm 2019a) carried out by academic experts from South Africa who interrogated both positive and negative aspects of the relationships between faith and violence against children to offer recommendations for faith communities' unique theological role in ending violence against children, including tackling harmful social norms and underlying beliefs (Palm & Eyber 2019).

Children have not always been served well by religious precepts. The expression 'children should be seen and not heard' is an old English proverb dating from the 15th century[2] which was recommended by religious leaders of the day and transported elsewhere on colonial ships. This harmful legacy of quiet obedience by children who were expected to know their place, was often accompanied by religiously infused dictates that 'to spare the rod would spoil the child'. These are

---

1 While this article focuses on Christian faith communities as the majority faith in South Africa, some of its premises may apply to other faith communities present here and who were also included in the global 2018 study.

2 Recorded in a collection of homilies by an Augustinian clergyman John Mirk in Mirk's Festial, circa 1450.

just two ways that religious values can entangle with existing cultural norms in ways that reinforce harmful attitudes to children. In a context of violence against children, these religious legitimations, still used today by some, endanger their safety and protection.

Christian faith communities in South Africa are, therefore, faced with an ethical challenge which requires them to reshape inherited harmful interpretations of theologies still used to legitimise certain forms of violence against children. Only if this takes place, can they effectively collaborate with the wider children's sector at many levels within the child protection system to help re-orientate how children are treated. This chapter will point to the promise within child liberation theologies that can help to underpin this ethical task. This can assist local churches to place children at the centre of their faith as full citizens of the beloved community of God whose suffering needs to be seen and whose voices must be heard.

THE GLOBAL CONTEXT OF VIOLENCE AGAINST CHILDREN

The UN Convention for the Rights of the Child celebrated its 30th Anniversary in 2019. According to Marta Santos Pais, the UN Special Representative on Violence against Children, freedom from violence sits at the heart of this Convention as a violation that compromises children's rights and hinders social progress (Pais 2014:7). Yet UNICEF statistics show that half of all children globally experienced some violence in the last year with nearly 300 million two-to four-year olds regularly subjected to violent discipline (UNICEF 2017:7).

Violence against children is an umbrella term that includes the abuse, neglect, maltreatment and exploitation of children (Mathews & Benvenuti 2014:27)[3]. Witnessing violence as a child can also have

---

3   The UN defines violence against children as all forms of physical or mental violence, injury and abuse, neglect or negligent treatment or exploitation, including sexual abuse. The World Health Organization expands this to include the intentional use of physical power or force, threatened or actual by an individual or group that results in or has a high likelihood of resulting in actual or potential harm to the child's health, survival, development or dignity (World Health Organization 2016:14).

far reaching and intergenerational effects and is increasingly seen as a form of violence in its own right (Mathews 2018:n.p.). Despite their inherent vulnerability, violence against children has often been rationalised as necessary or inevitable. It can also be tacitly accepted or minimalised due to the familiarity of the perpetrators (UNICEF 2017:6). Physical violence frequently begins when children are very young, first in their homes and then in schools and it is often shrouded under the ethical veneer of 'punishment' or 'discipline'. Over time, this can translate to similar physical and emotional patterns of bullying by children as forms of punitive disciplining of their peers in schools. Secrecy around patterns of family-based child sexual abuse can also travel forward into adolescent and adult forms of sexual violence. A 2018 study across 40 countries including South Africa notes that only a tiny proportion of children who experience sexual violence ever receive professional help and highlights that in nine out of ten cases of sexual abuse the perpetrator is known to the child (Economist Intelligence 2019:n.p.). It estimates the cost of this to the world economy as up to US$7 trillion. Child sexual exploitation has been recently declared a silent emergency across Africa with particular concern around its digital aspects (Africa Child Policy Forum 2019:15).

Since 2006, there have been some promising developments around ending violence against children with an intensification of global efforts to better understand its key drivers and to develop long-term prevention strategies (UNICEF 2014:5; WHO 2016:8). The Sustainable Development Goals, launched in 2015, address this issue directly in their political targets with Article 16.2 committing states to end all forms of violence against children by 2030. Article 5.2 focuses on violence against women and girls and Article 8.7 looks at child labour and trafficking (UN 2016:n.p.). In the light of these policy commitments, the focus must be on translating this new knowledge into effective protections on the ground. In this task, the meaningful participation of children has been identified as critical (Pais 2014:8).

Over the last ten years, an evidence base has developed around what works to end violence against children (Fulu, McCook & Falb 2017:1). Initiatives like the INSPIRE package of the Global Partnership to End Violence against Children (WHO 2016:8) offer a holistic approach around which all stakeholders can gather to bring their unique contributions. Harnessing local faith communities, especially in the key area of social norms change, has been identified as an important component of many effective violence prevention models on the African continent (Röhrs 2017:20). This is needed in the South African context to which this chapter now turns.

VIOLENCE AGAINST CHILDREN: A MULTI-PRONGED PANDEMIC IN SOUTH AFRICA TODAY

In 1995, South Africa ratified the Convention on the Rights of the Child and embodied it in the Children's Act and other national legislation. However, 25 years on, child abuse and neglect remain endemic. There is a saturation of violence in the everyday lives of many South African children (Richter et al. 2018a:181; Mathews & Benvenuti 2014:33), who regularly experience multiple forms of violence which also often intersect. A recently completed longitudinal tracking study of 2 000 children over 22 years (Richter et al. 2018a:181) shows that nearly 40% were exposed to five or six different forms of violence across the home, school or community. Recent studies suggest that over half of all children in South Africa report physical abuse by caregivers, teachers or relatives over their lifetime (Meinck et al. 2016:910). Violence against children violates their human rights under Section 28 of the Constitution of South Africa, and under the international rights conventions to which South Africa is a signatory. Academic experts have demonstrated that this causes personal suffering and a range of long-term consequences including health challenges, social difficulties and negative generational effects (Mathews & Benvenuti 2014:29; Jamieson, Matthews & Röhrs 2018:83).

According to the 2014 South African Child Gauge, the most common forms of violence encountered by children here are physical and sexual forms. These take place primarily in homes and schools and overwhelmingly at the hands of people that they know (Mathews & Benvenuti 2014:27; Jamieson et al. 2018:81). The severity of family violence in South Africa is particularly concerning. In a 2016 national study with 9 730 youth, one in three reported being hit, beaten or kicked by their caregiver (Burton et al. 2016:42). More than half of all parents here have admitted that they hit their children and over a third termed this a severe beating[4]. In this study, most of the cases of physical abuse resulted from punishment of children which had gone too far. Staff interviewed in this study noted that most of these perpetrators did not recognise what they were doing as abuse and that it often took place because of frustration with children who were perceived by them to be disrespectful. It was, therefore, hard to change as the abuse was seen as culturally acceptable by the perpetrators (Burton et al. 2016:59).

South Africa's violent colonial and apartheid history has left a legacy of a culture of violence still being meted out in homes and schools to women, boys and girls. Boys are particularly vulnerable to physical violence which can influence later perpetration (Richter et al. 2018b:2). It shapes negative internalisations, especially when accompanied by ethical justifications of the child's 'badness' as this comment by a young male survivor (in Jamieson et al. 2018) makes clear:

> I saw him (my father) with the strap, I realised there is major trouble. I do not remember him saying anything … He took me by the one arm, he beat me with his left hand, that's right, he was left-handed. He beat me over my neck over my back until I was lying on the floor and his words to me was 'I will beat you to death you too bad to be alive'. This had a huge impact on me, after this in a way I developed an inferiority complex. (p. 82)

---

[4] Regional differences also exist. An earlier study showed that over 90% of male and female youth in a large sample in the Eastern Cape reported physical punishment by caregivers before 18, the vast majority with hard objects (Jewkes et al. 2010:833).

Corporal punishment (chapter 3 deals with this matter in more detail) has been identified as a key aspect of the high levels of violence against children in South Africa (Jamieson et al. 2018:82; Mathews 2018:n.p.). In many families, the punishment of children, often viewed as inferior to adults, becomes religiously and culturally justified as an accepted form of discipline. It forms part of a patriarchal household model that underpins endemic patterns of violence against children with links to other domestic violence in the home (Mathews 2018:n.p.; Miller 2019:n.p.). Child homicide rates in South Africa are double the global average. Almost half happen in the context of home-related child abuse and neglect, with children under four most at risk (Röhrs 2019:5; Mathews & Martin 2016:1160).

Violence against South African children also varies across their life span with young children particularly vulnerable to physical injury and corporal punishment, school-going children to sexual abuse, and adolescents to gendered forms of intimate partner violence and sexual exploitation (Mathews & Benvenuti 2014:29). This requires targeted awareness and interventions at key risk points in a child's development. In some areas in South Africa, nearly half of the children also report having witnessed domestic violence against their mothers in the home (Jamieson at al. 2018:82), leading to an early socialisation into patterns of violence. Economic and emotional violence is less well documented but also shapes many children's lives where a refusal to pay for basic needs or fear of being homeless requires compliance with violence.

The frequency of sexual offences in South Africa has gained global attention in recent years with the rape and murder of girl children as a particular feature of crime here. Studies suggest an estimated 40% of reported sexual violence crimes in South Africa take place against children, with one in three women and one in five men reporting experiencing sexual abuse whilst under 18 (Mathews & Benvenuti 2014:31; Jewkes et al. 2010:833). There is also a need to look beyond the graphic extremes of sexual violence only, and to better understand the prevalence of everyday instances of unwanted sexual touching. For example, one in five 15- to 17-year olds here have experienced some form of sexual violence over their lifetime, both boys and girls, with girls twice as likely to experience forced penetration (Burton et al. 2016:12). This is significantly higher than the global average of 12.7% but in line with the highest rates in other parts of the world (2016:12).

Community level patterns of physical and sexual violence also take place and can include so-called harmful traditional practices, such as virginity testing or male circumcision which are often imposed on children without their full consent. Legal loopholes still exist around many customary laws here, as well as social practices of underage marriage (Moore & Himonga 2018:63). For example, an estimated 6% of girls in South Africa are married while they are still under 18 (Girls Not Brides 2017:n.p.). Claims of religious freedom are often used to protect these loopholes. Peer violence in adolescence also includes child-on-child bullying and gang-related violence. Risk factors for these patterns by children include witnessing violence at a young age and living in unsafe environments (Miller 2019:n.p.). Violence against children is now shown to have long-term consequences over the whole lifecycle and can also form a vicious intergenerational cycle. In the next section, this aspect will be discussed further.

THE COSTS AND CONSEQUENCES OF AN INTERGENERATIONAL CYCLE OF VIOLENCE

Longer term consequences and costs of violence against children in South Africa (Mathews & Benvenuto 2014:29; Hsiao et al. 2018:3) include a range of concerning effects on children's emotional, health and educational abilities. Save the Children's *Violence Unwrapped* study estimated that in 2015 alone, violence against children cost South Africa R23 billion, or nearly 5% of the country's GDP (Fang et al. 2016:5). The impact of violence against children often continues long after physical wounds may have healed, with lasting social and emotional consequences across their adult lifespan and ongoing risks of aggressive interpersonal behaviour as a result, especially by boys

(Richter et al. 2018b:1). Patterns of violence experienced can be re-enacted and boys who experience violence are at an increased risk of becoming perpetrators later in life (Richter et al 2018b:3). Jamieson et al. (2018) note:

> [t]here are significant, often gendered, pathways between exposure to violence in childhood and later victimisation or perpetration. Childhood trauma increases the risk of men perpetrating physical/ sexual IPV and women experiencing IPV; and of both men and women using corporal punishment against their own children … the effects last for generations. (p. 90)

This intergenerational cycle shows complex connections between violence against women and against children in the home (Miller 2019:n.p.). These are often tied to a gendered hierarchy of power with the man seen as the head of the household, a theme also reflected in global studies (Fulu et al. 2017:2). In South Africa, domestic violence and corporal punishment are associated with social norms that reinforce male dominance and accept violence as a reasonable means to resolve conflict (Röhrs 2017:10; Miller 2019:n.p.). Strong beliefs, often partially shaped by religious texts, can lie beneath these accepted social norms. Röhrs (2017:10) notes that women who believe husbands are justified in hitting wives, and that physical punishment is a necessary form of discipline, were up to eight times more likely to report that their children had experienced psychological aggression, physical violence, and severe physical violence in the last month when compared with women who did not hold these beliefs. Young children are then exposed to physical punishment in the home (Jamieson et al. 2018:84) at an age when this is likely to cause damage that affects the whole lifecycle. It also often sets up an early punitive pattern between caregiver and child that continues as the child gets older.

Women are frequently the primary caregivers of, and, therefore, are some of the main perpetrators of early home violence against children. However, a displaced aggression cycle (Jamieson et al. 2018:83) has been identified where women, often victims of domestic violence themselves, can then take out their frustrations on their children, often tied to ideas of justified punishment where men are allowed to punish women and then women punish children. This cycle legitimises multiple patterns of violence and can be internalised as normal by the one being punished. Taking a gendered lens to child violence is also important to make sure that boys do not become invisible in a narrow focus only on women and girls. Abuse is prevalent among boys as well, including their sexual abuse which often remains a deeply taboo subject in society (Burton et al. 2016:32; Jamieson et al. 2018:82).

What lies beneath this culture of violence against children? Social norms are consistently identified as a key factor underpinning the social tolerance of, or silence around, certain forms of violence against children, such as corporal punishment or family-related sexual violence. These norms and silences can act as a major factor in the ongoing vulnerability of children and in the continuation of repeated violence. Jamieson et al. (2018) note:

> Social norms that consider children as the property of their parents and not as rights holders can place children at risk of physical violence and promote a culture of silence that hinders reporting. The low status of children, evidenced by the widespread belief that children should not question the authority of their elders, disempowers children and leaves them vulnerable to abuse and neglect. (p. 38)

Changing the social norms and family attitudes that support violence is essential. It is here that the faith sector may play a particularly vital role in South Africa. Violence against children is often complicated by religious and cultural justifications with their roots in patriarchal attitudes where women and children can be viewed as inferior to men, and children are viewed as the possessions of their parents (Palm 2019a:36). This forms the ethical crux of many forms of violence that children face, and which also socialise them into its acceptability. Harmful beliefs that support the idea that children sit at the bottom of a hierarchy of value and that those higher up in the chain are allowed, or are morally required to either 'beat the naughty' out of them as a parental duty or ensure they are married off early to prevent the religious sin of pre-marital sex, must be explicitly challenged and not implicitly reinforced by faith leaders.

PROMISING DEVELOPMENTS IN SOUTH AFRICA

Important opportunities for change exist here. On 19 October 2019, South Africa's Constitutional Court unanimously declared the legal defence of "moderate and reasonable chastisement" by caregivers unconstitutional, effectively banning all corporal punishment in the home. This is an opportunity to shift endemic to social norms and practices in homes here.

South Africa is also placed 15th on a list reporting on child sexual violence in 40 countries. Its legal framework is identified as a significant strength, but implementation remains a concern (Economic Intelligence 2018). To tackle sexual violence at its roots, social norms around sex, sexuality and violence against women and girls will have to be transformed. This requires critical engagement with entrenched religious ideologies which place men as unquestioned heads of households and silence the women and children within them. An Africa-wide report on Child Sexual Exploitation (ACPF 2019:87) points to the urgent need to build the capacity of children to enhance their resilience to sexual harm, their readiness to report violence and their ability to protect themselves by using school curriculums to break the silence and start a sustained public conversation. This is a strategy being developed further in South Africa, despite vocal pushback from selected conservative Christian faith voices (Naidoo 2019:n.p.).

In 2017, South Africa signed up as one of 26 'Pathfinder' countries as part of The Global Partnership to End all Forms of Violence Against Children and as such has committed to take public action to accelerate change[5]. Local faith communities in South Africa can play a potentially important role in this task and it is to this area that we now turn.

WHAT IS STILL NEEDED?

There is a need for a sustained, large-scale shift in social norms and attitudes around violence against children (Röhrs 2017:23). Laws are important, but they are not enough on their own. Corporal punishment in schools here has been prohibited for decades but remains endemic (Mathews & Benvenuti 2014:28). An ethical commitment to end violence against children must build a shared conviction that it is neither justifiable nor inevitable, and that it can be prevented (Niekirk & Makaoe 2014:35). South Africa needs primary prevention approaches that tackle a complex interplay of multiple factors and require all stakeholders to work together with a shared agenda. Two areas identified as key are: changing social norms on violence and shifting attitudes to corporal punishment (Niekirk & Makaoe 2014:37). Extreme abuse is often the tip of a larger iceberg of sustained violence that still goes unchallenged. Despite high level commitments to end violence against women and children, there remains a lack of political will to implement these (Jamieson et al. 2018:87). Stopping violence requires an integrated approach that shifts social norms and gender relations at a fundamental level and supports families to better care for children. This requires intentional interventions at multiple levels of the socio-ecological model at the same time – not just a belief in a 'trickle down from the top' approach (Mathews & Benvenuti 2014:30). South Africa can learn from successful community social norms change programmes in Africa that prioritised engaging with faith leaders, such as TOSTAN in Senegal and SASA! in Uganda (Röhrs 2017:24). South African child experts have acknowledged the important role of faith communities and the need to bring religious leaders to the table.

---

5   For more on this initiative see https://www.end-violence.org/impact/countries/south-africa

However, more needs to be done to make this engagement a sustained local reality.

ROLE OF FAITH IN ENDING VIOLENCE AGAINST CHILDREN

UN child protection experts Robinson and Hanmer (2014:602) note that religions contain protective aspects which can offer important contributions to the task of ending child violence. Religious actors can play important roles in both changing harmful attitudes and in providing a range of community services.

Since 2006, different faith communities have mobilised internationally to reflect on their roles in ending violence against children. The 2006 Kyoto Declaration, signed by religious leaders from around the world, committed religions to play an active role in implementing laws on all forms of child violence including corporal punishment (Religions for Peace & UNICEF 2006).[6] Faith leaders pledged here to change theologies seen to legitimise any violence and to work alongside other sectors to end all violence against children. Since then, a range of contextual religious resources have been developed to help faith communities address specific forms of violence against children as an integral part of their faith mission. In 2013, at the 10th Assembly of the World Council of Churches (WCC) in Korea, the statement "Putting Children at the Center" was endorsed as part of God's mission for the churches to uphold children's dignity. This included actions, such as:

- Encouraging positive non-violent parenting with respect, love and compassion

- Working with others in a global movement to eliminate child corporal punishment

---

[6] Article 6 of this Kyoto 2006 Declaration states "[w]e call upon our governments to adopt legislation to prohibit all forms of violence against children, including corporal punishment … Our religious communities are ready to serve as monitors of implementation."

- Using sacred texts to promote peace, justice and non-violence in living with children

- Building partnerships with inter-government organisations, ecumenical partners and other faith communities and networks for promoting children's rights.[7]

In 2017, the Panama Declaration committed religious leaders across all faiths to actively work together for legal, policy and social change on violence against children in their respective countries, with a focus on local faith communities playing more active roles in preventing and ending this violence (Arigatou 2017:n.p.).

However, a gap remains between global religious declarations and lived experiences of many children in local faith contexts. An opportunity exists for faith communities to play an important role in bridging this gap but if this is to take place, harmful theologies must be reimagined in local congregations. Faith communities need to acknowledge that their spaces have often been complicit in justifying patterns of violent punishment and turning a blind eye to sexual harms (CRIN 2014:5; Palm 2019a:27). This task is urgent in South Africa today.

FAITH AND ENDING VIOLENCE AGAINST CHILDREN IN SOUTH AFRICA

Over eighty per cent of South Africa's population identify as Christian. Surveys carried out by the Human Sciences Research Council show high unquestioned beliefs in God across all racial groupings with a strong preference towards literalist interpretations of sacred texts (Rule & Mncwango 2010:186). Churches remain the most trusted

---

7   The statement in full can be found at churchesfornon-violence.org/wp/wp-content/up-loads/2012/02/Putting-Children-at-the-Center.

institution for the majority of South Africans (Rule & Mncwango 2010:196), making them an important social factor for change.

The South African context, therefore, offers an opportunity for Christianity, in particular, to play an influential role in ending violence against children. Faith communities can play an important role in dismantling harmful philosophies of child rearing in particular, often underpinned by the selective misuse of certain sacred texts and theological doctrines that has also shaped South African history. These need urgent divesting of any aura of religious morality, in the light of evidence that these approaches do harm both to children and to the parent/child relationship. Faith communities can also offer regular spaces for direct support to child victims and for playing a triage role in the recognition, referral and response to child abuse, if they are connected into a wider child protection system, and do not try to manage alone.

At the start of the new South Africa in the 1990s, South African theologian Albert Nolan (1995:155) called for a Reconstruction and Development programme of the family to become a place where the rights of women and children are deeply respected. And yet, over 24 years on, South Africa has some of the highest rates of violence against women and children in the world. Many religious organisations here still seek to reinforce models of the family that legitimise patriarchal power and adult patterns of violent discipline (Palm 2018:n.p.; Palm 2019b). South Africa has also inherited a problematic conflation of religion and culture, tied to a history of colonialism. This can translate into patterns of legitimised violence against children as one child expert here notes (quoted in Palm 2019a)

> It is also a conflation, particularly in Africa ..., there is a conflation of "God says I must" and "it's my culture"..., there is no history of corporal punishment of children in Africa until the slave traders and the missionaries and the colonisers arrived. (p. 31)[8]

---

8 All direct quotations referenced in this way are from Palm (2019a), a study commissioned by the Joint learning Initiative for Faith and Local Communities at Stellenbosch University South Africa.

Many Christian faith groups and organisations across South Africa, such as the South African Council of Churches and the Catholic Bishops Conference of Southern Africa have aligned with commitments to end all forms of violence against children. Archbishop Emeritus Desmond Tutu is an ambassador for ending corporal punishment to counter entrenched religious legitimisations that child discipline requires violence. Tutu (2006) notes that:

> [p]rogress towards abolishing corporal punishment is being made, but millions of the world's children still suffer from humiliating acts of violence and these violations of their rights as human beings can have serious lifelong effects. Violence begets violence and we shall reap a whirlwind. Children can be disciplined without violence that instils fear and misery ... If we really want a peaceful and compassionate world, we need to build communities of trust where children are respected, where home and school are safe places to be and where discipline is taught by example. (p. 11)

However, this faith mandate has not always translated consistently into ordinary local congregations. Vocal resistance has been seen by organisations, such as Freedom of Religion South Africa (FOR SA), who claim to represent 6 million South Africans of faith (Palm 2018; Palm 2019b:180). They have played an obstructive role in legal reform on corporal punishment[9]. Some of their partners have even called families to disobey the law (Baptist Union 2016):

> [h]oly Scripture has clear instructions on the discipline of children ... including spanking ... It is outrageous to propose spanking as administered by loving Christian parents committed to the best interest and welfare of their children ... State legislation

---

9   In October 2019, a protracted legal battle in which certain religious arguments were publicly deployed by FOR SA to appeal the High Court decision to remove this parental 'loophole' in the law. Their appeal was overruled.

forbidding this would be a direct rejection of biblical authority … we must obey God rather than men.[10] (p. 1)

These conflicting religious messages, in the light of the 2019 Constitutional Court judgement on corporal punishment, create a haze of ambivalence for many ordinary Christian families. They may do harm by creating moral resistance by parents, as well as fuelling fears which may encourage parents to hide their negative parenting practices rather than to seek help. After this decision, FOR SA claimed publicly that this ruling, celebrated by local child activists, reduces the 'toolkit of options' that parents need to fulfil their faith obligations, by suggesting not only that parents should be allowed to hit their children but that they may be religiously required to, by drawing on so-called "Biblical mandates to smack" (Swain & Palm 2019).

This chapter claims instead, that faith leaders should employ their religious freedom in South Africa in alignment with other human rights to call churches and people of faith forwards into progressive social action on all forms of violence against children, in the light of high levels of family violence tied to harsh punishment. Careful contextual engagement with sacred texts, such as the Bible, rather than a literal approach, offers an alternative to calls for a return to hierarchical theologies of superior and inferior groups often inherited from South Africa's chequered religious past where the Bible was misused to justify slavery, racism and apartheid. Questions around violence against children and faith reflect an internal crisis of religious freedom within South Africa which requires attention being paid to the theologies that lie beneath these varied claims (Palm 2019b).

Corporal punishment is also not the only site of struggle between faith and strategies to end violence against children. South Africa has recently launched a comprehensive sexuality education curriculum for schools aimed specifically at preventing child sexual abuse and exploitation by equipping young children with more information and life skills. However, this has been vocally denounced by selected

---

10 'Response to the South African Human Rights Commission.'

religious voices here, such as the Family Policy Institute, who term it a "diabolical plan" designed to change the sexual and gender norms of South African society (Naidoo 2019). Until voices such as these are consistently challenged publicly by other faith leaders, Christian faith may be seen as a liability by many other stakeholders working to end violence against children. This is a missed opportunity. South African child experts Chames & Lemovsky (2014:49) point to the potentially important role of religious leaders within South Africa in the child protection systems. They can play a "pivotal role" in raising the awareness and support of the public, especially in rural areas, and in challenging religiously endorsed patriarchal systems that make children more vulnerable. This call is in line with many religious communities who have recognised their important role in ending violence against children and stand together to counter a rise in religious fundamentalism which reinforces a deeply problematic patriarchal household model.

Faith-based support in South Africa can be an essential factor in eliminating violence against children as both an ethical and a religious imperative. However, the Churches' Network for Non-Violence (2015:1) notes that this involves "changing an often deeply entrenched culture of acceptance of physical punishment and challenging those who use their sacred texts and teachings to justify it." It requires embracing alternative ways of imagining children in South Africa that align with the 2018 World Council of Churches movement to place children at the centre of local churches through commitments to child protection, child participation and a future environment fit for children. Organisations such as The Warehouse Trust in Cape Town have developed resources to equip church workers with guidance about children, churches and the law (Palm 2018:n.p.). But these tools must become embodied in the lives and attitudes of local congregations if they are to challenge long held social norms about children needing to be quiet, punished and knowing their place that often also become internalised by children.

CHAPTER 2

FAITH'S CROSS-CUTTING ROLES ACROSS THE SOCIO-ECOLOGICAL MODEL

Recent consultations with faith-related child protection experts across the world (Palm 2019a) have focused on the complex interconnections between faith and violence against children and highlighted the two areas of corporal punishment and sexual abuse as primary concerns. Lessons can be drawn from this for the South African context where these two issues are prominent concerns. The study highlighted that faith is currently a "mixed blessing" (Eyber & Palm 2019:1) on ending child violence and notes the role that religiously infused beliefs play in shaping diverse interpretations of sacred texts that can harm or help children. This reality requires faith leaders to be uniquely engaged in the task of ending violence against children (Child protection expert, Panama, cited in Palm 2019a):

> We need to involve faith leaders not only because they are influential but first and foremost because of underlying beliefs … in many cases there are underlying beliefs and social norms and values that are somehow highlighted in or by the religious sector that need to be changed. (p. 29)

Two insights can be particularly valuable for South Africa. The study suggests that faith leaders can play important roles at each level of the socio-ecological model used by child protection experts in South Africa (Mathews & Benvenuti 2014) to address violence against children. It also highlights the cross-cutting "spiritual capital" role that faith can uniquely play (Palm & Eyber 2019). This is depicted in the diagram below:

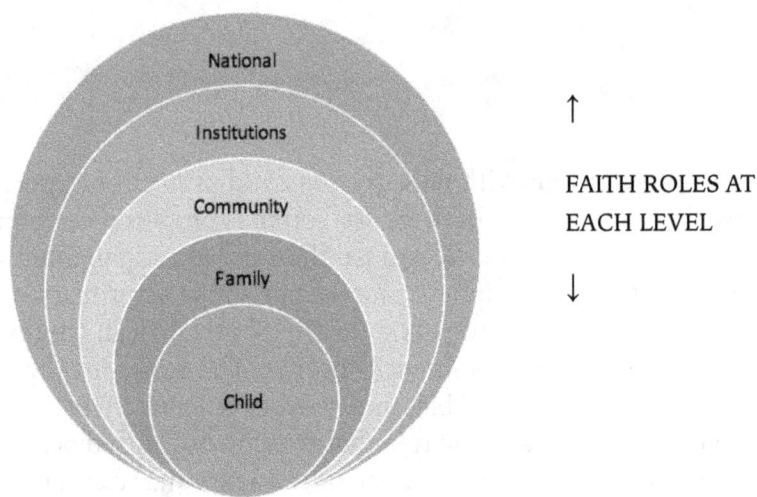

Diagram based on insights from Palm 2019a:17.

Faith communities can contribute at all levels of this model and play multiple roles across the child protection system to both prevent and respond to violence against children. However, child protection experts need to assist them to develop minimum standards of care and to build capacity to prevent and respond to violence effectively. Faith communities can provide care at a low cost but need to support families and children among themselves. Faith leaders can engage formal child protection systems and have crucial roles to play in the prevention of and referral of child abuse.

At the level of the child, faith communities can ensure that children are both seen and heard by creating regular spaces for their voices within child-friendly churches, and by engaging with sacred texts and traditions through a child-centred lens to ensure that they do no harm. These offer opportunities for meaningful child participation, identified as a key mechanism for sustainably changing social norms. However, faith responses must also move away from merely rescue and rehabilitation approaches to nurturing child-centred approaches that link protection and participation, and equip children as active agents who can be empowered as recent evidence has highlighted (Eyber &

Palm 2019:4). Faith leaders in South Africa do not have to be child protection experts to play an important role in protecting, recognising, and referring children identified as at-risk. Sunday schools and church youth programmes can also engage children directly around their innate value tied to the primary prevention of abuse, and offer a safe space to report child abuse rather than becoming havens for adult abusers to hide as recent reports have highlighted (CRIN 2014). Children can experience feelings of guilt and shame when abused, especially sexually. Faith communities can develop new ways to help children understand that they are not to blame and that their bodies belong to them. This will, however, involve tackling historic taboos on discussing sex within religious spaces. Faith communities can also play a role in building resilience in children as a regular presence through childhood and in supporting their safe nurture and their human dignity:

> [T]he real thing that we need to do is change childhood to being a place where children are nurtured and cared for and helped to grow to their full potential. Not beaten, denigrated, put down and humiliated and made to feel small and stupid and useless. (Interview with child expert in South Africa, cited in Palm 2019a:180)

At a family level, faith can offer practical hope and support rather than legitimise harms or ignore children's needs. Eyber & Palm (2019:2) note that religious leaders have unique trusted access to family life. They can play a critical role in identifying children at risk or victims of violence. They can potentially act as interlocutors between the child and potential perpetrators, raising awareness about child rights and caretaker obligations (:8). Religious leaders can also play a role in engaging perpetrators within religious frames of reference and offering counselling and accountability, using their ethical and spiritual authority in the lives of families to help perpetrators of violence against children to understand and change their patterns.

Families have significant potential to protect children from harm and give them a safe container, as well as forming a socialising container for society. However, in the light of the unsafety often experienced by children within the family unit, it needs to be critically engaged. Faith leaders can offer targeted support to families to change harsh parenting practices, end corporal punishment and build nurturing relations of trust across the child's life span:

> (O)ne of the most important roles that churches can play, or faith groups can play is prevention. They can support new parents, they can support parenting by helping people, parenting is a difficult thing to do ... there is no manual of how to do this ... If parents can be supported ... to create nurturing and caring environments for themselves and their children, then we will go a long way to preventing abuse and neglect. I think that is a key role. (Interview with child expert South Africa, quoted in Palm 2019a:17)

At a community level, faith leaders have influence in reshaping harmful social norms, and in increasing protective factors within the community. They need to make concrete links into the wider system to ensure a coordinated response that engages with other agencies rather than seeking to be the solution on their own. They can, however, provide important, informal roles to bridge the gap between a child and the formal system. Faith communities can also look out for particularly vulnerable children, such as those with disabilities, migrants or orphans, and form a safety net for vulnerable children who may fall through other formal systems of care.

At national and international levels, faith leaders can also join together to support, rather than resist, legal reforms around ending violence against children as seen, for example, in the Churches' Network for Non-Violence (2015). They can help hold governments accountable for acting on their policy commitments and as transnational communities of faith they can align with global commitments and be held accountable by the wider faith community. Faith leaders in South Africa can help provide needed moral authority to end violence against children by making a sustained contribution at multiple levels of the

CHAPTER 2

socio-ecological system that surrounds children rather than focusing on parental rights at the expense of the needs of children.

A second key insight of the scoping study was that although there are many ways in which faith communities can play important roles at each level of the socio-ecological model, the cross-cutting, unique contribution of spiritual capital is critical. Its religious resources and mechanisms of faith in the form of doctrines, practices, rituals, experiences and structures within faith traditions can play a very important role in the formation of protective norms, beliefs and attitudes about how children are seen and treated. Faith communities should not just be instrumentalised to access communities, run programmes and implement projects, but be supported to develop their spiritual capital for children: an area which is often still overlooked (Palm & Eyber 2019). Eyber & Palm (2019) note, however, that faith can also be complicit in certain forms of violence against children. This needs to be publicly challenged in the South African context if greater trust is to be forged between faith organisations and the wider children's sector. According to Eyber and Palm, harmful religious beliefs and a misuse of selected Biblical texts can

> (a)ssign children to a position of inferiority in comparison to adults, with fewer social rights and less legal protection. This is a root cause of violence against children. Faith communities must take responsibility for their role in perpetuating these norms and take active steps to challenge and change this. (p. 1)

Faith-based approaches could instead develop positive connections between child protection and faith by using a child rights lens that connects to religious themes and enables sacred text reflections on dignity, justice and peace with children involved as a central part of these reflections. Faith communities can also help develop alternative religious and cultural rituals that do not endorse harmful practices but place the best interests of the child at the centre. These can range from a zero-tolerance policy by all religious leaders on issues, such as child marriage, to the use of baptismal rituals and family counselling spaces to reinforce positive parenting and challenge existing religious justifications of negative practices, such as corporal punishment. Religious structures can engage with and share alternative sacred text reinterpretations and rituals with their adherents and help equip faith leaders at their formation stages to think about children as congregants and as citizens of the kingdom of God. It is to this unique theological task in challenging overarching harmful beliefs and promoting positive beliefs, in specific relation to ending violence against children that the final part of this chapter will now turn.

WHEN FAITH DOES VIOLENCE TO CHILDREN

Ancient sacred texts take patriarchy (the 'rule of the fathers') for granted. As a result, literal readings of these texts today can be highly damaging for children (as well as for women and other marginalised groups). There is a tendency to make children voiceless, invisible and the property of their parents. As a result, harms to children within sacred texts often remain hidden and can even be justified. The Biblical stories of Abraham and Isaac (Gn 22), of Jephthah's daughter (Jdg 11), Tamar's rape (2 Sm 13) and even the story of Jesus himself (Mt 2) all contain descriptions of extreme forms of violence against children and hint at the fear it creates for those children. At the root of much abuse of children in South Africa today, lie entrenched social norms that perpetuate hierarchical ways of viewing children as patriarchal property. This places adults in a superior position over children and makes vulnerable children more voiceless and invisible. Local faith communities must critically re-interrogate these traditions in the light of their ethical obligations to children today to ensure that they are seen and heard. Church complicity in the physical and sexual abuse of children is emerging all over the world, including in South Africa. Abusers here must be systematically held to account. In an interview with a South African child expert, the following opinion was expressed (in Palm 2018):

CHAPTER 2

> The church needs to take responsibility for its own complicity … a long, terrible history of abusing children … (T)o the extent that faith organisations do not stand up against violence against women and children, they are part of the problem. (p. 27)

Underpinning entrenched patterns of children not being seen or heard can be harmful beliefs that tell children that they are bad, mere objects or adult property. These fuel the root cause of violence against children by presenting them as 'less than' adults. This can be especially strong in contexts like South Africa that are deeply shaped by Calvinism and a history of religious family national education scripts that often support both a literal belief in hell and a strong sense of being born bad (into original sin). Faith leaders must take an active role in challenging damaging ways of understanding punishment through the lens of a violent, angry patriarchal God figure if they are to play a role in building a human rights culture that includes children. In an interview in 2018, a South African child expert noted (in Palm 2019):

> The way that certain patriarchal religions conceive the world is that there is a hierarchy … someone at the top … in charge, they are punitive, powerful, in control and if you don't do what they say you are going to get thumped in one way or another … the church and parenting needs to move away from punishment to discipline … Faith groups should be helping parents see that and raise their children in caring, nurturing environments. (p. 29)

Certain theological themes reoccur in discussions of faith's complicity in violence against children. These include an *angry and punitive God, eternal damnation,* and the *inherently sinful nature of humans.* These are used to instil fear and guilt in children or in their parents (Rutledge & Eyber 2019; Palm 2019a). When children are viewed religiously as small creatures whose will needs to be "broken" by their parents, Scripture becomes a source of harm and needs reinterpretation (Trofgruben 2018:57). Religious belief systems often shape what many adults believe is best for their children because they see it as God's will. This can become entangled with cultural norms and has to be tackled directly by faith leaders. South Africa also has complex slave owning, colonial and apartheid histories which have invoked God to seek to justify violence against groups that have been seen as 'less than' or subordinate.

Theologian Trofgruben (2018) highlights that God is still invoked today to justify some child violence and must be named, like apartheid, as a blasphemous reading of sacred texts. He notes:

> [w]here biblical interpretations endorse hatred, abuse, or violence against other human beings created in God's image, especially the most vulnerable and powerless, such readings become acts of blasphemy. They contradict the spirit of the One who taught love for the neighbour, welcome to the child, and special divine concern for "little ones," wherever and whoever they may be. Such acts take God's name in vain, justifying violence against the most vulnerable among us. (p. 56)

A vision of God as both judgementally punitive and mercifully loving can provide religiously legitimated underpinnings for the ethical role that the parent is expected to play in relation to their child. In the light of harsh parenting practices that lead to abuse, these parental motifs need to be rethought with an interpretive key to which the final section of this chapter will turn.

TOWARDS A LIBERATING THEOLOGY FOR CHILDREN

Craig Nessan (2018:12) notes that "child liberation theology takes seriously the research and social analysis that conclusively demonstrates the serious and lasting harm done to children through these forms of oppression." Ryan Stollar (2017) points out that ignoring children's suffering is often shaped by a philosophy of "adultism" where faith beliefs are seen from an adult perspective rather than paying attention to whether they are liberating for children. He suggests that faith communities can, however, work together to dismantle systematic prejudice and discrimination against children in and outside the church. To do this, they must lift up the voices of children and engage them in meaningful participation (Stollar 2017:n.p.; Eyber & Palm 2019:3). This involves reclaiming the invisible or silenced voices of children within sacred texts and in their interpretations. Children must be both seen and heard in all spaces.

At the heart of reshaping attitudes and behaviours that often lie beneath violence against children in South Africa, is a shift away from hierarchical relationships of fearful respect, ownership and power over children seen as second class persons who are 'less than' to instead build trusting relationships of child nurture and growth. These can open spaces for children to participate as citizens in families, communities and nations and enable them to speak up without fear of punishment. Ingrained notions of one-way respect and obedience shaped by religious and cultural scripts will need to be recalibrated to shape new patterns of mutual respect and listening between adults and children within a shared container of doing no harm.

This need for a liberation theology for the child is not a new idea. As early as the 1970s, Janet Pais was identifying children as an oppressed group who are inherently disadvantaged due to their lack of access to power or resources that is equal to the adults around them and because they can also be socialised into normalising the violence around them. She (Pais 1971) notes:

> The case of children as an oppressed group is unique … An outstanding feature of their oppression is that their feelings and perceptions of reality are often denied; abused children are often denied the ability to know what is happening to them or that it could possibly be any other way. (p. 17)

Christians need to find ways to reimagine God as Child and not only as Father or Parent in order to speak about God from the lived experience of suffering children (Pais 1971:16; Nessan 2018:7). This requires refusing to read faith traditions and texts through the eyes of adults only but also paying close attention to how they are seen from a child's perspective. Surfacing and elevating the silenced and unheard voices of children in this respect, both within sacred texts and in today's society, are brought together. Seeing children as created in the image of God, forms an important part of respecting their bodily and emotional integrity. Here, 'God as Child', seen most clearly in the incarnation of God in Jesus, becomes an interpretive key for reimagining all theology from the vantage point of child suffering and for exploring what is good for children as full persons in the eyes of God (Pais 1971:23; Nessan 2018:12).

A child liberation theology has been developed further by a number of Western scholars in ways that are beyond the scope of this chapter to explore[11]. But their insights need to go beyond the Northern academic world into the lived embodiment in South Africa in the light of high levels of child violence here (Nessan 2018:12). This theological reorientation has radical implications for reimagining the core stories of Christian tradition through the eyes of the children who suffer in some of those stories and it may be a sobering task. It will also require reflecting far more critically on interpretations of the atonement that emphasise an angry parent God punishing a son to instead centre on the core belief that God comes as a vulnerable child and that "when we receive a child in Christ's name, we receive Christ … we receive God the Child incarnate" (Pais 1971:23).

Jesus himself extended a warm welcome of open access to children which was at odds with many of his own followers and also transgressed the social norms of his day (Nessan 2018:11). We should not see this as a glorification of childhood purity and innocence but as a placing of those from the very bottom of his society into the centre of faith. Jesus placed children at the centre of his new vision of a beloved community and warned of dire consequences to those

---

11 Scholars in this area include David Jensen, Joyce Mercer, Marcia Bunge and Bonnie Miller McLemore, and they provide helpful suggestions. However, they all sit within Anglo-American contexts. The need is for more South African liberation theologians to do this work and connect it to the specific challenges of violence against children here.

that harm children. Nessan points out that Jesus related to children as full persons, enabling them to approach him safely, be touched with tenderness and to leave blessed, saying to his followers "[t]ruly I tell you, whoever does not receive the kingdom of God as a little child will never enter it. And he took them up in his arms, laid his hands on them, and blessed them" (Mark 10:15-16). This offers a way to reimagine theology (Nessan 2018:12), a point also reinforced by the Churches' Network for Non-Violence (2015) who played an important role in South Africa:

> (A)ll recorded encounters between Jesus and children were kind, gentle and respectful with children seen as central to the new social order that Jesus initiated. By blessing and laying his hands on children, Jesus received children as people in their own right and gave them status, respect and dignity. (p. 3)

At the centre of Christian faith, is the confession that God experienced human life, including the early terrors of a refugee childhood at risk of violent death. This God then not only welcomes children but makes the child a sacrament of the kin-dom or community of God and insists that it is only when adults honour and respect children and identify with the child in themselves that they can know how to participate in kin-dom existence (Nessan 2018:12). The theme of a pilgrim child is used by theologian David Jenson to view children as offering unique gifts to adults which must be respected in all their "graced vulnerability" (2005:44).

Jesus makes the child's status the touchstone for Christians seeking abundant life. If we take seriously Jesus' words to receive each child in his name as Christ, then all Christians share responsibility for the fate of all children (Nessan 2018:13). This child-centred theology has practical implications for child protection and for freedom from child abuse and violence (Stollar 2017). But it requires radical revisions to many traditional interpretations of some scriptures and traditions that can, if taken literally, support the denigration of the status of children. Theologies of original sin, the fourth commandment to "obey your parents" and some ancient parenting proverbs need critical revision if children are to belong fully within the life-giving shalom of God. Questions will need to be engaged in new ways to make this real for congregations. For example, what violence does Jesus witness as a child where an edict is made for his child death before the age of two? He grows up, however, not to become a king, gang leader or warlord, but an adult victim of more political and religious violence. How do we re-imagine the images of God that lie beneath our sacred stories about a God who comes not as a mighty warrior but as a vulnerable boy-child? What might it mean to see the Holy Spirit re-imagined as a little girl child full of graced vulnerability who is skipping and dancing along laughing at the creation of the world? South African faith leaders have an important theological task if their beliefs are to help prevent and not enable violence or domination over children.

CONCLUSION

Many South African faith leaders have a proud history of developing liberation theologies to challenge the harmful theological underpinning of racism and apartheid. This took place in the light of sobering failures of many churches to challenge theologically legitimised, yet harmful racial categorisations of white people as superior to black people, under both apartheid and colonialism. At the start of the new dispensation, many of these liberational voices called for the churches to play an active role in building a human rights culture in South Africa. The family and violence in society were two key areas of engagement identified in the 1990s as needing new liberating theologies if the rights of women and children were to be respected.

However, if faith communities in South Africa are to play this role in ending all violence against children, its faith leaders will need to reject theological interpretations that do harm to children and publicly name them as blasphemous. Only then can they nurture liberating theologies that reimagine faith through the eyes of those children experiencing violence. In this way, they offer what Dutch scholar of religion Gerrie Ter Haar has termed positive spiritual capital that mobilises their unique cross-cutting resources across the legal, political and civil society spaces. This is a theological-ethical contribution to making ending all violence against children a reality, in ways envisaged by the 2018 World Council of Churches movement for child-friendly churches that places child protection, child participation and a world fit for them at their heart. As an interview with a South African child protection expert notes (cited in Palm 2019a):

> (T)here are a huge number of people for whom their faith is a critically important part of their lives ... it is the role of leaders within different faiths to set an example above all else but also to talk about things like respect for human dignity, appreciation of diversity, your obligations, we all have rights ... We need churches and faith leaders to search their texts and hearts for ways to make humankind nicer to each other. To forget about power and control and dominance. (p. 23)

This chapter has suggested ways in which religious leaders in South Africa can play a role across many areas of the child protection system but especially around primary prevention at child, family and community levels. They can use special spiritual occasions, such as childbirth, baptism or marriage, to provide new and existing parents with information on abuse and neglect, and to incorporate messages around the protection of children. They can offer ongoing pastoral support for overstretched caregivers and connect them to informal support or formal services. Opportunities for parents to share their challenges and accomplishments and to support each other in positive parenting without resorting to violence can also be rooted in faith communities. Theologians must explore how diverse forms of violence against children are understood in their faith traditions and highlight sacred texts and teachings that can promote the protection of children from abuse and neglect, as well as challenging those that still do harm.

Christian theologies must become liberating for all children if churches are to become spaces of freedom for the most vulnerable in society. These beliefs can then help churches to play their unique spiritual role in the shared struggle to end violence against children. If all local churches consistently dismantle harmful beliefs that legitimise any violence against children, and instead witness to and enact a theology that places the dignity and personhood of every child at the centre of their followers' faith and ethics, they will play a unique and important role. But these beliefs need active embodiment in the hearts, minds and hands of all those of faith living on South African soil and not just in the abstract proclamations of its senior faith leaders. Only in this way, can our legal skeletons for protecting children from violence take flesh in the homes, families, streets, schools, churches and communities where it really matters. 2020 marks the 30th anniversary of the African Charter on the Rights and Welfare of the Child but many of these child rights still need to take firm root on South African soil. In the words of former South African President Nelson Mandela in 2002, "[w]e owe our children – the most vulnerable citizens in society – a life free from violence and fear" (Mandela 2002:ix).

CHAPTER 3

THE CONTENTIOUS ISSUE OF CORPORAL PUNISHMENT IN SOUTH AFRICA

Jan Grobbelaar & Chris Jones

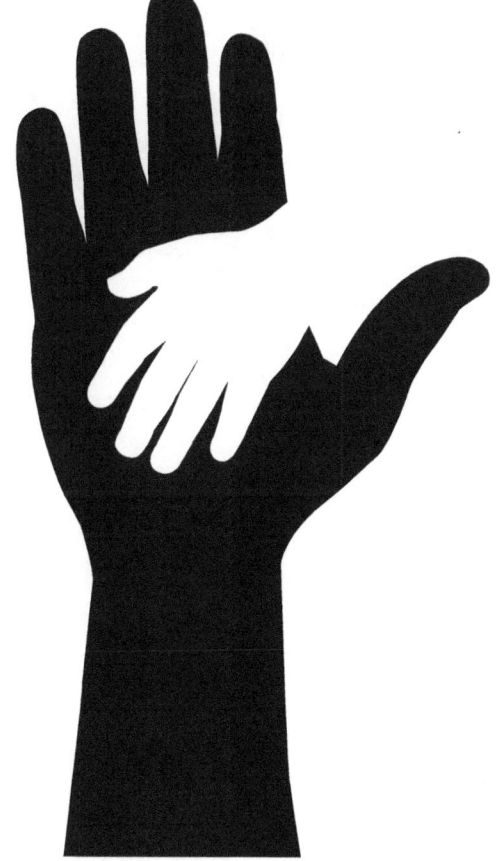

If a child can't read ... we teach,

If a child can't spell ... we teach,

If a child can't swim ... we teach,

When a child can't behave ... we punish

Greg Jansen and Rich Matta

CHAPTER 3

INTRODUCTION

This chapter will focus on how children should be treated and raised in a culture where the distinctions between discipline and punishment have been blurred for decades. Why should a rights conception of discipline matter? The chapter will navigate these and other issues when it comes to disciplining children in a democratic, but often violent society. It will firstly attend to the legal framework for discipline in South Africa, especially regarding school discipline. Then it will describe the current situation in South Africa and also look at recent developments regarding corporal punishment and the continuing struggle against violence that children experience and are exposed to on a daily basis. Lastly, positive alternative ways of disciplining children in order to behave better and how people responsible for children can be assisted in this regard, will be addressed.

LEGAL FRAMEWORK REGARDING DISCIPLINE AND CORPORAL PUNISHMENT

In any discussion of the contentious issue of discipline and the use of corporal punishment regarding children in South Africa, it is important to take the legal framework and current legal position regarding discipline into consideration (Reyneke 2013:123). In this regard, the first question to ask is: How is corporal punishment officially defined in South Africa? The South African Department of Education (Department of Education 2000) defines corporal punishment as:

> [A]ny deliberate act against a child that inflicts pain or physical discomfort to punish or contain him/her. This includes, but is not limited to, spanking, slapping, pinching, paddling or hitting a child with a hand or with an object; denying or restricting a child's use of the toilet; denying meals, drink, heat and shelter,

pushing or pulling a child with force, forcing the child to do exercise. (p. 6)

This formulation should be read against the legal background of the Constitution of the Republic of South Africa [Act 108 of 1996]. Chapter 2 of the Constitution, under the heading Bill of Rights, states in Section 7 points 1 and 2 the following (Republic of South Africa 1996a):

(1) This Bill of Rights is a cornerstone of democracy in South Africa. It enshrines the rights of all people in our country and affirms the democratic values of human dignity, equality and freedom.

(2) The state must respect, protect, promote and fulfil the rights in the Bill of Rights.

Furthermore, it declares in Section 10 about human dignity: "Everyone has inherent dignity and the right to have their dignity respected and protected" (Republic of South Africa 1996a).

Reyneke (2013) interprets the provisions in Section 7 (2) as follows:

To "respect rights" means that the state has an obligation not to violate rights or to limit rights unlawfully. In the context of school discipline, this would mean that the state, organs of state and employees of the state should not infringe on the rights of learners and others, such as educators. To "protect rights", on the other hand, requires the state to prevent the violation of rights; hence measures such as legislative provisions must be put in place to prevent the infringement of rights. To "promote and fulfil rights" means that the state must take active steps to make it possible to exercise rights and to prevent the infringement of rights. This implies that the state must put measures in place to ensure that, while discipline is maintained, rights are promoted and fulfilled. (p. 125)

Moreover, Section 28 1(d) states: "every child has the right to be protected from maltreatment, neglect, abuse or degradation" (Republic of South Africa 1996a).

Reyneke (2013:128), opined that the Bill of Rights (Republic of South Africa 1996a) provides in section 28(2) the benchmark for school discipline:

A child's best interests are of paramount importance in every matter concerning the child.

The implication of the above-mentioned sections of the Constitution is that teachers have to respect the human rights of learners and, therefore, may not use corporal punishment under any circumstances. It also obliges state organs to take steps to prohibit corporal punishment and to ensure that it is not used (Reyneke 2013:126).

In 1995, in *S v Williams*, juvenile whipping was found to be unconstitutional because it contravenes the human dignity of the offender, and the punishment was described as inhuman and degrading (Reyneke 2013:160). This precedent was followed by accepting the *National Education Policy Act* of 1996 which outlawed corporal punishment in schools (:160). Section 3(4) provides as follows:

[N]o person shall administer corporal punishment or subject a student to psychological or physical abuse at any educational institution. (p. 6)

In response, the *South African Schools Act* of 1996 (Republic of South Africa 1996b) provided in Section 10 the following:

(1) No person may administer corporal punishment at a school to a learner.

> (2) Any person who contravenes subsection (1) is guilty of an offence and liable on conviction to a sentence which could be imposed for assault.

It was followed up with the *Abolition of Corporal Punishment Act* 33 of 1997 (Republic of South Africa 1997) that repealed all laws which authorised corporal punishment by a court of law, including a court of traditional leaders. Hereby corporal punishment was banned in South Africa.

But the efforts to create a culture of non-violent school discipline was not accepted and supported in all quarters. Christian Education SA, a voluntary association of 196 independent Christian schools, took the Minister of Education to court (cf. *Christian Education SA v Minister of Education* 2000 (4) SA 757 (CC)) in a bid to make an exception to the prohibiting of corporal punishment on grounds of religious conviction. They declared that

> its member schools maintain an active Christian ethos and seek to provide to their learners an environment that is in keeping with their Christian faith. They aver that corporal correction – the term they use for corporal punishment – is an integral part of this ethos and that the blanket prohibition of its use in its schools invades their individual, parental and community rights freely to practise their religion. (p. 2)

The judge of The South-Eastern Cape Local Division of the High Court found that

> section 10 of the Schools Act did not constitute a substantial burden on religious freedom. He also held that corporal punishment in schools infringed the children's right to dignity and security of the person and was accordingly not protected by section 31 of the Constitution. He therefore dismissed the application. (p. 7)

What is very interesting of this judgement, is that the Judge found that "the scriptures relied on provided 'guidelines' to parents on the use of the rod, but did not sanction the delegation of that authority to teachers" (*Christian Education SA v Minister of Education* 2000 (4) SA 757 (CC):5). He also expressed the view that "the authority to delegate to teachers was derived from the common law and the approach adopted by the appellant was merely 'to clothe rules of the common law in religious attire'" (:5). He then declared that "in the circumstances it had not been established that administering corporal punishment at schools formed part of religious belief" (:5). A careful reading of Proverbs established that the Judge was technically correct in his observation that the scriptures used said nothing about the delegation of authority to use the rod from the parents to teachers.

The association then took the judgement on appeal to the Constitutional Court which found the following (*Christian Education SA v Minister of Education* 2000 (4) SA 757 (CC)):

> When all … factors are weighed together, the scales come down firmly in favour of upholding the generality of the law in the face of the appellant's claim for a constitutionally compelled exemption. The appeal is accordingly dismissed. (p. 57)

Reyneke (2013) summarised the factors for this verdict as follows:

> although the restriction on corporal punishment was not in line with the religious beliefs of the parents concerned, the court still had a duty to promote respect for the dignity and physical and emotional integrity of all children; that language, culture and religion cannot shield practices that are unconstitutional; that an exemption, even on religious grounds, would not be in line with the equality clause; that upholding corporal punishment would disturb the symbolic, moral and pedagogical purpose of the prohibitive measure and would undermine the state's duty to protect people from violence.

The prohibition of corporal punishment, stated the court, is designed to transform national civic consciousness in a major way. In this regard, it held that the broad community has an interest in reducing violence wherever possible and in taking active steps to protect children from harm.

In addition, it considered the best interests of the child to be of paramount importance. Parents' religious beliefs, it said, could not limit children's best interests, and, if parents' beliefs are not in the child's best interests, the child should be protected, even if this means infringing the parents' religious beliefs. (pp. 161-162)

In the light of this legislative situation, how does the current situation regarding corporal punishment look in South Africa?

THE CURRENT SITUATION

Although corporal punishment in schools has been banned in South Africa, Angie Motshegka (Joubert 2019:n.p.), the Minister of Basic Education, is of the opinion that it is still being used unlawfully by teachers. This is confirmed by the Committee on the Rights of the Child[1] as well as other human rights treaty bodies such as the Human Rights Committee (Global initiative to end all corporal punishment of children 2019a:4-5).

In the 2016-2017 financial year, according to Motshekga (:n.p.), 229 letters of advice were sent to teachers who were convicted of corporal punishment. In 2017-2018, it increased to 233 but in 2018-2019 dropped to 194 (:n.p.). The fact that some teachers continue to inflict corporal punishment even after receiving advisory letters as a warning, became clear from the fact that the South African Council of Educators (SACE) – which is the country's watchdog for acceptable

---

1   27 October 2016, CRC/C/ZAF/CO/2, Concluding observations on second report, paragraphs 35 and 36.

teaching practices and with whom all teachers must be registered if they want to teach in 2016-2017, found seven teachers guilty of inflicting corporal punishment (:n.p.). In 2017-2018, 24 teachers were found guilty in a disciplinary process, and in 2018-2019, the number increased to 33. The penalties imposed by SACE varied. Some teachers' names have been deleted from the roll. This only happened in cases where pupils were seriously injured by the teacher. Some of the other guilty teachers' punishment was that the deletion of their names from the role was suspended on condition that they were not convicted of corporal punishment again (:n.p.).

If one goes further back to a social audit of school safety and sanitation that was conducted in the Western Cape (one of the nine South African provinces) during September-November 2015, involving 912 learner questionnaires, 220 administrator interviews, and 229 physical inspections, the audit (Global initiative to end all corporal punishment of children 2019a; Equal Education 2016) found

> [t]hat despite a ban on corporal punishment in South African schools, learners [were] beaten at 83% of schools sampled. Learners [reported] that it [occurred] daily in 37% of schools and at least once a week in 59% of schools. Of the learners sampled, 64% have personally been abused or seen a fellow learner abused by a teacher weekly, and 39% [experienced] or [witnessed] corporal punishment daily. (p. 8; n.p.)

In some of the schools where corporal punishment occurred, learners reported "teachers using a weapon (stick, baton, pipe, etc.) to abuse them in 91% of these schools. The most common means of assault by teachers on children in their charge [was] with a ruler or other small stick (75%), their open hand or fist (61%), or a pipe (44%)" (Global initiative to end all corporal punishment of children 2019a:8).

In a qualitative study done by Marumo and Zulu (2019) in Mahikeng Township secondary schools of the North-West province on teachers' and learners' perceptions of alternatives to corporal punishment, they found:

> Although some teachers and learners felt that alternative forms of discipline were effective to a certain extent, the general perception was one of scepticism. Both teachers and learners expressed the need for a return to corporal punishment in cases of serious misconduct. (p. 46)

The reality described above raises the question: Why does corporal punishment, despite its banning as unlawful, persists in some schools? Morrell (2001) already partially answered this question by stating:

> Reasons for the persistent and illegal use of corporal punishment include the absence of alternatives, the legacy of authoritarian education practices and the belief that corporal punishment is necessary for orderly education to take place. A neglected explanation is that corporal punishment persists because parents use it in the home and support its use in school. There is a tension between the prohibition of corporal punishment in schools and the increase in parent involvement in the affairs of schools. (p. 292)

Although more attention was given to identifying alternative discipline methods since the publication of Morrell's article, it seems that it does not make much of a difference. In Marumo and Zulu's (2019:46) research, teachers indicated that their negative perceptions can be attributed "to a lack of adequate training in the implementation of alternative forms of discipline." Morrell (2001:292) also expresses the opinion that there exists, amongst teachers, parents and pupils, many different local understandings concerning discipline and corporal punishment. In a qualitative case study among high schools in Pretoria East, South Africa, Joubert and Serakwane (2009:127) draw the conclusion that the educators in these schools viewed discipline differently, stating: "Some perceived it as the formation of moral character, some perceived it as control over learners, some perceived it as preventive and corrective measure, some as self-discipline, whereas some understand it more narrowly as punishment."

It seems that about 20 years after Morrell's article appeared, some of these same complicating factors still exist, as will come to the fore in the discussion in the next section on another case before the Constitutional Court of South Africa in 2019.

Another possible reason for the struggle to change the culture surrounding corporal punishment in South Africa come to the fore in Reyneke's (cf. 2013, 2014, 2016, with Pretorius 2017) research, emphasising the importance of the best-interest-of-the-child concept as a right and guiding principle for discipline in schools. Although the Constitution clearly pronounces that in every matter regarding children, their best interests should be predominant, and the Constitutional Court has already delivered various judgements concerning this concept (cf. Reyneke 2014), it is still not incorporated in the stipulations concerning school discipline (Reyneke 2016:1). After scrutinising section 8 of the School Act, Reyneke and Pretorius (2017:112; cf. 2017:118-123) concluded that from "the lack of prescriptions ensuring that sanctions serve the best interest of children, the insufficient provision for support measures and structures for counselling, the undue focus on the best interests of the transgressor and the lack of guidance concerning the appointment of an intermediary", it is evident that the approach followed and the disciplinary processes is incompatible with the right of the best-interests-of-the-child. In spite of "the fact that the Constitutional Court continuously directs decision makers, in different contexts, to focus on the best interest of children" and "also provides guidance on how the best interests of the child should be considered" it repeatedly happens that "decision makers fail to heed this call of the Constitutional Court and consequently infringe on children's best-interests right" (Reyneke 2014:137).

As long as this situation endures, it will be difficult to establish the concept of the-best-interests-of-the-child as part of the South African culture regarding corporal punishment and the illegal use of corporal punishment will persist. Laws and even a stricter application thereof will not on its own stop the violence against children and their abuse through corporal punishment. This situation is a great ethical challenge for the Church in South Africa to establish a culture of human dignity towards children in the South African society and morally responsible conduct in disciplining children, not only in schools, but also in every child's home. This challenge is stressed by some recent developments concerning the use of corporal punishment towards children in South Africa.

RECENT DEVELOPMENTS REGARDING CORPORAL PUNISHMENT IN SOUTH AFRICA

On 18 September 2019, the Constitutional Court of South Africa ruled that the defence of "reasonable and moderate chastisement" was unconstitutional. This effectively means that all corporal punishment of children was banned. But what led to this prohibition? Adriaan Mostert, an IT specialist and his wife Hannah, unknowingly helped set this landmark order in the Constitutional Court. It all started with the charismatic Joshua Generation Church, which in 2013, posted a 38-page manual on its website of the thickness and length of the rod with which a parent should educate a one-year-old. In the *Raising Children* manual, that has since then been removed from their website, the church recommends that the stick with which a one-year old should be punished, should be 25-28 cm long and 3 mm thick. For an older child, the couple who wrote the manual, recommended a wooden or plastic stick of about three rulers in length. According to them, a hiding should cause pain otherwise it will be useless and will leave your child unchanged. When the Mostert couple saw this manual, they lodged a complaint at the Human Rights Commission asking them to prohibit the church from allowing their members to hurt their children. In 2016, the Human Rights Commission ruled against the Joshua Generation Church. The church's promotion of corporal punishment at home was found to be unacceptable by the commission. The Joshua Generation Church appealed on procedural grounds and the Human Rights Commission undertook to review the report, which has not happened (Brümmer 2019:n.p.).

In 2016, a Muslim father, known as YG, was convicted in a Johannesburg regional court for assaulting his wife and 13-year-old son after the boy was caught watching pornography on the internet. This case was reviewed in the High Court, after which this court found that the defence of reasonable and moderate chastisement is unconstitutional. Freedom of Religion South Africa[2] (FOR SA), admitted as a friend of the court (*amicus curiae*), took it on appeal after which it was referred to the Constitutional Court. In September 2019, the Court decided that all forms of corporal punishment are unconstitutional (Brümmer 2019:n.p.). The implication is that corporal punishment in any form and at any place is prohibited in South Africa. Indeed, activism by ordinary citizens of a country, also in South Africa, can make a huge difference in the lives of people, especially children.

THE CONTINUING STRUGGLE AGAINST VIOLENCE IN THE LIVES OF CHILDREN

A further very important factor that led to the outlawing of all corporal punishment of children, has to do with the violence many of the 19 million children in South Africa (UNICEF 2015) are exposed to on a daily basis. For Shanaaz Mathews[3], director of the Children's Institute[4] at the University of Cape Town, positive parenting is not about being permissive, but about raising your children in such a way that they know what respect is, not only for others but also for themselves.

---

2   More information about this legal advocacy organisation working to protect and promote the constitutional right to religious freedom in South Africa is available at https://forsa.org.za/

3   http://www.ci.uct.ac.za/shanaaz-mathews.

4   http://www.ci.uct.ac.za/.

Mathews (Brümmer 2019:n.p.; Mathews & Martin 2016:1160-1163), among others, conducted a national study on child murder, in which they found that more than 1 000 children are murdered annually – and half of these happen in the context of fatal child abuse. Even softer forms of chastisement make children feel as if they have no control over what is happening to them, because they don't know whether it is punishment or abuse. It is often just a grey area. The problem is that when you are angry as a parent, you do not always have control (Mathews in Brümmer 2019:n.p.). Earlier in her career, Mathews (in Brümmer 2019:n.p.) conducted a national epidemiological study on intimate femicide and found that a woman was killed by her intimate partner every six hours. And it has more to do with corporal punishment than one might think. Children who grow up with physical corporal punishment easily become aggressive and violent later in their lives. It made her understand how violence in the form of discipline has this incredible lasting effect on who we are and who we become as human beings.

A study called Birth to Twenty Plus [Bt20 +] (Brümmer 2019:n.p.; Richter et al. 2018:181-186), of which Mathews was part, revealed that half of the children received corporal punishment within the first five years of their lives. By the time they were 17 years old, about 70% of them had experienced some form of physical punishment or violence in their homes. "Birth to Twenty Plus is a unique birth cohort study which started enrolling pregnant women from Soweto, Johannesburg, in 1990 and has followed them and their children for more than 27 years" (Mathews 2018:n.p.). This study shows "the extent to which children are exposed to violence in their homes, at school, in their communities and in their intimate relationships with peers and the long-term effects of violence in their lives" (:n.p.). According to this study, "[o]nly a handful (1%) of the nearly 2 000 children studied across their childhoods had not been exposed to severe forms of violence at some point in their lives" (:n.p.). Large numbers of children are affected by violence. The report (Matthews 2018) stated:

[t]wo thirds of parents report that they regularly beat their 4-5-year-olds with sticks, belts, straps and shoes. More than 80% of children in their primary school years, and more than 90% during their secondary school years report being a victim of violence at home, school, in their community, or in their intimate relationships … Violence is concentrated in the lives of mainly poor Black children, where criminal, community and school violence spills into their homes and leaks into their close relationships. (:n.p.)

Children growing up in chronic violent circumstances, according to the report (Matthews 2018) mentioned above,

are … at risk of becoming desensitised to violence, uncaring towards others and potentially violent themselves. In fact, the study points to already high levels of violent behaviour, with more than two thirds of school-aged in the study reporting that they themselves have behaved violently towards others … (:n.p.)

This study further highlights that when children are physically punished, "most children … experience increasing stress and helplessness. This can lead to poor mental health, impaired social relationships and substance abuse, with implications for their educational progression, work productivity and social stability" (Matthews 2018:n.p.). Therefore, according to Mathews (n.p.), it is essential to reduce "children's experience of and exposure to violence … to prevent the long-term negative consequences for children growing up in South Africa's townships." Louise Laskey (2015), lecturer in the Faculty of Education at the Deakin University, Australia, states in this regard that

[h]arsh punishment has been found to negatively affect children's emotional and language development, academic progress and parental attachment. Disruptive, anti-social behaviour may result … Reviews considering long-term outcomes typically

identify mental health issues such as internalising problems (like depression), or externalising problems (like aggression), and increased vulnerability to substance and alcohol abuse in adolescence and adulthood ... There are also concerns about cognitive impacts due to the potential stress and trauma involved. (:n.p.)

Bernadette Saunders and Bronwyn Naylor (2012:n.p) confirm this by referring to a study authored by Tracie Afifi and her colleagues who "investigated the link between children being hit, pushed and shoved, and the development of psychological problems later in life. They found that harsh physical punishment was associated with depression, anxiety, substance abuse and personality disorders." Afifi (2012:n.p.) and her fellow researchers go so far as to argue that "reducing physical punishment may help decrease the prevalence of mental disorders in the general population."

Mathews (in Brümmer 2019:n.p.) argues that their research shows that if children receive corporal punishment, especially from a young age, they cannot distinguish between what is loving and what is not loving. And when you hit a child, they consider it a normal reaction if you don't like someone's behaviour. They are, therefore, more likely to act aggressively towards their peers from a young age. Children who experience violence at home become aggressive. According to her, it is crucial that the cycle of violence in a country like South Africa should be broken. Researchers know there is an intergenerational cycle of violence and that the parallels must be drawn between what children experience early in their lives and how it later affects them in terms of who they become. If we want to change behaviour, we must start at home. We all have a responsibility to think about how we can reduce the levels of violence ourselves (Brümmer 2019:n.p.).

Mathews further reasons that we know corporal punishment leads to immediate response. If you hit a child on his hand if he did something wrong or naughty, he'll probably stop it immediately. But it will only have short-term results. This kind of action does not teach children why this behaviour was dangerous or why you didn't want them to act like that. This is confirmed by Laskey (2015:n.p.), stating: "Perhaps the most seductive aspect of the traditional method is that it has an instantaneous effect of discouraging undesirable behaviour. Not only that, but it can have a cathartic effect on the frustrated, stressed parent." Furthermore, according to Saunders and Naylor (2012:n.p.), "many parents admit that they resort to hitting their children when they are tired, angry or distressed, and that they later feel regret and remorse." Parents may even apologise to their children. "However, change over the longer term is entirely another matter. Research does not support the efficacy of physical punishment in achieving lasting behavioural change" (Laskey 2015:n.p.). It seems thus, that corporate punishment is used by parents to vent their own discomfort and emotions, the shame and perhaps aggression they experience themselves about their children's behaviour, rather than to effect long-lasting behaviour change in their children. If that is the case, then it is not even corporal punishment but abuse, even if it is just a 'light' spanking.

Many parents say, in light of the abovementioned judgment by the Constitutional Court regarding corporal punishment, that it takes away their control, and that they do not know what to do. According to Mathews (in Brümmer 2019:n.p.), it should not be about exercising control, but rather about building better, positive relationships with your child. Most child abuse happens in the context of wrong forms of discipline. Mathews (in Brümmer 2019:n.p.) further states that she has never come across an extensive peer reviewed study in favour of corporal punishment. Furthermore, using religion to justify corporal punishment is wrong. She thinks we have advanced enough in our thinking about human rights. We all have our own forms of religion – but we are now living in the year 2020, the Bible was written centuries ago and we need to start thinking differently about what the Bible's message means in our contemporary context with our unique challenges (Brümmer 2019:n.p.).

ROLE OF THE CHURCH

Jones (2019:4) emphasises that churches are the institutions most trusted by South Africans, therefore, it is possible for faith groups to make a big difference to the problematic culture surrounding discipline and corporal punishment in South Africa. In 2017, an Ipsos Mori poll (Ipsos 2017:n.p.) confirmed this view of the church with its finding that 88% of South Africans indicated that religion or faith is an important part of their lives. When you take this into account, you realise what a huge impact religious leaders and believers can make through spiritual capital at individual levels, in terms of stopping corporal punishment and violence against children. It can also be done in families, communities, institutions and the wider community. Unfortunately, this does not happen (effectively) when you look at the violence statistics of our country (:14).

Statements, like the following, especially coming from FOR SA (Brümmer 2019:n.p.) in light of the decision of the Constitutional Court regarding corporal punishment, that loving God-fearing parents will now have to go to jail for punishing their children, certainly do not help us in this regard. Continuous awareness should be raised about the negative effects of corporal punishment, and religious and cultural attitudes will have to be changed to ensure that discipline is administered in a manner consistent with children's dignity and their other human rights. The right to dignity indeed "means that children are independent and autonomous right-holders who may not be subjected to shameful and undignified treatment" (Landmark moment for child rights in South Africa 2019:n.p.).

In the current situation in South Africa, churches should play a more active role in advocating against the use of corporal punishment in homes and schools by teaching their members to interpret the Biblical verses allegedly justifying corporal punishment, in a more responsible way, in and for our South African context. Verses from the book of Proverbs (e.g. 13:24a; 19:18; 22:15; 23:13–14; 29:15 & 17) are regularly cited as justification for corporal punishment (cf. *Christian Education SA v Minister of Education* 2000 (4) SA 757 (CC):3-4). Although "the act–consequence relationship" (von Rad 1972), expressed in retributive rhetoric (Sandoval 2013:102), is present in Proverbs, we should be very careful of a simplistic reading of these texts from an ancient cultural context as if they are literally applicable today. Proverbs is not a simple promise of "good things to those who pursue wisdom's way and bad things to those who stray onto folly's path" (:102). This simplistic reading should be countered by teaching people to read these verses about discipline in the light of the prologue of Proverbs with its emphasis on "righteousness, justice, and equity" (Pr 1:3) and that the beginning of wisdom and living a wisely life begins with the fear of the Lord (Pr 17).

A better understanding of the Hebrew words related to discipline, the verb *'yāsar'* and the noun *'mûsār'* should also be considered. These words are used in a variety of ways in Proverbs and can express different sides of the concept 'discipline': chastisement, correction, instruction, wisdom (Branson & Botterweck 1990:127-128; Fox 2008:n.p.; Sæbø 1997:714-715; Von Rad 1975:53). Although the use of *mûsār* with rod (Pr 13:24; 22:15; 23:13-14; 29:15) can indicate that physical methods were used to discipline children (Sæbø 1997:715), we should take the fact that the rod was used in the Bible for different tasks into consideration more seriously. It seems that a rod's function in the Old Testament was mostly to protect, to support, to help, and not to inflict physical pain (cf. ed. Youngblood 2014:989; cf. Brady 2000:1134). According to Brown (2008:72), in not one of the proverbs is the language of punishment present. The use of the rod is not penalty or punishment or punitive. "Hence, 'corporal punishment' does not technically apply in Proverbs ... Retaliation, even retribution, does not figure in the act of discipline. 'Rod and reproof yield wisdom' (29:15a)." (:72).

The use of the rod "is meant to edify, that is, to save the child from, literally, grave danger. Love, not anger, is the fundamental reason or motivation" (Brown 2008:71). Actually, Proverbs 19:19 prohibits using discipline out of anger and the loss of control. In Proverbs, anger is seen as "a violent emotion, likened to a flood (27:4) that destroys relationships (22:19)" (:72). Therefore, in Proverbs, a clear preference for verbal discipline rather than using the rod for physical discipline is expressed: "A rebuke strikes deeper into an intelligent person than a hundred blows into a fool" (Pr 17:10). "Reproof or rebuke in Proverbs is to be equated not with mere scolding or harsh denunciation but rather with convictive, cajoling, urgent words of wisdom ... The word, thus is mightier than the rod" (:76-77). Words, and only words, expressing care and love, is the medium of discipline. Brown (2008:77) states that "[i]n Proverbs 1–9, the rebuke has replaced the rod."

In light of the above remarks, it is difficult to justify the use of the rod for disciplining children in our time. The "misuse" of these texts as if they still literally apply today, can easily leave children voiceless (Jones 2019:14). As South Africa is seen as a pathfinder country in fighting violence against children, the churches in South Africa should urgently work together to change the culture surrounding discipline in our country.

SOUTH AFRICA RECKONED AS A PATHFINDER COUNTRY IN FIGHTING VIOLENCE AGAINST CHILDREN

On 18 September 2019, as already indicated, the South African Constitutional Court ruled that the "common law defence of 'reasonable and moderate chastisement' is unconstitutional under articles 10 and 12(1)(c) of the Constitution"[5] (Global initiative to end all corporal punishment of children 2019a:1). Previously, common law acknowledged parent's "power 'to inflict moderate and reasonable chastisement on a child for misconduct provided that this was not done in a manner offensive to good morals or for objects other than correction

---

5   18 September 2019, Freedom of Religion South Africa v Minister of Justice and Constitutional Development and Others, Constitutional Court, ZACC34; confirming 19 October 2017, YG v. The State, High Court of Gauteng Local Division, Case No. A263/2016.

and admonition'"[6] (:1). In their report, the Global Initiative to end all corporal punishment of children states that "under South Africa's common law system, this decision from the Constitutional Court is equivalent to repealing the defence in legislation. With this decision, the Court effectively banned the use of all corporal punishment in the home, as criminal provisions against assault now apply equally to children" (:1). According to this initiative South Africa is a "pathfinder country with the Global Partnership to End Violence Against Children, which commits it to three to five years of accelerated action towards the achievement of Target 16.2 of the Sustainable Development Goals" (:2).[7] This prohibition by the Constitutional Court includes all settings, implying the home, and alternative settings, such as day care, schools, and penal institutions (:2-4). According to the Global Initiative to end all corporal punishment of children (2019b),

> only 12% of the world's children are fully protected in law from all corporal punishment … [g]overnments of 87 states have not yet made a public commitment to law reform … and in 67 states, corporal punishment has not been fully prohibited in schools … 58 states have now achieved prohibition in all settings, including the home. 54 more states have committed to reforming their laws to achieve a complete legal ban … In 32 states, corporal punishment – whipping, flogging, caning – is still lawful under state, traditional and/or religious law as a sentence for crimes committed by juveniles. In 17 states, corporal punishment is not fully prohibited in any setting, including as a sentence for crime. (:n.p.)

---

6   R v Janke and Janke 1913 TPD 382.

7   Various forms of violence against children persist. In 83 countries (mostly from developing regions) with recent data on the subject, nearly 8 in 10 children from 1 to 14 years of age were subjected to some form of psychological aggression and/or physical punishment at home. In all but seven of these countries, at least half of children experienced violent disciplinary methods. Sexual violence is perhaps the most disturbing of children's rights violations. Based on the limited data available, in 14 of 46 countries with comparable data, at least 5 per cent of women between the ages of 18 and 29 experienced sexual intercourse or other sexual acts that were forced, physically or in other ways, for the first time before they were 18 years of age.

As a pathfinder country, we have to find answers on what the best ways are to discipline children in order to live wisely.

SEEKING BETTER WAYS TO DISCIPLINE CHILDREN IN ORDER TO LIVE WISELY

It is not so easy to develop new discipline strategies that are effective. It is quite a complex challenge to accomplish such a goal. What always makes it difficult is "the broad scope of what constitutes discipline and the multifactorial etiology of behavior problems" (Howard 1996:809). Therefore, it is essential that the whole South African society should together seek for these better ways. Together we have to develop a new culture regarding discipline and violence, in general, in this country. This new culture should be developed in both our homes and schools, and in broader society. Parents and teachers should work together on this. One of our first challenges is to establish a mutual understanding of what discipline is. Your discipline strategy always flow from your view of what discipline means. Only if we can create a broader consensus on our understanding of the concept of discipline, can we really work on applying such an understanding in our different contexts. There are some general principles applicable to both the home and the school contexts, but there are also different challenges present in each of these contexts. These different challenges can only be addressed effectively if educators, parents and children can find mutual ground around what discipline really is. Is this a farfetched dream, or can it be achieved by starting more open conversations about discipline in our local communities, schools and families?

According to Lewis and Short's *Latin Dictionary. Founded on Andrew's edition of Freund's Latin Dictionary* (in Reyneke 2012:2; cf. Reyneke 2013:42-43) our word discipline originates from the Latin word *disciplina* meaning: "instruction, tuition, teaching in the widest sense of the word ... are the objects of instruction ... Subject: a custom, habit." In her (Reyneke 2013:43) discussion of related Latin words derived from the concept '*disciplina*', it is clear that 'instruction', 'teaching', 'learning' and 'learner' are the focus of this concept. What is interesting, is that there is no reference to discipline as punishment.

In a study on the classical approaches to discipline in the Athenian, the Roman and Christian traditions, Oosthuizen, Roux and Van der Walt (2003) confirm the above views. They draw the following conclusion:

> The notion of punishment, chastisement, retribution or justice does not appear in any of the Greek words discussed ... (although *paideia* implies a degree of chastisement, if and when necessary). It also does not form part of the meaning of the Latin roots of the word "discipline" or "disciple". (p. 387)

In a discussion on the root and meanings of *discipline*, the Merriam-Webster online dictionary (n.d.) indicates that the reference to discipline as punishment was actually a fairly late evolution in the development and understanding of this concept. The dictionary states:

> *Discipline* comes from *discipulus*, the Latin word for *pupil*, which also provided the source of the word *disciple* (albeit by way of a Late Latin sense-shift to "a follower of Jesus Christ in his lifetime"). Given that several meanings of *discipline* deal with study, governing one's behavior, and instruction, one might assume that the word's first meaning in English had to do with education. In fact, the earliest known use of *discipline* appears to be punishment-related; it first was used in the 13th century to refer to chastisement of a religious nature, such as *self-flagellation*. (n.p.)

Brendtro, Brokenleg and Van Bockern (1990:82) confirm this view. According to them the original concept was the "purest form of discipline", meaning the adult provided guidance through teaching to the young. Over time, this understanding mutated up to the point that many dictionaries now indicate 'punishment' as synonymous with discipline. They opined:

> The joining of discipline with punishment creates a psychological oxymoron. ... Discipline is a process of teaching, not of coercion. It seeks to involve youth in learning social responsibility and self control. Discipline is impeded by the unilateral exercise of adult authority and control. (p. 82)

In summary, it can be stated that discipline is not about punishment to establish an adult's control and authority over children, but rather instruction in which knowledge and skills are transferred and children are also helped to attain self-control and self-discipline. "This entails guiding them on the right way, correcting inappropriate behaviour in a loving and caring way, and warning and supporting learners where necessary" (Oosthuizen, Roux & Van der Walt 2003:44). The task of the educator is to build a good relationship with every pupil, as well as creating an environment which will enhance teaching and learning and enable children to achieve the realisation of their full potential. To achieve these goals, it is important to take cognisance of and apply the following differences which Le Motte (in Reyneke 2012:3) makes between discipline and punishment:

- Discipline is intrinsic, while punishment is external.
- Discipline is educative, while punishment is punitive.
- Discipline is about self-control for the sake of self-actualisation, while punishment is the exercise of control over people for the sake of compliance.

In the light of the above basic understanding of the concept of discipline, the focus can now turn to discipline in the contexts of the school and the home.

CHAPTER 3

DISCIPLINE IN OUR SCHOOLS

After the use of corporal punishment in schools in South Africa was outlawed by legislation, the Department of Education (2000) introduced alternatives to corporal punishment (ATCP) which can be employed in classrooms. These alternatives are based on the principals of Positive Discipline which want to enhance non-violent measures of discipline. The question to ask is: Does ATCP work?

Already in 2007, Badenhorst, Steyn and Beukes (2007:302) expressed the opinion that "[t]he apparent inability of many educators to manage learner behaviour is cumbersome. They seemingly lack the skills to bridge the gap between reactive and pro-active discipline ..." Since then, various researchers have expressed their concern about the disciplinary situation in South African schools and teacher's struggle to survive in these circumstances. Joubert and Serakwane (2009:126) found that "some of these [new] methods are perceived to be ineffective by the majority of educators and they battle to find alternatives that works" (:129). With their study on disruptive behaviour in the Foundation Phase of schooling, Marais and Meier (2010:41) confirm this view that teachers find it hard to uphold discipline in the classroom and that learners keep on with disruptive behaviour. Increasing cases of learner indiscipline after the introduction of ATCP in 2000, suggest that teachers are not capable of effectively implementing these substituting disciplinary measures (Maphosa & Shumba 2010:387).

In a study on the relationship between school discipline and the legislative banning of corporal punishment, Ntuli and Machaisa (2014:1781) came to the conclusion that the result was "indeed a decline in the level of discipline in schools." They also state: "One of the key findings of this research is that educators and principals find it difficult to apply the alternative" (:1788). This maybe a reason why some educators still persist in using corporal punishment (cf. The current situation above) or are pressing for bringing it back, at least as an option. Although Marumo and Zulu (2019:46) found in their study on the perceptions of teachers and learners on alternatives to corporal punishment that "some teachers and learners felt that alternative forms of discipline were effective to a certain extent, the general perception was one of scepticism." They also draw the conclusion that "[b]oth teachers and learners expressed the need for a return to corporal punishment in cases of serious misconduct" (:46). Marumo & Zulu (2019:61) is of the opinion that "[t]he majority of calls for the reintroduction of corporal punishment stemmed from desperation on the part of teachers as a result of their inability to handle 'out of control' learners." During their research, one teacher commented: "Corporal punishment should be re-introduced in order to curb ill-disciplined behaviour by learners" (:61).

How did this situation develop? Many answers can be given to this question. One of the answers which are regularly given is that educators was not properly prepared and trained for the changed situation and how to apply ATCP effectively, and still do not receive enough training in this regard (Joubert & Serakwane; 2009; Busienei 2012; Ntuli & Machaisa 2014; Mulaudzi & Mudzielwana 2016; Marumo & Zulu 2019). This led to a lack of knowledge, skills and motivation to apply ATCP among teachers. Related to this reason, is the claim by teachers "that they were never consulted on their views when the strategy was initiated and this could be a contributing factor to the continuous use of corporal punishment and the partial or non-use of ATCP" (Moyo, Khewu & Bayaga 2014:9). Joubert and Serakwane (2009:130) indicated that "[i]t is important to note that strategies that are employed by educators to establish discipline in the classroom will be based on the knowledge, skills, attitude and values they acquire in one way or another." It seems, thus, as if the planning and implementation of ATCP was done haphazardly and that not enough attention was given to these important factors. If people are not consulted and not trained, they will not buy into a new strategy, nor adhere to it. In such a scenario, it will be very difficult to change a school's disciplinary strategy and culture. The disturbing result was that many educators and schools could not cross the bridge from reactive to proactive discipline with positive-orientated measures (Badenhorst et al. 2007:306).

Although other factors also played a role in creating the situation where ATCP is not working effectively in many schools, it will not be discussed here because it does not change the fundamental questions to be asked: Is ATCP a suitable strategy for inculcating discipline in schools? (Moyo et al. 2014:3). The more probing question is: What is the theoretical basis and values of ATCP?

In answering these questions, it can be helpful to identify the disciplinary method that is used by educators in the place of corporal punishment. Some of these methods are: verbal warnings, written warnings, demerits, time-out, small tasks like tidying the classrooms, giving learners extra work, exclusion from certain activities, detention and suspension from school. In their research amongst teachers from 335 schools, Lessing and de Witt (2011:413) found that detention was the most used disciplinary method, used by 44.9% of the respondents. What was especially worrisome for them was that only 0.7% of the respondents referred to the importance of a value system in the punishment process (:413). Although Lessing and de Witt are positive about the movement to ATCP and away from viewing discipline as punishment, it is a bit ironic that they still use vocabulary of the old dispensation in their article, Afrikaans words referring to punishment (straf), for instance, 'strafproses' (punishment process), 'strafmaatreëls' (punishment measures) and 'strafmetodes' (punishment methods). To change a culturally embedded system, the change of language plays a very important role and should get more attention in our discussions about discipline.

From the above, it is clear that many teachers are still working with an authoritative mindset, control orientated, re-active, with punitive measures, retributive, and with no clear distinction between discipline and punishment. It seems that in order to counter this situation, a new approach to discipline has to be developed and implemented. In this regard, Reyneke made a very important contribution with her work on a restorative approach to discipline (cf. Reyneke 2012, 2013, 2016, with R Reyneke 2020). Reyneke and Reyneke (2020) declare about restorative approach to discipline:

to implement this approach, a complete mind-shift is required. This mind set requires an understanding that to discipline learners is to teach socially acceptable behaviour. The restorative approach entails moving away from an approach that merely focuses on the ill-disciplined learner to an approach that focuses on preventing disciplinary problems, changing the culture of the school and restoring the harm done to those affected by the misconduct. The restorative approach involves focusing on finding solutions to address the needs and interests of all the role-players in the school community, rather than finding suitable punishments. Thus, focusing on the best interests of every learner and the interests of educators. Restorative discipline is a value-driven approach that respects the human rights of every stakeholder and also protects, promotes and fulfils everyone's human rights. (back end of book)

This approach is in line with the understanding of the concept of discipline stated above. Although it will not be easy, with this approach, a new culture regarding discipline can be built in South Africa, which will enhance the best interests, not only of children, but also of all citizens of South Africa. But to build this new culture, it is of the utmost importance that parents should also implement this new approach in disciplining the children in their homes.

DISCIPLINE IN OUR HOMES

According to Saunders and Naylor (2012:n.p.)

> [m]ost parents love their children and want to be the best parents that they can be. Children are more likely to respect parents who treat them with respect and teach them constructive ways to behave. Children thrive on positive recognition that motivates the repetition of behaviours parents want to see, and also enhances children's self-esteem.

CHAPTER 3

A joint press release by respondents and amici curiae in the case of *Freedom of Religion South Africa v Minister of Justice & Constitutional Development & others* [Children's Institute (UCT); Quaker Peace Centre; Sonke Gender Justice; Centre for Child Law; The Parent Centre; Global Initiative to End All Forms of Corporal Punishment of Children; Dullah Omar Institute for Constitutional Law, Governance and Human Rights], states that the "court's approach to parents' entitlement to chastise their child was guided by the best interests of the child in respect of protection from potential abuse" indicating that the best "interests of the child would be to achieve discipline and achieve the same result without causing harm or unduly undermining the fundamental rights of the child" (Sonke Gender Justice 2018:n.p.). Furthermore, the court "also found that reasonable chastisement was neither necessary nor justifiable in light of the fact that there are non-violent methods for disciplining children such as 'positive parenting'" (:n.p.). Marta Santos Pais (in Saunders & Naylor 2012:n.p.), a Portuguese lawyer who served as Special Representative of the United Nations Secretary-General on Violence against Children from September 2009 until May 2019, said: "Legislation provides an ethical and normative framework to promote values of respect, tolerance and human rights."

Rightly so, Laskey asks (2015:n.p.): "So how do you then make your children behave?" She then refers to the following alternative techniques to discourage misbehaviour: "providing consequences; withdrawal of privileges; exclusion (time out) or quiet time; setting and enforcing boundaries; [and] saying 'no' firmly but avoiding hostility" (:n.p.). According to her, desirable behaviour over the longer term depends on the quality of our relationships. Research and practice confirm, according to Laskey, that positive outcomes can be enhanced by the following:

- spending focused time together in activities of the child's choosing, while demonstrating patience, support and warmth;

- educating ourselves about appropriate expectations (in line with the child's level of development). For example, aggression in toddlers is normal (peaking at 24-42 months). A child's ability to concentrate when following adult-directed activities can be estimated at 3 minutes per year of age (4 years x 3 = 12 minutes);

- being warm, affectionate, consistent and encouraging with children;

- minimising the need for discipline with preventive strategies. Provide a high-interest novel toy on occasions where coping with the environment will be challenging (such as aeroplane travel) or plan brief excursions to retail environments when the child is neither fatigued nor irritable, involving the child in the experience. This could be finding and placing suitable objects in the shopping trolley. If the children feel involved, they are less likely to lose interest and act out;

- providing appropriate, active supervision and involvement in activities (avoiding distractions of technology such as mobile phones so the parent is completely available);

- explaining why certain behaviours are inappropriate, including their impact on others;

- teaching empathy by supporting children in identifying emotions and responding sensitively;

- offering choices – for example, letting the child choose what colour they would like to wear (but not presenting 'not wearing a hat' as an option);

- modelling appropriate behaviours and responses, providing support and guidance (alternative strategies) when frustration occurs;

- redirecting the young child to other activities when tensions arise; [and]

- developing rules appropriate to children's developmental level. (:n.p.)

The challenge for parents remains that we "teach children internalised self-regulation, ethical choices and consideration for others, and ultimately, to interrupt the generational cycle of violence in child discipline" (Laskey 2015:n.p.).

CLOSING REMARKS

According to the joint press release, as referred to earlier, by respondents and *amici curiae* in the case of *Freedom of Religion South Africa v Minister of Justice & Constitutional Development & others*, "[c]orporal punishment is one of the key drivers of the high levels of violence against children in South Africa" (Sonke Gender Justice 2018:n.p.). They refer to the Constitutional Court that "acknowledged the intergenerational cycle of violence" by stating: "[w]e have a painful and shameful history of widespread and institutionalised violence" (:n.p.). Furthermore,

> violence against women and children are inextricably linked. They occur in the same households and share the same drivers. With the current attention to the high levels of gender-based violence in South Africa, it is important to note that this ruling is not aimed at criminalising parents. This is only the first step in protecting children more from physical violence in the home. The real work begins now. Raising public awareness on the ruling is accompanied by momentum from the Department of Social Development to drive a national parental awareness campaign on Positive discipline. Positive discipline is not an alternative form of punishment: it avoids the use of punishment. Instead, it assumes that children want to behave well but need

help understanding how to do so and that children learn best through cooperation. (:n.p.)

South Africa must also concentrate on introducing wide-ranging programmes to support families and teachers at national level to alter attitudes and behaviours that promote the use of harsh and abusive forms of discipline against children. We need programmes that have proved effective in "changing both individual attitudes and social norms around child discipline and we need to teach caregivers alternative, non-violent forms of discipline that can replace smacking and spanking" (Sonke Gender Justice 2018:n.p.).

CHAPTER 4

RECONCEIVING CHILD THEOLOGY FROM A QUEER THEOLOGICAL PERSPECTIVE: FOR LGBTIQ+ PARENTED FAMILIES AND CHILDREN

Hanzline Davids

INTRODUCTION

In this chapter, the focus will be on LGBTIQ+ children and LGBTIQ+ parented families from a Christian sexual ethics perspective. The traditional notion of family is contested by a variety of different structures of family. The traditional view of family is often equated to a heteronormative structure in service of patriarchy through procreation. This family consists of a mother and a father who reproduce children that defined the family unit. The family became the space where sexual and gender norms were constructed along societal, religious and cultural belief systems. In recent years in South Africa, literature scholars looked critically at the notion of family, especially pertaining to how the traditional view excludes Lesbian, Gay, Bisexual, Trans, Intersex, Queer and other (LGBTIQ+) parented families (cf. Lubbe-De Beer & Marnell 2013; Morison, Lynch & Reddy 2018). Furthermore, little research exists of children in LGBTIQ+ families and LGBTIQ+ children in heterosexual family units. In theological discourse, sexual and gender identities of LGBTIQ+ parented families and LGBTIQ+ children in heterosexual family units are even less studied.

Since the beginning of the twentieth century, Child Theology has emerged as a global movement with the focus of moving children from the margins to the centre of theological discourse. The focus of this theological interest is influenced by the theoretical lenses and methodologies of liberation and feminist theologies. Theologians from Africa too, contributed to the development of this theological focus on children. Contributors to this theology are also critical that the theology thus far has been constructed by adults rather than children. This criticism highlights that, children do theology, already, from their own embodied experiences. However, within a hierarchical system of power, in many cases patriarchy, their theological contribution is often ignored and denied. Before I outline this chapter further, I want to acknowledge that as a self-identifying gay man of colour, I am not a father and neither in a civil union. In this chapter, I theologically journey with LGBTIQ+ children and LGBTIQ+ parented families as an activist-theologian working in the intersection of sexuality, gender and faith in mainline churches and higher theological education training centres in South Africa.

In the following section, the struggles that LGBTIQ+ children and LGBTIQ+ parented families experience will be discussed from various literature sources, my own embodied experiences and the multiple contexts I am exposed to in my work at Inclusive and Affirming Ministries. Hereafter, Child Theology will be briefly outlined to see whether theological principles exist that can assist theological imagination to explore life-affirming theologies for LGBTIQ+ parented families and LGBTIQ+ children in heterosexual family units. Lastly, this chapter will examine whether Queer Theology as a liberation theology can perhaps contribute to the development of Child Theology that are life-affirming towards LGBTIQ+ parented families and LGBTIQ+ children in heterosexual family units.

LGBTIQ+ CHILDREN AND FAMILIES: CONTESTED EMBODIMENT

LGBTIQ+ children in heterosexual families and LGBTIQ+ parented families in the South African context is greatly under reported and studied.[1] The embodied realities of LGBTIQ+ children and LGBTIQ+ parented families are non-normative and for this reason they face multiple challenges to their sexual, gender and family identities.

STIPULATIVE DEFINITIONS OF SEX, SEXUALITY AND GENDER

It is important to pause here for a moment and gain some clarity on sex, sexuality and gender. Ugandan human rights activist and law professor Sylvia Tamale discusses in her chapter 'Researching

---

1   Though these embodied realities are understudied in academia, numerous ontological works were published in the last few years by LGBTIQ+ persons. These include, but are not limited to: Kumalo 2018; Mabenge 2018; Windvogel & Koopman (eds.) 2019.

and theorising sexualities in Africa' (2011:11-36) the intersectional struggle of African sexualities (gender) through colonisation, medicalisation, sexual culture, violence and HIV & AIDS. Even amidst these challenges Tamale (:11-36) is of opinion that African sexualities (and gender) can be rewritten from an ethical perspective that gives voice to the corporeality of African bodies. I want to point out that these epistemologies are influenced by Western discourse. However, there is no reason why it should be diminished from an African perspective. Rather, these epistemologies provide the space to engage our own cultural and religious discourse from the African continent (:26). Theorising our contextual embodied experiences become part and parcel of the African church's justice work.

North American ethicist Jams Nelson (1978:17) describes sex as "a biologically-based need which is oriented not only toward procreation, but, indeed, toward pleasure and tension release." In other words, this definition pertains to 'having sex' as a wholistic well-being of bodies while the same word also has a different meaning. Sex also refers to the biological composition that differentiate human beings in male and female (Thatcher 2011:4). It was also believed that male and female are the only biological sex bodies that exists (:4-14). On the contrary, intersex bodies today is also understood as being part of the biological sexes.[2]

For South African ethicist Louise Kretzschmar (2013:51), sexuality "is a very basic element of our humanness and is closely tied to our self-understanding and the way in which we relate to others and the world around us."[3] Gender, according to Cranny-Francis, Waring, Stavropoulos & Kirby (2003:4; cf. Boonzaaier & van der Walt 2019), "is the culturally variable elaboration of sex, as a hierarchical pair

---

[2] "A general term used for a variety of conditions in which a person is born with a reproductive or sexual anatomy that doesn't seem to fit the typical definitions of female or male. For example, a person might be born appearing to be female on the outside, but having mostly male-typical anatomy on the inside. Or a person may be born with genitals that seem to be in-between the usual male and female types, for example, a girl may be born with a noticeably large clitoris, or lacking a vaginal opening, or a boy maybe born with a notably small penis, or with a scrotum that is divided so that it has formed more like labia" (Thatcher 2011:12 cf. DeFranza 2015; Cornwall (ed.), 2015.

[3] Ola Sigurdson (2016:429-445) argues that sex and sexuality in the Christian tradition has a painful past. However, Sigurdson develops a convincing argument that Christian sexual ethics can learn from the past in order to contribute to meaningful theological understanding of sexuality in the post-modernity.

(where male is coded superior and female inferior)." Sex, sexuality and gender are contested terms and, therefore, Thatcher's point that these definitions ought to be understood along stipulative lines is important. Throughout this chapter, these definitions will be the theoretical basis on which the argument of this chapter rests. In conjunction with this definition, Kretzschmar's (2013) view of the importance and function of sexuality (and gender) in Christian ethics will furthermore provide a theoretical framework:

> … our sexuality is not simply a private matter. It has family and social consequences and cannot be separated from our relatedness to God. Humans need to have an openness to life and the integrity to exercise self-control in the interests of inter- and intra-personal wholeness and the willingness to live their sexual life in terms of their love for God. (p. 69)

The embodiment of gender and sexuality cannot be divorced from God. Our bodies are the sites through which we experience God's self-revelation, grace, salvation and love. Kretzschmar (2013) urges us to think theologically about sex, sexuality and gender. Theologians like Jordan (2002), Coakley (2013), Thatcher (2011), Althaus-Reid (2000, 2003), Stuart (2002), Isherwood & Stuart (1998), Loughlin (2007) and Williams (2002) have already started thinking theologically about sex, sexuality and gender. Therefore, contributing to new understandings of sex, sexuality and gender from a scriptural and dogmatic perspective, rather than relying solely on modern science.

SEXUAL AND GENDER PERFORMATIVITY OF THE FAMILY

Contrary to theological inroads that have been made to see sex, sexuality and gender in a new light, heteronormative discourses still exist that dehumanise bodies, especially pertaining to LGBTIQ+ children and LGBTIQ+ parented families. Heteronormativity structures the world based on a hetero-binary worldview that divides the world between masculine and feminine (Butler 1990:22-23) and structures gendered bodies according to "[g]ender norms [that] are often written into the constitution of the family, reflecting hegemonic discourses around the ideal reproductive unit" (Sanger & Sanger 2013:55). Blood ties become a normalcy marker that excludes families that do not meet these blood-related criteria (Breshears & Le Roux 2013:2).

In his book, *Theology and Families* (2007), Adrian Thatcher thinks "theologically about families and children" (:ix) based on the doctrine of the Trinity (:3). Thatcher defines family according to Lisa Sowle Cahill's definition as "an organized network of socio-economic and reproductive interdependence and support grounded in biological kinship and marriage" (:6).[4] These two definitions of 'blood-related criteria' and blended kinship differ fundamentally and how the heteronormative definition highlights it as "the family is a key site for hetero-sexualisation …" (Sanger and Sanger 2013:53). As a site of hetero-sexualisation, the family "operates as a performative space where gendered subjects recreate various roles that help sustain and reproduce imaginary notions of an ideal family" (:61). These "imaginary notions" put LGBTIQ+ children (:61) and LGBTIQ+ parented families at risk. For this reason, Breshears and Le Roux (2013:2) point out that "[l]esbian/gay parents are actively aware of the complex implications their 'different' family identity may have on their children." Furthermore, "the negative discourses with which their children struggle most often come from outside the family unit and that these can impact upon the development and maintenance of a healthy family unit" (:2).

These sexual and gendered norms that are advocated by heteronormativity is fundamentally formed by patriarchy. Patriarchal belief systems stratify bodies hierarchically according to set values

---

[4] Thatcher (2007:6) elaborates on this definition stating: "This definition draws on historical family forms while also accommodating some of the contemporary changes to families. 'Organized' implies social custom and domestic authority, neither of which is fixed. 'Network' implies a common residence. 'Socio-economic' implies the wider resources of work, social interaction and exchange, necessary for families to survive. 'Reproductive' includes children as a raison d'être of families: 'interdependence and support' implies both mutuality between members and the dependence of some on others. 'Grounded' allows for the extension of families beyond their reproductive base to include adopted and fostered children, elderly relatives, and even residing companions and friends. 'Marriage' accommodates within the definition the expectation that the core of the family unit still remains the married couple." This definition makes room for all different forms of families.

and norms. LGBTIQ+ children and children from LGBTIQ+ parented families face even more challenges. As an example, Breshears and Lubbe-De Beer (2016:90-93) in their empirical study, focused on lesbian and gay parented family (children included) experiences in South African schools. The study found that these children and families faced numerous challenges. Even though challenges exist, schools that include LGBTIQ+ sexual and gender identities in their curricula, impact the embodied experiences of LGBTIQ+ children and LGBTIQ+ parented families significantly (Breshears & Le Roux 2013:12). Intervention practices of anti-bullying and anti-homophobia contest the dominant cultural, religious and societal heteronormative discourse of binary sexuality and gender identities.

In the southern African region, Francis et al. (2019) analysed gender and sexuality diversity in schools in five countries (Botswana, Lesotho, Namibia, South Africa and Swaziland). Francis et al. (2019:30) points out that in the "Southern Africa region, the viability of inclusive learning environments is compromised by the ongoing denial and exclusion of gender and sexuality diversity which results in more violent and less inclusive educational spaces." Contributors to the violence and denialism according to Francis et al. (:30) are "[p]atriarchal values, Christian values, and a tension between African and western values …" These value systems hinder the inclusion of sexual and gender diverse bodies in the curricula and negatively impacts the holistic well-being and development of all children.

The South African government revised the Comprehensive Sexual Education (CSE) curricula. This decision was met with backlash from especially religious conservative groups. Haley McEwen (2018) in her article 'Weaponising Rhetorics of "family": The Mobilisation of Pro-Family Politics in Africa', states how religious conservatives from America advocate against CSE. According to McEwen (2018:149), these pro-family activists promote "its politics in African countries [as] part of the movement's broader efforts to advance anti-gay agendas globally." For McEwen (:145), this movement has three core focus areas namely: "The use of a rhetoric of 'love' in order to disguise an ideology of intolerance[5]; the couching of hate speech in the rhetoric of 'free speech;'[6] and the positioning of the 'natural family' as congruent with development imperatives."[7] Children, who are clearly caught up in this phobia, who are on their own journey of sexual and gender diversity self-discovery are exposed to an environment that is contrary to their holistic development. Because "the cultural productions of Western societies is the bourgeois nuclear family, it is very difficult for other family formations to be granted legitimacy and the material and other support which make it possible to operate" (Cranny-Francis et al. 2003:13).

CONTESTING HETERONORMATIVE FAMILY NOTIONS

Contrary to religious conservatism, the Johannesburg Declaration (JD)[8] advocates for an inclusive understanding of family that contributes to the well-being of children. The Global Interfaith Network for People of all Sexes, Sexual Orientations, Gender Identities and Expressions (GIN-SSOGIE), convened "rights defenders, scholars, researchers, and religious leaders from diverse family backgrounds and traditions, including African traditional religions, Islam and Christianity, for its first dialogue on Family and Traditional Values" (GIN-SSOGIE 2018). Throughout the five sections of the declaration, the importance of family is discussed through international and continental rights charters, reclaiming of sexualities and culture, interrogation of sovereignty

---

5   "in disguising 'hate' as 'love,' Western and Okafor attempt to create ambiguities about the exclusionary and oppressive intentions of the pro-family movement by softening its oppressive edges and inoculating the movement against being labelled as a 'hate' group. Yet, violent undercurrents of the movement become evident in such efforts to eradicate and 'invisibilize' hated bodies so that other loved bodies (namely, Christian, heterosexual, cisgender, middle class bodies) can retain hegemonic social status" (McEwen 2018:159 -160).

6   "Here, the pro-family movement exploits the idea of 'freedom of speech' in order to protect their ideology and policies that exclude, oppress, and engender multiple forms of violence against LGBTIQ+ people" (McEwen, 2018:161).

7   "... neoliberal imperatives of economic growth and individual wealth are given as reasons why individuals should choose the 'natural family' model" (McEwen 2018:166).

8   Global Interfaith Network, Johannesburg Declaration, viewed 10 October 2019, from http://www.gin-ssogie.org/johannesburg-declaration/

and the reclaiming of faith. The JD correlates with Thatcher's understanding of the fluidity of family and particularly acknowledges a contextual understanding of family.⁹ The JD provides a basis for a contextual understanding of family not only as fluid but a life-space for the nurturing and well-being of children, family and society.

In the following section, Child Theology will be discussed and analysed to provide possible insight to reconceive Child Theology towards the inclusion of LGBTIQ+ children and LGBTIQ+ parented families.

CHILD THEOLOGY: A BRIEF OVERVIEW

French philosopher Michel Foucault's (1990) analysis of power led him to understand that power is both repression and resistance.¹⁰ Those who are repressed always resist the discursive practices of

---

9   "1. That the definition of the "natural family" as being limited to the nuclear family, which is promoted by the extreme religious right and the proponents of so-called cultural and traditional values, does not reflect the diversity of family life in contemporary Africa. 2. That family has always evolved and today manifests itself in many forms such as the nuclear family, single parent (mother/father/caregiver) family, cross-generational (grandparents-grandchildren) family, same-sex (parents) family, childless family, and child-headed family. All these models of family can and must find their place in the African family and policy-making processes. 3. That these diverse forms of extended family into which members are born, married, formally or informally adopted, or invited, is the true, natural African family. 4. That extended families are communal, characterised by interdependence, and are constituted by mutual love, care and accountability, especially for their most vulnerable members. 5. That we recognise that the family has always been more than biology, both historically and in our sacred texts. 6. That all our sacred texts present the family as a unit that provides social, psychological, economic and emotional support and security to all its members, as well as a place of belonging, which is in line with the African understanding of family. 7. That the African family is grounded in the concept of ubuntu – "I am because we are"; "I relate therefore I am" – which does not imply the domination of the one by the many but entails the achievement of balance between the one and the many. Therefore, we affirm Article 18 of the African Charter on Human and Peoples Rights. 8. That it indeed takes a village to raise a child and therefore the communal nature of family, within the diversity of family systems and parental models, promotes the child's own understanding of being in community. 9. That the natural African family was attacked and undermined by colonialism, Christianization … and now is under attack from the extreme religious right; and these are, in fact, the forces from which the institution of the family requires protection."

10 In the History of Sexuality: Volume 1, Foucault describes power as repression and resistance as follows: "[…] Where there is power, there is resistance, and yet, or rather consequently, this resistance is never in a position of exteriority in relation to power" (Foucault 1990:95). Power, therefore, can be viewed as not only negative but also positive. See Grobbelaar and Breed (2016a and 2016b) – in various chapters, contributors reflect critically on how power construct the lived realities of children, their powerlessness as well as empowerment.

knowledge formations that concretises bodies and identities. Those who are repressed, stand on the margins of meaning making and resist the centre forces. In recent years, children, who are on the margins of theological meaning making, were brought into the centre by Child Theology, for example in the Child Theology Movement (CTM) (cf. Bunge 2006). Children were not regarded by theological disciplines, especially in systematic theology and ethics, as a priority (Bunge 2001:3). Child Theology was born, and children became a theological "lens through which some aspects of [God's] revelation can be seen more clearly" (White & Wilmer 2006:6). In other words, "the child is like a light that throws existing theology into new relief" (:6). Children moved from the theological margins of theological meaning making into the centre (cf. Grobbelaar 2016a:51-91).

DOING CHILD THEOLOGY FROM THE MARGINS OR CENTRE?

The movement from the margins to the centre urged Jan Grobbelaar (2016b:63-70), to pose critical questions to Child Theology that describes children as theological lenses[11], similarities with theologies of liberation[12] and the impact of Child Theology on the lived realities of children.[13] From these critical questions Grobbelaar proposed a possible shift in the epistemology and methodology of Child Theology.

For Grobbelaar (2016b:71), the epistemological change of Child Theology starts with the acknowledgement that children are sites of revelation. Grobbelaar's starting point connects Child Theology with

---

[11] "'The child' tends to become only an object or instrument, an analytical tool, a utility in the hands of adults to serve, hopefully improving and liberating, their own thinking about God and God's kingdom. In the process, children tend to become only a means to achieve a goal: a better understanding of God and God's kingdom" (Grobbelaar 2016a:65).

[12] "In liberation theology in South America it is the poor people who are doing feminist theology rather than liberation theology. In Black theology it is black oppressed people who are doing Black theology in reaction to colonialisation and some aspects of the mission history in Africa. In feminist theology it is women who are doing this type of theology to overcome gender bias in church and society. The moment one uses the concept Child Theology, it creates the impression that it is similar to other liberation theologies and is thus theology done by children" (Grobbelaar 2016a:65).

[13] "Therefore, Child Theology has to become doing theology, not just about or for children, but with and by children. As long as it is done only by adults it will tend to be only self-centred adultism" (Grobbelaar 2016:70).

CHAPTER 4

Body Theology where the body's experiences are taken seriously as "occasions of revelation" (Nelson 1992:9) which "creates theology through the body and not about the body" (Isherwood & Stuart 1998:22). The body becomes the subject of revelation through the incarnation of God in Jesus. Grobbelaar's incarnational theological approach lays bare the perceptions, bias and power of adults over and against children.

Grobbelaar's epistemological approach, from a theological perspective, I would perhaps argue, recalls the kenotic hymn in Philippians 2 in the New Testament which describes "[i]n Jesus Christ, God and humanity are united in mutual self-giving love" (Migliore 2014:186) through Jesus's self-emptying. This hymn inspires and teaches followers of Christ to follow the triune God's example of "a union … in which there is reciprocal self-limitation and total openness of each to the other" (:186). A kenotic discipleship entails a letting go of perceptions, bias and power whereby space for the other, in this case, the child, is made. Making space, ought not to be perceived as a hierarchal power structure that would still be in place when the adults 'decide' to surrender their power. Earlier, it was pointed out that power could be, through a Foucauldian lens, understood as both repression and resistance. Therefore, in the making space process, contestation will transpire through children's multiple creative ways of resistance. For this reason, Grobbelaar sees in this letting go or rather self-emptying process of adults, a space where children are doing "their own liberating theology" (2016b:76). Doing theology requires a methodology.

Methodologically, Grobbelaar proposed some of the core Contextual Bible Study (CBS) method values as outlined by South African biblical scholar Gerald O. West. Though Grobbelaar indicates that some of the values will be discussed, three other values that characterises CBS are excluded without Grobbelaar providing sound reasons why the other values like criticality, change and contestation were excluded. These values, criticality, change and contestation, are explained by West (2015) in the following way:

- "Criticality: 'analyses the self, society, and the biblical text, using a range of structured and systematic questions; [that facilitates] a critical dialogue between a critical reading of life (the first text) and a critical reading of the Bible (the second text)' (p. 239).

- Change: '… primary focus of transformation is the structural and systemic, and the … ideo-theological' (p. 240).

- Contestation: 'recognises that struggle is a key characteristic of reality, and so CBS takes sides with the God of life against the idols of death …'" (p. 241).

For West (2015:242), these core values, including community, collaboration and context, as discussed by Grobbelaar (2016b:78-82), "inhabit a collaborative nexus, captured by the six core values, between the epistemology of the poor and marginalised and the critical capacities of socially engaged biblical scholarship." Although one could argue that Grobbelaar's proposal of implantation does entail subtle nuances of criticality, change and contestation, omitting these values from the pillars of doing Child Theology create serious questions about the methodology, as proposed by Grobbelaar. Furthermore, criticality, change and contestation are part of the making-room process of a radical hospitality that sees the embodied lived experiences of children as sites of the triune God's revelation.

INTERSECTING CHILD THEOLOGY AND QUEER THEOLOGY

Child Theology, as a liberation theology, does not stand alone in reclaiming marginalised embodied experiences. In recent years, LGBTIQ+ people too had to reclaim their bodies as sites of God's revelation. Intersectional similarities exist between marginalised groups. West (2015:241) points out that in their CBS work, even though the traditional focus was on the poor, an intersectional reality began to form part of their work.[14] If Child Theology devises a methodology based on CBS's core values, intersectionality[15] will have to be taken into account. For this reason, I want to point out that sexuality and gender diversity as an intersectional reality does not feature in Child Theology. In *Children and childhood in world religions: Primary sources and texts* edited by Don Browning and Marcia Bunge (2009), as an example, the Christianity section made little mention of the sexuality and gender diversity of children, although holistic child development should be focusing on the complete well-being of children. An indicator of this theory is the decision of the Department of Basic Education to implement Comprehensive Sexual Education (CSE) in the South African school curricula.[16] However, the church (Smit 2016:15; Davids & Jones 2018:101-103) and theology (West, van der Walt & Kaoma 2016:1-2) are institutions that are dominated by patriarchal ideologies and, therefore, new insights into sexual and gender diversity must go a long way before being incorporated into the Church's teachings. The family, according to Cranny-Francis et al. (2003:13-14), is an example of patriarchal ideologies. Thatcher points out that sexual theology, in this case 'queer theology', "for all their liberatory intent, generally collude with the hiddenness of children" (2007:144). It is interesting that children are hidden in queer theology since religious conservatives use the notion of children and traditional family as strategy against LGBTIQ+ parented families.

---

14 West (2015: 241) describes the intersectional themes that they have encountered in their work as follows: "Bible reading movements, in both Brazil and South Africa, have given priority to economic dimensions of reality – because it is the primary reality of 'the poor' – there has been increasing recognition of the intersectionality of marginalisation, including class, race, gender, HIV status, disability, sexuality, etc.in our work."

15 "Intersectionality means that discrimination is both vertical and horizontal and takes place at multiple levels among various identities. Thus, racists are likely to be homophobes and sexists. Multidimensionality suggests that oppression takes place in multiple dimensions. We can be oppressed as women but also women who are lesbians" (Mutua 2011:461).

16 Cf. Department of Basic Education, 2019. Comprehensive Sexuality Education, viewed 14 November 2019, from https://www.education.gov.za/Home/ComprehensiveSexualityEducation.aspx; Department of Basic Education, clarifies comprehensive sexuality education to Portfolio Committee, viewed 14 November 2019, from https://www.gov.za/speeches/sexuality-education-portfolio-17-sep-2019-0000.

QUEER THEOLOGICAL PERSPECTIVE ON CHILD THEOLOGY

The hiddenness of children, as discussed above, is the result of value systems that hierarchically positions children. Proponents of Queer Theology like Marcella Althaus-Reid (2002, 2003) focus on sexual abuses that children endure in Latin-America, however, the embodiment of children's sexual and gender diversity are hidden. The hiddenness of children in queer theology, is a fundamental challenge to this liberative theology. In the discussion that follows, I am cognisant of the limitations of doing queer theology as an ally in the absence of LGBTIQ+ children and LGBTIQ+ parented families. However, what will be discussed, is broad contours that might consist of insights that are able to facilitate conducive theological investigations that can assist Child Theology in collaboration with LGBTIQ+ children and LGBTIQ+ parented families in hopefully various contexts to critically contest current patriarchal and heteronormative embodied experiences.

DOING QUEER THEOLOGY

Doing theology was always regarded as the privilege of a few elite heterosexual men, from developed countries. In developing countries, doing theology was subsequently modelled after the style of the developed countries. These theologies complimented the church as a heteronormative institution (Davids & Jones 2018:93). Queer theology contrary to these homogenous heteronormative theologies privilege the embodied experiences of LGBTIQ+ people. Patrick Cheng (2011) provides the following definition of Queer Theology:

> First, queer theology is [LGBTIQ+] people 'talking about God.' Second, queer theology is 'talking about God' in a self-consciously transgressive manner, especially in terms of challenging societal norms about sexuality and gender. Third, queer theology is 'talk about God' that challenges and deconstructs the natural binary categories of sexual and gender identity. (p. 9)

CHAPTER 4

West et al. (2018:4) articulate Cheng's definition that LGBTIQ+ people and their allies do theologies from their lived experiences through engaging developments in the African faith contexts. West et al. point out the following benefits:

> we must draw on other established African forms of biblical and theological hermeneutics, such as those found in inculturation, liberation, feminist/womanist, and postcolonial theologies. These theologies offer communal and systemic perspectives and resources ... Each of these overlapping and intersecting theologies seeks to interrogate the Christian faith from the perspective of the oppressed as opposed to the powerful. (p. 4)

West et al. (2018:4) state the intersectional benefit of doing queer theology by taking African faith tradition seriously. However, West et al. (:4) also point out the non-transgressive manner of "inculturation, liberation, feminist/womanist, and postcolonial theologies." These liberation theologies, Isherwood and Althaus-Reid (2004:3) remark, "have been traditionally gender- and sex-blinded", however, "much of theology has developed forms of sexual orderings into doctrinal reflection or the reading of the Scriptures" (:5). For this reason, Queer theology "takes seriously the queer project of deconstructing heterosexual epistemology and presuppositions in theology, but also unveiling the different, the suppressed face of God amidst it" (:5). Davids and Jones (2018) unveil the "suppressed face of God" by looking at the doctrine of Christology from a queer African theological perspective based on holism and ubuntu, stating:

> [f]rom a Christological perspective, holism and ubuntu finds theological meaning in the incarnation-crucifixion-resurrection of Christ. Christ's incarnation brings interdependence between human beings. (p. 116)

INTERSECTING SEXUALITY AND GENDER: FROM A QUEER TRINITARIAN PERSPECTIVE

In the doctrine of the Trinity, the interdependence that Davids and Jones speak of, is elaborated on even more. British theologian Sarah Coakley (2013:6), for example, provides a "trinitarian ontology of desire". Throughout her book, Coakley analyses Christian texts to discover how the Trinity function in prayer (:100-151) and Christian art (:190-265). Coakley's (2013:55-56) exegetical analysis of Paul's well-known exposition on prayer in Romans 8 lead her to conclude that the triune God invokes desire in human beings when our words are failing us. Thus, desire and sensuality begin in God and are known in our bodies through God's incarnation. For Jordan (2002:168), "[o]ur intimate encounters with God through prayer are erotic because they are pleasurable intimacies of creatures with bodies." Prayer according to Sigurdson (2016:438) is, therefore, "... an instruction in the art of love." Jordan (2002) argues that prayer as an art of love also sheds light on masturbation, although self-pleasure is frowned upon. Prayer also transpires in private as masturbation, however, persisting in prayer "often find [that we] are led out of this selfish insistence into generous intimacy with God and with others" (:167).[17] This intimacy of growth is for the former archbishop of the Anglican Communion, Rowan Williams, the body's grace. Williams understands desire through the doctrine of grace and argues that as human beings we discover how God desires us.[18] Thinking theologically about the

---

17 Parents were told in the 19th century how to surveillance their children. Foucault's analysis of 19th century surveillance led him to understand that this "was the sexualising of the infantile body, a sexualising of the bodily relationship between parent and child, and a sexualising of the family domain ... sexuality is far more of a positive product of power than power was ever a repression of sexuality" (1980:120). In Christianity, especially in the Catholic and Protestant tradition, masturbation is viewed as sin based on Natural Law in the case of the former and in the latter based upon the reading of Genesis 38:8-10. Thatcher (2011:185) points out: "Onan's capital offense, of course, was his failure to perform his duty, under the law of Levirate marriage (Deut. 25:5–10), to provide children for his dead brother and his dead brother's wife. He was practicing the earliest known form of contraception".

18 "Grace, for the Christian believer, is a transformation that depends in large part on knowing yourself to be seen in a certain way; as significant, as wanted. The whole story of creation, incarnation, and our incorporation into the fellowship of Christ's body tells us that God desires us, as if we were God, as if we

CHAPTER 4

sexuality of LGBTIQ+ children and LGBTIQ+ parented families to experience their bodies grace and contest the rigid hold of biological reproduction as the only criterion for sexuality is an act of justice.

Marcella Althaus-Reid (2003), a bisexual, liberation theologian from Latin-America, proposed a more radical understanding of the Trinity pertaining to sexuality and gender. In the *Queer God* (2003), Althaus-Reid argues that the doctrine of the Trinity could be understood as gender-fluid and God as a polymerous Being. This analogy of Trinity is a critique against heteronormativity and monogamy (2003:52-58). In the current state, Althaus-Reid (:58) points out, the Trinity is nothing else than a "restricted polyfidelity". Althaus-Reid's theological reconceiving of the Trinity strikes a chord with Thatcher's (2007) discussion of two influential figures' understanding of the Trinity as analogy for children and family. Analysing theological texts of the Swiss Reformed theologian Karl Barth and the late pope John Paul II, Thatcher (:88-94) concludes that both Barth's and the Pope's theological premise is entrenched with masculine bias and excludes same-sex relations and gender diverse identities from communion. Thus, Althaus-Reid's queer theological understanding of the Trinity as gender-neutral, non-sexed, but as an example of mutual indwelling, reciprocity and love, ought to constitute the relations and the identities of human beings, especially in this case of LGBTIQ+ children and LGBTIQ+ parented families.

The Trinity, therefore, consists of a fundamental reconceiving of sexuality and gender, moreover of family from an *Imago Trinitatis* perspective. If human beings are created in the Image of the triune God, does this mean that masculinity and femininity could be found in God? According to Miroslav Volf (2003), we project masculinity and femininity onto God through our human language. Volf (:169), for this reason argues that the Trinity "serves as a model for how the content of 'masculinity' and 'femininity' ought to be negotiated in the social process." The Trinity for Volf (:169) is an example of the self-giving

---

were that unconditional response to God's giving that God's self makes in the life of the Trinity. We are created so that we may be caught up in this, so that we may grow into the wholehearted love of God by learning that God loves us as God loves God" (Williams 2002:311–312).

love and mutual indwelling of the three persons in one another. In the Trinity, there is no hierarchical ordering of the persons, for the Trinity as a model rather shows how equality between human beings can be embodied (Volf 2003:164-169). The Trinity as a radical model of equality "is an eternal dance, a perichoresis of grace" (Stuart 2007:72). This understanding of the Trinity as dance and grace leads Stuart (:72) to conclude that sexual and gender identities will eventually cease and that our baptismal identity is the one identity that will never cease.[19]

When sex, gender and sexuality of LGBTIQ+ children and LGBTIQ+ parented families are reconceived from a trinitarian perspective, heteronormativity that places a high premise on reproduction and bloodlines cannot and may not water down theological reconceiving by toxic doctrines of exclusion, prejudice and bias.

CONCLUSION

LGBTIQ+ children and LGBTIQ+ parented families ought to form part of doing Child Theology. As indicated in the introduction earlier, the shortcoming of this chapter is the lack of the voices of LGBTIQ+ children and LBGTIQ+ parented families that ought to speak on their own behalf. As an ally, I hope this chapter will stimulate robust discussion that leads to justice for LGBTIQ+ children and LGBTIQ+ parented families in theological discourse.

Bearing in mind that culture and colonial history rests firmly in institutional practices of our continent, West (2019:57-79) argues convincingly though that all CBS core values contribute to a process

---

19 "The church is the only community under a direct mandate to be queer, and it is only within the church that queer theory reaches its telos, with the melancholia of gender replaced by the joy born of the death and resurrection of Christ – into which the Christian is incorporated through baptism – and the delight of sacramental growth, whereby the Christian is conformed more and more closely to the body of Christ – which parodies and subverts all culturally constructed identities. Queer flesh is sacramental flesh nudging the queer performer towards the Christian eschatological horizon and sacramental flesh is queer flesh nudging the Christian towards the realization that in Christ maleness and femaleness and gay and straight are categories that dissolve before the throne of grace where only the garment of baptism remains" (Stuart 2007:75).

that empowers ordinary readers to interpret the text. Biblical texts usually used to discriminate against sexual and gender diverse bodies, could be read in a liberating manner.

The reconceiving of Child Theology from a queer theological perspective ought to remind us that we are created in the Image of the Trinity. The createdness of LGBTIQ+ children and LGBTIQ+ parented families in the Image of the Trinity, paves the way for theological imagination that can contribute to responses of justice by the Christian church in Africa.

CHAPTER 5

THE STIGMATISATION OF CHILDREN LIVING WITH FASD AND THEIR BIOLOGICAL MOTHERS

Leana Olivier, Lian-Marie Drotsky and Jaco Louw

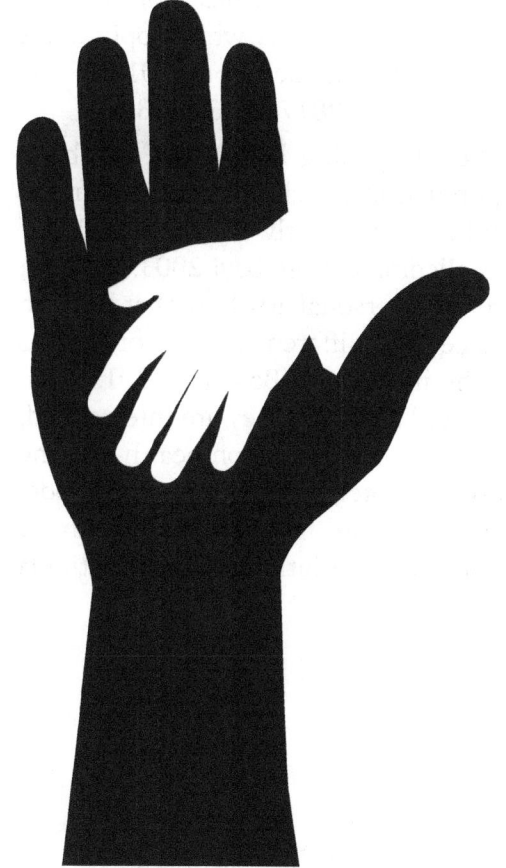

INTRODUCTION

The harmful consequences of alcohol exposure in utero are the most common cause of preventable intellectual disability (Gibbard, Wass, and Clarke 2003:72-76). It can lead to various sequelae collectively referred to as Fetal Alcohol Spectrum Disorders (FASDs). These disorders are directly linked to the negative health behaviour of alcohol consumption during pregnancy (Riley et al. 2011:73-80). Ideally it should, therefore, be preventable through positive health behaviour.

Alcohol exposure is not the only risky health behaviour that can have negative impacts on children during pregnancy and afterwards. Many of these dangers, including FASD, can be minimised and managed if a mother, father or caregiver is willing to search out assistance from healthcare providers or other professionals. There are, however, significant barriers in the way of this kind of help-seeking behaviour. Frequently, there are no services available, or the parents/caregivers cannot access these services due to practical, logistical or financial reasons. There are also personal reasons why people don't seek help, with a major reason being stigma (Bell et al. 2016:65-77; Choate & Badry 2019:36-52; Corrigan et al. 2017:1166-1173).

The impact of stigma on health-seeking behaviours has been demonstrated in a number of populations, including South African populations. However, these studies have mostly focussed on HIV/AIDS (Day et al. 2003:665-672; Kalichman & Simbayi 2003:442-447; Meiberg et al. 2008:49-54). Stigma is a personal attribute that leads to an individual being devalued and seen as different to the norm. This leads to negative perceptions of the individual (Bos et al. 2013:1-9). There are various forms of stigma, and although they are interrelated, they can have different antecedents and can impact on health-seeking behaviours in different ways. In this chapter, we will refer to a model that breaks down stigma into four separate manifestations, namely self-stigma, structural stigma, stigma by association and public stigma (Bos et al. 2013:1-9).

We will be looking at how children and women experience and perceive stigma in various contexts. To date, and to our knowledge, there have been no studies in the South African context looking at stigma associated with alcohol use during pregnancy. This chapter, therefore, looks at the qualitative experience of women in communities with high FASD prevalence rates (Olivier 2017). When it comes to FASD, it is not only the mothers who experience stigma with regard to their health and psycho-social behaviours. Children born with FASD are also stigmatised based on their disabilities. We will highlight the impact of the various types of stigma on them as well. It is important that the observations made here are taken further and used as the basis for thorough research on the impact of stigma on FASD prevention efforts.

In reading this chapter it is important to take cognisance of two important facts. In the first place, we admit that in the chapter there is much focus on FARR's work. This focus is necessary to understand the context of the data used in this chapter. As the data was gathered during an intervention by FARR's staff, the reader needs to be aware of the details of said intervention so that they can bear possible sources of bias in mind. These are not interviews conducted with a random sample of participants.

In the second place, the method and focus of the chapter are tied to the data available from the South African context to interrogate. In this case, only data on the mother's lived experiences are available. We admit that children's experiences cannot be understood only as derivative from adults' experiences and that they are part of a bigger system of influences. But, it is also true that the impact of stigma on children cannot be divorced from the impact on their mothers. Therefore, some interferences can be made from the available data about the mothers' experiences. It is important that the observations made in this chapter are taken further and used as the basis for thorough research on the impact of stigma on FASD prevention efforts. Further research into this area is necessary so that more in depth data from children's experience can be obtained.

FETAL ALCOHOL SPECTRUM DISORDER (FASD)

Prenatal alcohol exposure, even in small to moderate amounts, can cause a myriad of adverse pregnancy outcomes ranging from pregnancy losses, preterm labour, still births, neonatal and infant deaths, including Sudden Infant Death Syndrome (SIDS), pre- and postnatal growth retardation and FASD (Grinfeld 2009:179-200; Jones & Smith 1973:999-1001; Jones et al. 1973:1267-1271; Odendaal et al. 2009:1-8; Ornoy & Ergaz 2010:364-379).

The term FASD is used to describe a range of birth disorders, such as Fetal Alcohol Syndrome (FAS), Alcohol-Related Neurodevelopmental Disorders (ARND), Alcohol-Related Birth Defects (ARBD) and Partial Fetal Alcohol Syndrome (pFAS) (Hoyme et al. 2016:1-18). Neurobehavioural Disorder Prenatal Alcohol Exposed, is a psychological diagnostic category, separate from FASD (ND-PAE) and listed in the DSM-5 (Harris 2014:95-97). People with FASD present with varied degrees of cognitive impairment manifesting as life-long learning and behavioural problems, and can also have physical birth defects.

The first FASD studies in South Africa (1997-2001) were undertaken amongst farm workers in a rural, viticulture area in the Western Cape Province (Croxford & Viljoen 1999:962-965; May et al. 2000:1905-1912). The research results and findings were widely published in the lay media leading to the myth that farm workers, especially in wine producing areas, are at specific risk of having children with FASD. It was furthermore linked to the 'dop-system', whereby farm workers were partially paid with food, tobacco and wine (Olivier 2017:13-243). Despite numerous subsequent studies, reporting higher rates in non-viticulture areas and even cities, the misconception remains. It has furthermore led to significant stigmatisation of the condition and perpetuates the belief that others from different cultural and income groups are not at risk of having alcohol exposed pregnancies and children with FASD (Olivier, Curfs & Viljoen 2016:S103-S106).

CHAPTER 5

In a country with the highest reported FASD rates in the world (Popova et al. 2017:e290-e299; Roozen et al. 2016:18-32), this stigmatisation has had a severe impact on service rendering and health-seeking behaviour. With rates ranging between 27 to 282 per 1 000 (Olivier 2017:13–243), the true scale of the epidemic in the country is most probably higher and the urgency for prevention and early intervention therefore dire. Stigmatising the condition, in whatever way, is severely detrimental to prevention, adequate service delivery, help-seeking behaviour and management.

STIGMA AND FASD

Self-stigma happens when an individual internalises the negative stereotypes associated with their perceived negative attributes. This feeds into the fear of being exposed when seeking help (Bos et al. 2013:1-9). This has been shown to be especially relevant in the field of substance abuse, and is a significant barrier to seeking treatment (Hammarlund et al. 2018:115-136; Santos et al. 2016:1-16). Self-stigma also erodes the individual's sense of self-efficacy, one of the key determinants of whether behaviour change will be successful (Orji, Vassileva & Mandryk 2012:40-41).

Even in children with severe disabilities there can still be an awareness that they are different than their peers. This is reinforced by their difficulty in making and maintaining friendships (Sanders & Buck 2010:e308-e322). Mood disorders are also frequently co-morbid with FASD and can reflect low self-image, again possibly exacerbated by self-stigma (Gibbard et al. 2003:72-76).

Structural stigma refers to how stigma towards groups becomes entrenched in societies, institutions and ideology (Bos et al. 2013:1-9). This can be seen when individuals that are stigmatised are treated differently when they access services or ask for assistance. It is also reflected in the discourse around the stigmatised behaviour. Seeking help requires that a person reveals the fact that they have the attribute that is stigmatised (Cockroft et al. 2019:1-8). This also means that they need to put themselves in the vulnerable position of possibly being stigmatised due to the revelation. They may, therefore, opt to rather protect themselves than to seek help (Meiberg et al. 2008:49-54). This is especially problematic when the public discourse becomes punitive towards those struggling with substance use. With regard to FASD, calls for the incarceration of women have been particularly damaging (Choate et al. 2019:36-52; Pietro et al. 2016:726-732; Reporter 2018).

The future of children with FASD is frequently viewed as bleak and hopeless (Watson et al. 2013:76-93). These beliefs can impact on the amount of effort expended on their schooling and learning. Where these children remain in mainstream schools, they may be seen as lost cases. The system can, therefore, give up due to the label of FASD and not the actual profile of the child which has been shown to be amenable to interventions (Peadon et al. 2009:1-9; Pei & Kerns 2012:308-311).

Stigma by association refers to how those close to the stigmatised person are judged and it also refers to how people close to the stigmatised person feels about being associated with them (Bos et al. 2013:1-9). Stigma by association can erode the support structure of individuals seeking help. It can strain personal relationships and lead to problematic behaviours being hidden from view (Corrigan, Watson & Miller 2006:239-246; Van der Sanden et al. 2013:73-80).

Public stigma refers to the social and psychological reactions people have towards stigmatised individuals. Two factors associated with public stigma that are particularly important in terms of alcohol consumption during pregnancy, are perceptions of norm violation and perceived controllability of the condition's onset (Bos et al. 2013:1-9). The norm against which pregnant women are judged is one of protecting the unborn baby and ensuring their healthy birth. Exposing a fetus to a harmful substance is, therefore, a serious violation of this norm. When it comes to substance use, the perception is that the onset of substance use and substance use disorder can be attributed to the sufferer and is under the control of the sufferer (Yang et al. 2017:378-388). This leads to the perception that substance use during pregnancy is an active choice and the blame can, therefore, be laid at the mothers' feet, leading to stigmatisation. It is partly due to the fear of this perception that health-seeking behaviours are avoided and delayed.

There are unfortunately very negative narratives regarding individuals with FASD and the danger they pose to society. Even though some of the secondary disabilities associated with FASD includes conflict with the law (Brown et al. 2018:13-19), this is frequently sensationalised leading to statements like: "The nation's prisons are home to an untold number of convicted killers whose brains were damaged in utero when their mothers drank!" (FASfacts n.d.). This feeds into a narrative of children with FASD being dangerous and unpredictable, further alienating them and their caregivers (Watson et al. 2013:76-93).

It should be a priority to avoid having children born with FASD. However, where this is not possible, one should follow the principles of harm reduction. For this to be possible, we must be able to identify at-risk mothers and we need to be able to reach children already affected. Neither of these two goals will be reachable if we do not combat stigma. If a woman has a substance abuse problem and becomes pregnant, stigma can prevent her from reaching out and receiving effective antenatal care and assistance to cut down on or stop using alcohol. Effective interventions exist that can make a difference at this stage of a child's development.

If, on the other hand, a child has been born with FASD, there are interventions and support programmes that can improve on their life outcomes in terms of health and development. For these to be effective, the problems have to be identified as early as possible and assistance should be given as early as possible. The fear of stigma may prevent parents and caregivers from acknowledging concerns and make them hesitant to access services.

Tackling stigma surrounding the future prospects of children with FASD can help them better integrate into society. Putting them in a more sympathetic light can help build support networks around them and improve their life outcomes. Failing to do so, relegates them to the fringes of society and makes the idea that there is no hope for them a self-fulfilling prophesy.

FASD STIGMA IN THE SOUTH AFRICAN CONTEXT

Stigma is closely tied to public perceptions of behaviour. If a behaviour has been normalised, it is less likely to be stigmatised. South Africa has a particularly high per-capita level of alcohol consumption and a high prevalence of high-risk drinking behaviour (World Health Organization 2018). It is, therefore, not a given that the same stigma surrounds alcohol use, and as knowledge of FASD is not universal, it is similarly possible that the stigma against drinking during pregnancy is not as prevalent.

OBSERVATIONS AT THE FOUNDATION FOR ALCOHOL RELATED RESEARCH (FARR)

The Foundation for Alcohol Related Research (FARR) is an NPO focused on decreasing the prevalence of FASD through comprehensive awareness and intervention programmes. As part of our efforts, we have worked in five of the nine South African provinces. We, therefore, have access to communities where the prevalence of FASD was determined and where some level of awareness regarding FASD has been established. In all our project sites in these provinces, we are conducting research and implementing an evidence-based prevention programme, the Healthy Mother Healthy Baby© (HMHB©) Programme (Olivier 2017). In this brief motivational interviewing and support programme, pregnant women receive information, support and guidance to facilitate informed decision making in terms of health and psycho-social behaviours as to ensure healthier pregnancies and healthier babies. To alleviate stigmatisation, women are enrolled irrespective of their alcohol use.

At one of these project sites, in a study on parenting of children with FASD (Drotsky 2019:1-126), qualitative interviews provided rich information on parenting and on the experience of being a biological mother or caregiver of a child with FASD. Information obtained from these mothers, caregivers, as well as the Project Coordinators of the HMHB© Programme is shared below. Lastly, perceptions of FASD and prenatal alcohol use of participants in FARR's training sessions are also shared below.

CONTEXT OF STUDY POPULATION

In South Africa, unemployment rates as high as 80% are reported in some communities with up to 70% of inhabitants living below the poverty line (Stassen 2012). There are numerous financial, social and emotional pressures exerted on most households. This frequently leads to alcohol abuse and high levels of FASD (Olivier 2017:13-243; Stassen 2012; Urban et al. 2008:877-882). Often the main source of income in these households comes from South African Social Security Agency (SASSA) grants. These include child-care grants, old age pensions and disability grants.

Education is often limited in these communities and less than 65% of mothers of children with FASD have secondary schooling. Depression is common amongst women, with 30% of women presenting with severe depression (Davies et al. 2011:298-305). The combination of poor domestic life and low educational level results in a loss of hope with devastating impact on issues, such as school dropout rates, crime and substance abuse.

Mothering children with disabilities requires unique child-care practices filled with paradox (Bourke-Taylor, Howie & Law 2010:127-136). Mothers are often torn between others' opinions about their children's abilities and their own hopes for a miracle and progress. The mother has to embrace her child in spite of challenges associated with the disability (Larson 1998:865-875). This paradox may be aggravated for the mothers of children with FASD who also face public stigma, struggle with feelings of guilt and self-stigma.

THE EXPERIENCE OF THE BIOLOGICAL MOTHER OF THE CHILD WITH FASD
SELF-STIGMA

Zelda[1] joined the HMHB© Programme, during the last trimester of her pregnancy in 2010. At the time, she was alcohol dependent and worked hard to cut down on her alcohol consumption. At nine months her son was diagnosed with FAS. Zelda took her son to an early childhood stimulation group, offered by FARR, until he was three years old. For a number of years, while married to a much older, sickly man whom she cared for during most of their marriage, she was able to stop drinking. After his death she lost her secure home, becoming alcohol dependent again. During an interview in 2018, when her son was eight years old, she became tearful in her remorse for the damage she caused. When asked why she was sad, she stated: "My child is slow and could have been different if I did not use alcohol, but at the time of my pregnancy we knew so little about FAS." Zelda's sense of self-stigma seems to erode the sense of self-efficacy needed to change her drinking behaviour in the long term.

STRUCTURAL STIGMA

Women who are drinking are often threatened by service providers that their children will be removed from their care. Such removals are not uncommon in the communities where FARR works. Merely removing a child from the biological mother does not necessarily lead to behaviour change in the woman. Alcohol-dependant women, who are unable to abstain or cut down on drinking, often respond to this with their own fatalistic threat that they will then just produce another child. This narrative disempowers women with substance abuse problems and does not help to prevent children being born with FASD.

Service providers often become frustrated when they cannot change pregnant women's drinking behaviour and project these

---

1 Aliases are used to protect participants' identities.

frustrations on the very people they try to help. Health care workers commented in a recent focus group on FASD and stigma that "I want to strangle her", and "she should be locked up". Following a discussion, these health care workers recognised that such an attitude may be the reason why some pregnant women avoid them and their service completely.

STIGMA BY ASSOCIATION

The HMHB© programme described earlier, offers information, support and guidance for healthier pregnancies and healthier babies. In some cases, stigma by association becomes a barrier in the recruitment of clients. Zandi chose not to join the programme which she associated with women who use alcohol, because she did not drink any alcohol. After being diagnosed with HIV, also associated with stigma, she was unable to share her burden with anyone. The only way she could cope was by drinking alcohol to relieve her anxiety. When a community worker again invited her to join the HBMB© Programme, she joined. Although she was now much further along in her pregnancy, the support she received, did help her to abstain from alcohol for the rest of her pregnancy and she found alternative ways to manage her stress.

Even though Zandi herself exhibited stigmatised behaviour, the thought of being associated with those already stigmatised and others' perception, prevented her from seeking support for a long time.

PUBLIC STIGMA

Public stigma may be expressed in a variety of ways by various people including the partners of pregnant women. While raising FASD awareness on International FASD-Day (9 September) in a small community, on one of the project sites, FARR discussed the role of the partner in preventing FASD, with male partners in the community. A number of the men reacted by blaming the women for "drinking way too much". According to the men, for fear of conflict and domestic violence, the topic of alcohol abuse by the women was not discussed in their relationships. Education is needed to shift this view of blaming to one of collective responsibility where men lead by example, support pregnant partners, and select a partner who does not drink as the mother of their future child.

EXPERIENCE OF THE CHILD WITH FASD
SELF-STIGMA

Some children with learning challenges, avoided tasks by saying "I cannot" during intervention sessions with FARR's occupational therapist. These children seemed to have internalised the feedback from parents, educators and their peers to such an extent that they chose avoidance rather than experiencing another failure. In the South African inclusive educational system, children with FASD regularly experience failure of the curriculum's standards, resulting in a pattern of self-stigmatisation. This lack of explorative play has even been observed in pre-schoolers. When the same tasks were broken down into manageable steps and presented in a playful manner, children often surprised with their abilities.

STRUCTURAL STIGMA

During training offered by FARR, educators often blame mothers of children with FASD for being 'irresponsible' and 'damaging their innocent children'. They express hopeless frustration in the educational situation, referring to children as 'lost cases.'

After obtaining information about FASD and discussing myths, such as 'women choose to drink', 'children with FASD cannot learn' and 'people with FASD are violent and criminals', facts are put into perspective and lead to better insight and empathy.

CHAPTER 5

STIGMA BY ASSOCIATION

Where project funding allows, FARR offers support and/or intervention for children with developmental delays including FASD. In some cases, however, children with FASD avoid these programmes because they do not want to be associated with the 'dull' children. As one child put it: "FARR's children are dull. So, FARR is saying I am dull [by inviting me to their programme]."

PUBLIC STIGMA

Marie (aged 59) is a widow whose 23-year old biological daughter Filida was diagnosed with FAS when she was in Grade 1. Marie used alcohol during her pregnancy to cope with domestic violence. She was unaware of the harmful effect of alcohol. She described this time during an interview in 2018:

> I had a heavy battle with my husband. He humiliated me in public and even attacked me physically with a spade or anything he could lay his hands on. He always made sure he got me drunk first, because I could not defend myself when I was drunk.

Marie's daughter, Filida, was born prematurely and struggled for survival. After her birth, Marie stopped drinking and embraced the challenge of raising her daughter who had significant health problems. Marie stated:

> She was tiny, her body fit into my hands. One couldn't hear her crying, because she had no voice … only her tears flowing. So, I decided to pull myself together and stop drinking because she needed me.

Children with FASD often find it difficult to form and maintain friendships and can present with anxiety and depression (Gibbard et al. 2003:72-76; Sanders & Buck 2010:e308-e322). According to Marie,

Filida found school challenging and was often teased that she could not read, write or remember like her peers. She was aware of being different to her peers (self-stigma) and struggled to make and keep friends. Eventually she became so anxious and depressed at school that she dropped out.

Children with FASD are often perceived as being 'different' and are, therefore, bullied and/or humiliated by their peers and others. Marie explained how children teased her daughter for her learning challenges. She explained how she tried to comfort her child and how, with patience, she managed to teach her child to read and write functionally. She expressed her dream to support her child to 'become a success'.

Due to the public perception that children with FASD are 'dull', parents might decide not to seek the help that is on offer. One woman explained her reluctance to share her child's FASD diagnosis with anybody since she feared the effect and backlash on her daughter. She felt that the community might tease her and that she will be excluded from opportunities.

PERSPECTIVES OF FARR PROJECT COORDINATORS

Based on reports from project coordinators responsible for the implementation of the HMHB© Programme, it appears as if there is more stigmatisation in areas with very high levels of alcohol abuse and FASD. In these areas, participation in the HMHB© programme is seen as an indication that the pregnant woman might be a 'drinker'. In areas where there is a lower prevalence of alcohol abuse and FASD, it seems as if the community realises the benefits of the programme in terms of the health outcomes for mothers and babies. Of note is that the communities where the stigmatisation seems to be more prevalent are also the communities where the educational levels are lower and the unemployment and poverty levels are higher. This shows the risk stigma poses to intervention programmes and the value of including individuals not displaying the stigmatised behaviour.

In a number of the project areas, especially in areas where FARR has been operational for a couple of years, it seems as if the communities have grasped the importance and need for support for pregnant women and they, therefore, do not stigmatise participation. In some communities, alcohol abuse is so common that prenatal alcohol use may not appear to be of any concern. The prevalence of stigma varies greatly. Some community members 'with higher educational qualifications' have less empathy for pregnant women who are using alcohol. This is also the case in smaller communities with strong cohesion and pride.

On investigation, it seems as if stigmatisation of children living with FASD differs from community to community based on aspects, such as those mentioned above. In communities with higher educational levels, strong cohesion and knowledge about FASD (especially where FARR has been operational for a number of years) there is empathy towards the needs of the children, but also a strong push against children being born with FASD in the area. This sometimes aggravates stigmatisation. In areas with less knowledge and insight into the challenges pertaining to FASD, the communities seem to be unaware of the consequences and, therefore, do not stigmatise the children.

IMPLICATIONS FOR THE SOUTH AFRICAN CONTEXT
STIGMA AND INTERVENTION PROGRAMMES

In our sample, women were less likely to report feeling stigmatised for drinking behaviour. The general awareness about drinking during pregnancy and the dangers thereof did not necessarily translate into stigma. We are in the position of being able to capitalise on the lack of stigma and to work on preventing stigma from being established. An example of how this can be done is the HMHB© programme run by FARR (Olivier 2017:13-243).

Where women are not afraid of stigma, it is possible to recruit them, even in public settings, to take part in interventions. This is supported by not only recruiting mothers at risk of FASD births. Including the intervention into a general programme makes it impossible to attach the stigmatised behaviour to an individual with certainty. The training given to the individuals running the interventions emphasises a non-judgemental and safe environment. It is a foundational principal that all mothers are treated with respect and care, regardless of health behaviours. The importance of this cannot be overstated as, even though it appears to be less prevalent, there is still some stigma towards women with substance use problems and who drink during pregnancy. The insights from the FARR community workers and project managers show that there are women who avoid the programmes out of shame or fear.

CHILDREN AND STRUCTURAL STIGMA

Of the various forms of stigma experienced by children, structural stigma poses the biggest threat to long-term life outcomes. If the structures in the fields of education and social work pre-emptively identify them as possible criminals or as children with no hope for development, they are in effect being primed for exactly those outcomes. Part of FARR's intervention and prevention strategies include comprehensive training for professionals. In these training sessions, it is emphasised how our preconceived ideas about life outcomes must be challenged. It is possible to inculcate a sense of hope in teachers and allied professionals, and that has the potential to turn the narrative around.

DISCUSSION

Based on the literature, it was expected that mothers who used alcohol during pregnancy will be severely stigmatised. Our sample sometimes differed from this expectation since it seems as if stigmatisation was closely linked to the communities' level of knowledge and insight in terms of the harmful effects or prenatal alcohol use and the consequences of FASD. It appeared that in some communities, aspects such as unemployment, poverty and high levels of alcohol abuse in the general population masked the effects of having children with FASD. In communities with strong cohesion, described as 'proud' communities and in areas where a high value was placed on pregnancy and child well-being, women were more inclined to seek support for assistance during pregnancy.

In terms of children with FASD, it was expected that they would be seen as a burden on the community, resources and economy. In our context, it appeared as if this was the case in communities with higher levels of knowledge and insight into FASD and also in areas where the educational level and socio-economic status of the community was higher. Children were labelled as being 'dull'. In the others, there seemed to be a careless attitude towards children with FASD. This might, however, purely be because these communities are still unaware of the impact of FASD or because they are pre-occupied with daily struggles of basic survival.

This also highlights the questionable utility of diagnostic labels. As we see, the stigma associated with FASD can have a significantly negative impact on children. The ethical question must, therefore, be asked whether it is desirable to have diagnoses made in all cases. This is of specific importance when there are no, or limited resources, for FASD support and/or services. In cases like this, having a diagnosis with no access to services will not benefit the child or mother. By diagnosing a child with FASD, the family, especially the biological mother, is also implicated. The ripple effect thereof might even encompass the other siblings who could then also be under suspicion of having been affected.

It furthermore raises the concern regarding FASD prevalence studies and the publication of research results and rates. Although FASD prevalence rates alert governments and service providers to the existing problem and the extent thereof, especially in high-risk areas needing more resources and support, it can also stigmatise communities. In the past, it was acceptable to identify communities and rates in publications. With increased concern regarding stigmatisation, the current trend is to steer away from naming specific communities.

This unfortunately has a negative impact on the lobbying for resources in areas with very specific needs.

In a country facing the consequences of prenatal alcohol exposure, the need for evidence-based awareness programmes is obvious, but it is essential to acknowledge the double-edged sword aspect of these interventions as mentioned in the surveys above. At some stage, the level of community awareness regarding the link between prenatal alcohol use and the child born with FASD, inevitably leads to the blaming and stigmatisation of the biological mothers. These assumptions ignore other factors that can play a role in alcohol exposure like late recognition of pregnancy, lack of family planning (May et al. 2014:855-866) and unrealistic optimism with regard to the impact of alcohol on the fetus (Louw, Tomlinson & Olivier 2017: 212-229).

If FASD prevalence studies and awareness programmes are implemented without any prevention programmes, as well as lobbying for improved service delivery and a whole-of-society approach in terms of support to women of childbearing age and those already affected, the risk of doing more harm than good is evident. From FARR's experience, it appears as if the level of knowledge of the harmful effects of prenatal alcohol exposure and FASD in a community is coupled with the tendency to stigmatise and blame. With the implementation of evidence programmes and involvement of partners, family members, friends and service providers, the blaming and shaming should ideally be overtaken by a sense of collective responsibility towards the support of women of childbearing age, safe and alcohol-free pregnancies so as to ultimately result in the birth of FASD-free children.

As awareness regarding FASD increases, more government departments and non-governmental organisations are becoming involved in combating FASD. As we have shown, the danger exists that through confrontational language and policies and even the possible criminalisation of mothers, public and structural stigma is increasing. It is troubling that those in positions of power fall victim to the idea that punitive measures can make a positive impact while ignoring the best practice guidelines on improving health behaviours.

The responsibility to prevent this and to change the course of the current narrative falls on all parties involved in FASD prevention. As part of FARR's development, we have re-evaluated our messaging and use of language. Stigmatising messages and language can be subtle and South Africa is lagging behind the international community in acknowledging and condemning this.

These aspects highlight the need for research focused specifically on the South African context.

RECOMMENDATIONS

As indicated, little is known about the stigmatisation of children living with FASD and their biological mothers within the South African context. Surveys and reports from participants in existing programmes indicate considerable differences between communities. Reasons for this can only be speculative until research provides the empirical findings. As to facilitate improved prevention and care, research pertaining to the impact of stigmatisation on help seeking behaviour and utilisation of existing services is essential.

Experience indicates that essential components of service delivery include a non-judgemental service in a safe environment where the focus is not only on the women of childbearing age, but also extends to include her partner, family and friends. To adequately prevent children from being born with FASD, a whole–of–society approach is needed where all members of society embrace the concept of collectively protecting and caring for its off-spring. The African proverb 'You need a village to raise a child', can be adapted to 'You need a village to protect a child from being born with FASD'.

CONCLUSION

In South Africa, numerous children are affected by FASD and they face long-term difficulties because of it. It is, however, possible to make a significant difference in both the prevalence of FASD and in the life outcomes of those with FASD. However, the various forms of stigma are blocking the way. We have shown what some of the negative outcomes of stigma can be, and we have given a glimpse of how women in our country experience this. More importantly, we have also shown how this can be combated. It is up to all interested parties to reject stigmatising language and behaviours. Out of a sense of righteous indignation, we are preventing those who need help from seeking it, and we are putting those with FASD at even more risk of negative life outcomes. This cannot remain and we must have the courage to stand up to all spheres of society, both government and civil society, when they harm intervention efforts through stigma.

CHAPTER 6

MALE INITIATION AND CIRCUMCISION – A SOUTH AFRICAN PERSPECTIVE

Chris Jones

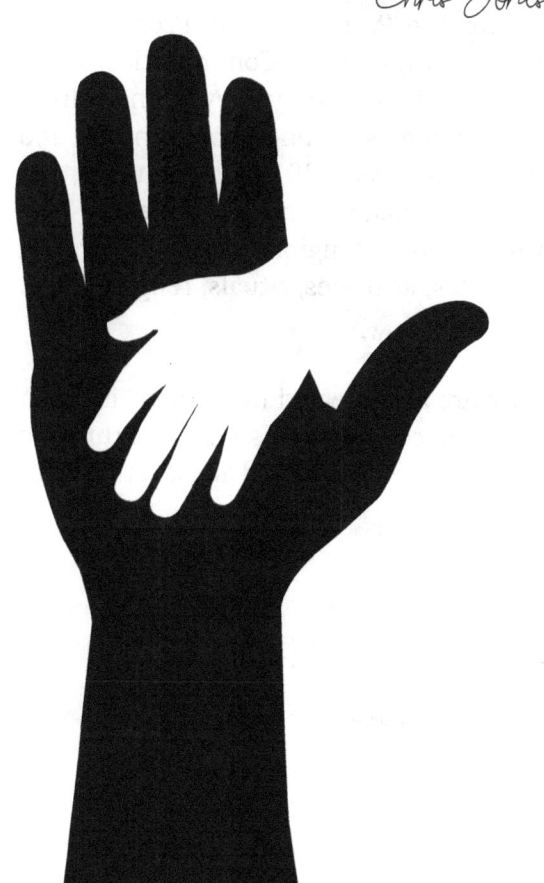

CHILDHOOD VULNERABILITIES IN SOUTH AFRICA: SOME ETHICAL PERSPECTIVES

INTRODUCTION

I have been interested in and following this rite of passage for a long time, knowing that it creates contexts and opportunities within which children can be extremely vulnerable[1]. On top of this, so many responsible individuals and institutions have been relatively quiet – especially since the dawn of our new democracy (1994) in South Africa – about botched circumcisions, dehydration, infections and the annual loss of lives during this ritual. This chapter does not rely on statistical and other data as its primary resource, which would be a typical social science approach, followed by a number of chapters in this book, but rather on presenting important views and contributions by mostly African people and scholars who are/were in different ways involved in this ritual, with its accompanying culture. The role of religion in this ritual will not be discussed. I will often refer to the significant report on public hearings on male initiation schools in South Africa, published by the Commission for the Protection and Promotion of the Rights of Cultural, Religious and Linguistic Communities[2] (CRL Rights Commission)[3]. In their executive summary, they define culture as "the totality of human creation and expression in both tangible and intangible forms" (CRL Rights Commission 2014:5). For them, the tangible forms of culture "include all material products created by a society as a result of human ingenuity. Intangibles comprise, among other things, language, beliefs, tastes, attitudes, rituals, religion" (:5). They further state that these

> intangible forms of culture are also created by humans in order to facilitate their individual and collective existence. Culture and cultural products are constantly being changed and altered. They

---

1 The author of this chapter did not experience this ritual of circumcision and initiation first hand.

2 Read more about the Commission's partners, how they view certain concepts, factors influencing male initiation, and what they recommend in their Report on public hearings on male initiation schools in South Africa, 2010, pp. 2-76.

3 This abbreviation will be used for all references to the resources of this Commission.

are handed over from generation to generation. Cultures are never static. (p. 5)

They are "dynamic realities which are in constant flux. Cultures diffuse and also absorb influences and traits from other cultures" (CRL Rights Commission 2014:5). It is reasoned by this Commission that "it is cultures which distinguish us from the rest of the animal kingdom. Cultures create humans, as humans create cultures" (:5). According to them "cultural rights, that is the right to live and practice one's culture without infringing on the rights of others" are today "acknowledged as a global human right, and enshrined in international human rights instruments" (:5).

Initiation practices occur in many cultures. They (CRL Rights Commission 2014)

come in many forms and institutional expressions. They are historical indicators used by human communities to mark the transit from one stage of life to another. It is in fact a rite of passage acknowledging the induction of an individual or individuals into a group or society. In a sense it recognises a social rebirth for the individual or individuals. The group into which the induction is made could be an open society or a secret society. Initiation rites are sometimes secret ceremonies with degrees of esotericism. (p. 5)

There are numerous universal examples of initiation such as Christian baptism and Jewish *bar mitzvah*. Puberty rites, common to some cultures, are another important set of initiation and attendant rites. These rites of puberty bear witness or testify to the transition from the state of being a child to adolescence and adulthood in some cases. Furthermore, shamans (witch-doctors or priests claiming to communicate with gods) or healers are initiated into their profession in many indigenous cultures throughout the world. These processes of initiation often involve specific rituals and rites of passage that (publicly) make known the advent of the new status of the individual involved. Male circumcision is, in many cases, a critical part of the initiation process. However, it may be an entirely separate practice in some cultures and societies (CRL Rights Commission 2014:5).

In South Africa (CRL Rights Commission 2014)

> male initiation is traditionally used as a transitional rite of passage from boyhood to manhood, conferring on the person the right to participate in the decision-making processes of the clan and the family; to share in the privileges, duties and responsibilities of the community and, in many instances, to marry a woman and raise a family. (p. 5-6)

Initiates may be as young as nine years old in some northern parts of Southern Africa (among the Venda, Pedi and Tsonga cultures). In these cases, the boy, however, is not expected to undergo additional rites before he eventually gets married. Furthermore, male initiation may parallel female initiation[4] as a rite of passage either from childhood to adolescence or from adolescence to adulthood in several different cultural communities. Initiation is seen as a tangible expression of both the person and the community's concepts, values, principles, ambitions and desires, embodied in the transmission of specific knowledge and practices during the rite. Initiation thus combines both personal experience and community values, expectations and heritage in a critical manner. The process of initiation and its protection,[5] properly and lawfully performed, is the cultural, spiritual and religious right of a community (CRL Rights Commission 2014:6).

With regard to the abovementioned statement that initiates may be as young as nine years old in some northern parts of Southern

---

4   Female circumcision is a well-known, documented and studied practice in some African cultures such as the Gikuya of Kenia (cf Githiga 2009:30). Also see Dora, 2018.

5   Read more about the factors influencing male initiation in the CRL Rights Commission's report (2010: 21-30). Some of the broader problems surrounding the practice of the initiation rite, are: 'challenges in setting up and running the initiation schools; diminishing appreciation of the cultural value of male initiation; inappropriate circumcision seasons; unfavourable health conditions; causes of death in initiations schools; negative public influence on the initiation rite; and the commercialization of initiation schools'. Also see Rijken & Dakwa's article (pp. 10-12).

CHAPTER 6

Africa, South African scholar Samuel Sindelo[6] (2019:n.p.) remarks that in some parts of South Africa, initiates must be, by law and tradition, 18 years and above but are rarely older than 23 years. However, boys of 16 and older may be circumcised with the permission of their parent/guardian. The logic for being 18 years old to be circumcised, is that a boy then normally is completing his high schooling years and will thereafter go and work or further his studies at tertiary level. "Way before the Xhosa speaking people made it fashionable to go to school, a boy would, once he drops out of school, go and work in the mines, and on his first home coming, would have accumulated enough money to pay for his passage to manhood" (Sindelo 2019:n.p.). It was unheard of that a "boy would be a multi goer to the mines (work) without being circumcised" (:n.p.).

According to the CRL Rights Commission, initiation schools are part of South African cultural practices and are protected by the Constitution. Such schools are considered to be cultural and educational institutions[7] where initiates are taught principles of the specific community inherent in courtship, social responsibility, discipline and acceptable behaviour as well as about their culture. Younger boys are taught filtered down values that are vital to their social and psychological growth and advancement (CRL Rights Commission 2014:6). Sindelo (2019:n.p.), in a nuanced way, emphasises that there is generally an acceptance in literature that circumcision and initiation processes are one and, therefore, often used interchangeably. However, there is a difference. The circumcision process relates to the procedure conducted by the surgeon (where some or all of the foreskin is removed from the penis), which takes a few minutes, and thereafter the traditional nurse, family elders and community take over to ensure that the healing process is expedited. On the other hand, the initiation process, much as it begins with circumcision, goes beyond circumcision. Strictly speaking, it is the induction of the initiate to the values, discipline, moral regime and ethics of a clan and a community at

---

6   He belongs to the clan of AmaCube which are descendants of uMadiba.

7   Read more about the communal, educational and cultural aspects of ritual male circumcision and initiation among others in Brunsdon (2016:262–269).

141

large. There can be no initiation without circumcision, but the reverse is true: there can be circumcision while initiation is done outside the clan and community. This prevails when the young man decides on his own, or through other factors, to abandon traditional initiation which culminates in the young man graduating from *ubufana* to a man (*ubudoda*) and ultimately to an old man (*ubuxhego*).

Be that as it may, initiation (usually) forms part of the culture, discipline and principles of a specific clan, and the community begin their teachings on the day of the home coming celebration(s) (*umphumo*). This is normally after three weeks of seclusion from the broader society – and of the three weeks, the first week is the most critical in the life of the initiate (Sindelo 2019:n.p.). "In the first week, normality of the outside world is thrown out and only the critical and sacred life is tolerated. Individual democratic rights are seen as both dangerous and not to be tolerated" (:n.p.). This first week, Sindelo (:n.p.) continues, "is akin to a sterilised environment in hospital, and not everybody is allowed inside the hut where initiates stay". To illustrate this point, he refers to "a man who had sexual intercourse the previous days who will not be allowed into and should not even come close to the hut, as there might be bacteria that could cause infections" (:n.p.), and "girls who are menstruating are also not allowed to come near the hut where the initiates are" (:n.p.). After seven days, "the community men converge in the hut (*boma*) to evaluate the progress with regard to the healing process of the initiate(s). It is only then that there comes some relaxation in the strict regime to the extent that it does not sacrifice sterility of the hut (*boma*)" (:n.p.). The traditional nurse is only at this time allowed to go and sleep at home, but he comes back to the camp on a daily basis to evaluate the progress of healing of the initiates, and in a situation where there is healing retrogression, he again sleeps in the camp to ensure that progress is made. "During the first seven days, initiates are taught how to take care of themselves in treating the 'wound'" (:n.p.).

The home-coming celebration is the "moment when a new man is put in front of the elders and specific people from the clan, as well as respected community members, who are allowed to begin instilling discipline, culture, and respect" (Sindelo 2019:n.p.) and show the initiates "milestones of which the first one namely circumcision, he has passed" (:n.p.). This happens in the kraal and ends up in a house where mothers do their part, imparting knowledge and thereafter presents the initiate with new clothes, bedding and other things. "At this point, all things like clothes, bedding, etc. of boyhood is donated to other (younger) boys and the young man starts a new life" (:n.p.). The process of initiation happens under the guidance of the clan members and community, and the boy is expected to be moral upright and must now learn from the elders.

Initiation is a much longer process than circumcision – even after home-coming has been celebrated, it continues until someone has gone beyond the young men group stage (*ubufana*). After this, there is another occasion which allows the initiate to graduate himself further to another level and be accepted by the next group. It is this occasion, strictly speaking, that ends the initiation process (Sindelo 2019:n.p.).

In the circumcision school, you are taught sacrifice, self-reliance and endurance through pain, but there are no cultural teachings or anything close to instilling clan and cultural values as during initiation, according to Sindelo (2019:n.p.).

Margaret Mead (1973), a cultural anthropologist, reasons that if adolescence is not monitored, individual adolescents, their families and their societies could be destructively influenced by it. This is, according to her, a delicate stage because the boy is neither child any longer nor adult during the intermediate phase of adolescence. Therefore, the role of initiation is vital in helping a young man to become a fully responsible person of dignity in his community. "This is the time when teenagers begin to look beyond themselves and they are in this stage faced with two choices: to join the ranks of responsible adults or follow the band with his peers in an alternative society" (Mead 1973:3).

THE CURRENT SOUTH AFRICAN SITUATION

While the practice of initiation has persisted over the years, it has become necessary to bring this emotive cultural and spiritual issue or tradition – with its ethos of sacredness and secrecy – in line with modern times and technology, and to address the challenges that have arisen in recent times.

As far as we know, 714 boys died in the Eastern Cape from botched circumcisions during 2006-2018, and, even more surprising, is the fact that more than 1 767 initiates have died in South Africa during initiation since 1994, equivalent to 160 soccer teams (Jones 2019:n.p.).

In June 2018, as reported by Lubabalo Ngcukana (2018), the Deputy Minister of Cooperative Governance and Traditional Affairs, Obed Bapela, said that since 2006

> at least 800 teens and men have had to undergo penile amputations after suffering complications related to traditional initiation. He also said penis transplants are expensive and unaffordable for government. We cannot run away from the issue of amputations. It is a very serious matter ... Suicides among those who are amputated is also a concern because when they have lost their manhood and they are in university, because of many challenges and pressures, they commit suicide. (n.p.)

Henry Mbaya (2020:n.p.), professor of Missiology at the Faculty of Theology at Stellenbosch University, reasons that it is important to refer to the 'healthy' and 'un-healthy' aspects of initiation. He states: "The death of many initiates relates to traditional male 'surgeons' not observing health rules" (:n.p.). According to the CRL Rights Commission[8] (2014), abovementioned cases

---

[8] Participants in the different provinces who took part in the hearings of the CRL Rights Commission attributed the following causes of initiates' deaths to among others: "dehydration, septicaemia, accidents during the operation, gangrene, kidney failure, and assaults on the initiates during initiation." (2010:24). It

are almost without exception due to the negligence of some traditional 'surgeons', some found operating under the influence of alcohol, while others have used unsterilized instruments, contributing to the spread of blood-related infections such as HIV and AIDS, as well as tetanus. In some cases, initiates have died from septic wounds, blood loss and/or other easily preventable result of unprofessional circumcisions. (p. 7)

They (CRL Rights Commission 2014:7) further state that "[s]ome initiation schools are also opened for pure profit, with initiates having to pay exorbitantly expensive fees", which means that poorer families cannot afford to initiate their sons. Some traditional or conventional 'surgeons' often misuse their power positions, while some 'surgeons' "are inadequately trained to perform traditional circumcision" (:7).

With the escalation of threats to the lives of initiates (CRL Rights Commission 2014),

some provincial governments and municipalities established legislation and by-laws to regulate certain aspects of the cultural practice. Different pieces of provincial legislation regulate medical, environmental and governance aspects of initiation, while municipal by-laws regulate community governance with specific reference to the role of traditional leadership ... surgeons and healers. (p. 7)

The Constitution of the Republic of South Africa "does make provision for cultural groups to practice their traditions, but also forbids cruel, inhuman and degrading behaviour" (Jones 2019:n.p.). The CRL Rights Commission (2014:7) reasons in this regard that our Constitution "guarantees people's rights to perform their cultural practices" and that it is "not neutral on values" whilst it "challenges

---

has also been "reported that the families of deceased initiates are often intimidated to withdraw complaints lodged at local police stations, resulting in perpetrators escaping prosecution" – CRL Rights Commission (2010:8).

South Africans to exercise their rights according to the values of, among others, respect, human dignity and freedom." However, these rights are sometimes in "conflict with some traditional practices, necessitating further discussion and further public education" (:7). In this regard, academic Luvuyo Ntombana (in Jones 2019:n.p) argues that "cultural practices can only have value as far as it promotes human well-being ... Therefore, cultural practices must be subjected to the test of Ubuntu." In my article 'Do more to eradicate illegal initiation schools', I argue that "[p]ower and material interests, often served by culture, may never be more important than human well-being" and that "initiation and circumcision should never be allowed to create a patriarchal hierarchy of authority – not between men, nor between men and women" (Jones 2019:n.p.).

The CRL Rights Commission (2014:7) makes the important point that "[c]ontemporary South African society requires initiation practitioners to re-examine their activities if they are to be responsive to their changing social environment." For them the

> challenge remains that cultural rights cannot infringe on the rights of others, e.g. unsafe traditional circumcision vs the right to health, bodily integrity, or indeed the right to life. Simultaneously, while cultural spaces are shared in the South African democracy, individual communities' specific cultural practices should not be infringed, provided these are legal and constitutional. (p. 7)

Although it won't be easy to design universal consensus on this matter, we must at all cost try to "reach viable solutions to inform individuals and communities to take action to stem the death toll and health consequences of bungled circumcision" (CRL Rights Commission 2014:7).

Sindelo (2019:n.p.) notes in this regard that, according to his knowledge, before 1990, the death of initiates was seen as a "legend in the Xhosa speaking communities. We only saw deaths of initiates after 1990 and a thorough study is still to be conducted on why initiates starting to die only after this period. The procedure was once safe and sacred."

In the process of circumcision, Sindelo (2019:n.p.) reasons that the following two forms of circumcision schools must be clarified, which is normally confused by those who have not undergone the process, namely:

- "Privately-owned circumcision schools" – this is owned by the surgeon and he charges a fee for initiates to stay there for anything between a week and a month depending on what the parent/guardian wants. The fee includes provision for food, nurses and the surgeon. This form has become a private business of the surgeon in more or less the same way as what a private hospital is to modern medicine. At this traditional circumcision hospital, there is always a group of initiates, sometimes up to 50 per any given point in time. It is specifically for boys whose parents are either not confident of doing it at 'individually built for purpose circumcision school' or those who don't have time and expertise to monitor their boys at the 'individually built for purpose circumcision school'. This is mainly preferred by single mothers as they often have no reliable brothers/relatives to handle this situation to their satisfaction. Even at this school, the surgeon rarely attends to the initiates, unless there is one initiate whose progress in healing is slow or retrogressing.

- "Individually built-for-purpose circumcision school" – this is a temporary structure built for the purpose of circumcision and, on the last day, it is razed to the ground. Here, the surgeon arrives on the day of the circumcision and conducts the procedure and then he leaves after he has been paid. After the procedure has been done, the surgeon is never seen again nor is he brought back. Sometimes, the surgeon does not even spend five minutes with an initiate, then he disappears and the initiate would probably never know the surgeon. The primary person responsible thereafter is a traditional nurse who is appointed by the family based on his experience in taking care of the boys. The nurse is called *ikhankatha*. Anything that goes wrong with the initiates, the nurse is held responsible for. Normally, this is an older person who is known to be strict in maintaining order and discipline at the school.

"It remains to be seen, as to whether botched circumcision is the negligence of the surgeons or nurses, but in my experience, surgeons play a little role or no role after the procedure. For three weeks, the nurse is the responsible person" (Sindelo 2019:n.p.). With regard to the abovementioned statement that poorer families cannot afford to initiate their sons, Sindelo (:n.p.) states that in the Xhosa speaking communities, there has never been a situation known to him that, where a boy from a poor family presented himself unannounced on the day of circumcision, was turned away. "The procedure is conducted and then elders are sent to the home of the poor boy to inform his parent/guardian that he has gone in and they should not look for him" (:n.p.).

THE SOCIALIZATION OF BOYS/MEN AND THE IMPORTANCE OF RITES OF PASSAGE IN AFRICAN CONTEXTS

According to Gary Barker, executive director, and Christine Ricardo[9], senior program assistant of the Gender and Health Initiative, at the Instituto Promundo[10] in Rio de Janeiro, Brazil, "gender is increasingly being used as a framework for analysis and program development

---

9   These two authors "(i) reviewed literature on men and masculinities, conflict and HIV/AIDS in sub-Saharan Africa; (ii) consulted with colleague organizations to identify promising program examples that apply a gender perspective to work with young men; (iii) carried out 50 key informant interviews with staff at organizations working with young men in Botswana, Nigeria, South Africa and Uganda; and (iv) carried out 23 focus group discussions and interviews with young men in Nigeria, South Africa and Uganda."

10 Promundo is a Brazilian NGO that works internationally to promote gender equality and child and youth development.

in youth and social development, HIV/AIDS and conflict in Africa" (Barker & Ricardo 2005:v). In the past, "gender has often referred to the disadvantages that women and girls face", and of course, this has been absolutely necessary "given [the] gender inequalities in the region", but all too often, the gender of men and boys has been overlooked by a gender perspective (:v). In this regard, White (1997:16) states the following with reference to men in Africa: "In the gender and development literature, men appear very little, often as hazy background figures. 'Good girl/bad boy' stereotypes present women as resourceful and caring mothers, with men as relatively autonomous individualists, putting their own desires for drink or cigarettes before the family's needs." Barker and Ricardo (2005:3) further say that "many of the problematic behaviors of young men – for example, the use of sexual coercion and violence against women, unsafe sexual behavior and participation in violence or local insurgencies – are often efforts by young men to publicly define or affirm themselves as men." According to Connell (2003), Gilmore (1990) and Pollack (1998), an almost universal characteristic of manhood is that it has to be achieved – it requires specific actions and behaviour before one's social group. "Achieving manhood is in effect evaluated or judged by other men and women; young men in diverse social settings frequently report a sense of being observed and watched to see if they measure up to culturally salient versions of manhood" (Barker & Ricardo 2005:4). Barker and Ricardo (:5) stress that the categories of manhood and the tensions that go with it, "are fluid and rarely mutually exclusive." They (:5) further say that young men experience various and, at times, contradictory ideas about what is meant to be a man – and generally believe that for their acts as men they are continually being judged and evaluated. They (:5) also emphasise "the multiple dimensions of young men's lives and identities" and that "African men have largely been seen as monolithic, and usually negative, and often seen as motivated purely by economic issues, including land use and work." According to Lindsay and Miescher (in Barker & Ricardo 2005:5), young men "have less frequently been examined in terms of their domestic lives – for example, as fathers and partners – or in terms of how motivation to work interacts with their other social roles."

Barker and Ricardo (2005:5) reasons in this regard that traditional gender analysis has often focused on criticising men's behaviour, emphasising their drug and alcohol use and violent actions against women and children. While it is important to highlight the negligence of men in their family responsibilities, it is also important to understand the complex nature of men's positions and roles in (their) households, as well as to take their cultural background and true functions and roles in social reproduction, into account (:5). In this regard, specifically referring to men's domestic lives as fathers, the latest South African statistics unfortunately say that only 42% of the 98% of living fathers are involved in the lives of their children, or the households in which they grow up. Of the 99% of living mothers in South Africa, 98% are involved in the lives of their children. Of all births that are registered in South Africa, 62.7% do not have information about the father (Jones 2018:12). "In the Western Cape, 35.6% of a total of 1.97 million children (approximately 650 000) live with their mothers only (Stats SA 2015:n.p.). In the 54% of homes where both parents are present, the level of engagement of fathers in the child's life varies considerably" (Jones 2019:n.p.).

WHAT DEFINES BEING A MAN?

According to Brunsdon (2016:264), "the main thrust of the process [of initiation] is instructional." Vincent (2008b:436) says that three main areas can be distinguished during the initiation process. Brunsdon (2016) indicates that except for the fact that "initiates are trained in the 'secret of the bush' to help distinguish them in future from unauthentic (hospital) initiates" and that "certain character traits such as courage, forbearance and strength are instilled upon them through deprivation, criticism and even physical punishment", they are (particularly) educated on

> what it means to be a man or adult in their culture. Especially this part contains instruction on how a man should conduct himself in marriage, family and social life, and it has a strong cultural and

sexual basis. The same pattern is discernible amongst the Gikuyu in Kenya[11] where knowledge on conduct in the community as adult and partner in marriage features prominently. (p. 264)

To briefly elaborate in this regard, the key mandate or social prerequisite for manhood in Africa, in other words to be a man, is to reach a certain level of financial freedom, work or wages, and then to start a family. If you're not married and have no children, you are seen as a boy, according to Barker and Ricardo (2005:5). According to the Social Sciences and Reproductive Health Research Network (in Barker & Ricardo 2005)

> [a] mature, but unmarried man is viewed with suspicion and often precluded from occupying certain social positions. He is also viewed as irresponsible and perhaps even a 'homosexual.' ... In the Eastern zone the consequences of not marrying are very serious for a man. He is forbidden to hold certain titles and in the event of his death, he cannot be buried like a married man. (p. 5)

To be employed, brings social recognition beyond the family, and this makes people respect you. Barker and Ricardo (2005) states in this regard that

> [a]mong ethnic groups in Africa that rely on cattle herding for subsistence, manhood begins when the father bestows land and cattle or other livestock to the son, which in turn can either serve as a bride-price, or enable him to achieve the status of manhood and form a family. In this way, achieving manhood depends on an older man – one who holds more power – deciding when a young man is able to achieve socially recognized manhood. (p. 6)

---

11 See Githiga (2009:39) for more information in this regard.

Furthermore, one has to support one's extended family. To be able to do this, one has to be an employed man. You're not only a breadwinner, but you must provide in the needs of your extended family too. Some men have a remarkable sense of obligation to their families. For this you must have a stable job, but this leads to massive migration (Campbell 2001:n.p.) with certain (sexual) consequences. Young men who do not achieve a sense of socially respected manhood seem more likely to engage in violence (Barker and Ricardo 2005:8).

RITES OF PASSAGE[12]

Brunsdon (2016:262) says that it "is generally accepted that ritual male circumcision forms part of a rite of passage that leads males from boyhood to manhood" and that this is how male circumcision is introduced in most literature.[13] Mtuze (in Brunsdon (2016:262) "depicts the completion of initiation as the 'greatest day' in a boy's life" and Githiga (2009:21) "describes initiation as a moment that youngsters 'yearn' for." Githiga (2009:21) is further of the opinion that "children knew that it was only initiation that would make them men and women."

Barker and Ricardo (2005) state that many

> cultural groups in Africa have developed and continue to carry out initiation practices, or rites of passage, some of which include male circumcision, as part of the socialization of boys and men. Such practices are widespread ... with tremendous local and regional variations. These initiation rites ... often include seclusion of young men from their families (and from women and girls), and some informal learning process, during which

---

12   Van Gennep (1960) coined the phrase "rites of passage" to "define the ritual practice, delineated it as a set of symbolic actions, either in ritual or ceremony, as a process intended to mark a transition in the human life cycle of both the individual and the community". According to Van Gennep "rites of passage are diverse, and are often recognised as such in the cultures in which they occur" - CRL Rights Commission 2010:12.

13   See Malisha et al. (2008); Meissner & Buso (2007); Westercamp & Bailey (2007); Broude (2005); Turner (1969).

older men pass on information and/or skills that are considered necessary to be an adult male in their societies. This information and skills may include how to hunt, how to treat women, how to build a house, warrior or fighting skills and historical information about the cultural group and its rituals. (p. 9)

Ellis (1997:6) refers to numerous studies that confirm the cultural power of these rites of passage as "agents of political and social incorporation, notably of young men who are most likely to be the warlike element in any society." These rituals may become particularly important when more formalised public institutions, such as education, institutional religion and political institutions are weak. Such rites of passage provide a mixture of social control, assistance, encouragement and guidance for young people to make the sometimes mixed-up and stressful transition from childhood to adulthood, as well as to create or reinforce a sense of cultural or tribal identity and social cohesion (Barker & Ricardo 2005:9).

Reinforcing a clear boundary or demarcation between children, or boys, and men, and between men and women, is a common factor in rites of passage. There are expectations or anticipations in many settings in Africa that boys need to be separated from their mothers. Once they reach puberty, boys are often taken to stay in a separate compound for boys. In some environments, it is expected from male children to be defiant, stubborn, and to refuse to take on tasks deemed female. Many of these rituals' elements contain references to giving up boyhood in favour of adult manhood. Some of the rituals include a cathartic moment of being out-of-control or drunk or under the control of evil spirits before a clearly outlined and mature, ripe and seasoned identity is achieved. Along with the initiation rituals, the age-specific peer groups, also referred to as secret societies, set parameters for conflict resolution, male–female interactions, family and community life, and adult roles. While some elements of this socialisation reinforce traditional (patriarchal) gender norms that have negative effects on men and women, they have deep cultural significance and often act as a form of positive social control. These practices of initiation are often viewed as fundamental to their personal development. Some of these rites of passages have been, and still are, ways of gaining access to elders, where people have met with the chief and other members to resolve conflicts and prepare grounds for taking up political power. While many of these rites of passage perpetuate conventional hierarchies of gender, they sometimes also serve as a form of social confinement. Ceremonies that go with rites of passage and secret societies, are at times co-opted for armed insurgencies. Charles Taylor is said to have relied extensively on these rites of passage in Liberia in order to legitimise his strength. His warlords used elements from traditional rites of passage – such as talismans and tattoos – which allegedly left young men immune against enemy fire. Cross-dressing that is part of traditional passage rituals has been subverted in such a way that rebels often were dressed as girls while committing their extreme wickedness (Barker & Ricardo 2005:9-10).

According to Ellis (1997:n.p.) several scholars have suggested that armed movements have simply become modern iterations of passage rituals, continuing to draw on traditional elements – such as tribal seclusion, men's and boys' supremacy, a cathartic or out-of-control moment, among others. While it is difficult to generalise about rites of passage in Africa, what is obvious is that they can simultaneously perpetuate strict sex segregation and gender inequalities, while also acting as a form of positive social control. Such practices often include sexuality-related information with consequences for HIV, violence against women and intimate relationships between men and women in general. It is also clear and obvious that rites of passage are dynamic – integrating new information and realities – making them resilient and lasting (Barker & Ricardo 2005:10).

BACKGROUND OF INITIATION AS A RITE OF PASSAGE IN SOUTH AFRICA

The CRL Rights Commission (2010:13) states that "even under conditions of colonial subjugation, the rite thrived in many African countries, including South Africa." Acculturation was a cornerstone in the colonial era and this meant "that Africans were forced to abandon their indigenous practices and structures and adopt the more, so-called 'enlightened' modern Western colonial belief systems and practices" (:13-14). Initiation practices were referred to as 'barbaric' and missionaries saw initiation as 'pagan belief' (:14). Christianisation made it "difficult for the institution of initiation to find legitimate expression" (:14). This ritual is deeply embedded in African culture and the community's[14] value of this rite gives it the strength and resilience that it enjoys today. Turner (1969) warns against the simplification of the notion of initiation. It is about more than moving from childhood to adulthood. According to him, the rite of initiation is firmly embodied in the values, beliefs, identity and spirituality of a community. With the dawn of the democratic and constitutional dispensation in South Africa (1994), "individual youngsters have now the right to choose not to participate in the initiation practice" (CRL Rights Commission 2010:15) although it was expected of them before 1994 to be initiated at a particular age. It must be stated that "many young people are finding ways of making money out of the initiation practice" because of unemployment and not having access to economic participation (:14). The media has the right to exercise freedom of speech responsibly (Anon. 2011:6), however, many cultural communities are convinced that the "South African media has played a role in portraying negatively African cultural practices, by promoting stereotypes, misconceptions and demeaning perspectives about South African culture in general and the practice of initiation in particular" (CRL Rights Commission 2010:15-16). In some provincial governments and municipalities, there are certain "legislation and by-laws to regulate certain aspects of the cultural practice. Different provincial legislations regulate medical, environmental and governance aspects of the institution, while municipal by-laws regulate community governance with specific reference to the role of traditional leadership, traditional surgeons and healers" (:17). Although governments express their concern "primarily with the health aspects of initiation", the initiation schools

---

14 Read more about the communal and familial aspects of ritual male circumcision among others in Brunsdon (2016:262-264); Vincent (2008b:431-446) and Turner (1982:20-60).

"require holistic rather than cosmetic intervention" (:18). The CRL Rights Commission says in its 2010 report that despite the fact that

> there is legislation or policy guidelines, there are still shortcomings when it comes to initiation, as legislation and policy do not address all the problems. They address only those relating to circumcision, without including the relevant social and cultural systems or their contexts. The overarching pitfall in all these legislative regimes is the presumption of the superiority of Western ways as reflected in the various powers given to government officials. The various legislations do not acknowledge and recognise the existence of indigenous problem-solving mechanisms. Most of the policy guidelines remove from the practice its cultural meaning; thus contributing in effect to cultural erosion. They give more powers to government bureaucrats, so they become like chief magistrates who regard themselves as 'bureaucratic potentates' directing everybody else under their unchallenged authority. (p. 19)

In this regard, it must be said that The National Assembly passed the new Customary Initiation Bill in December 2018 without any objections. Hereafter, it has been sent to the National Council of Provinces for agreement. According to Besent (2018) the "Bill seeks to regulate customary initiation practices to curb the deaths of male and female initiates due to the operation of some bogus initiation schools." The Bill will also "create various structures that can regulate initiation schools in provinces and local municipalities" (2018). During the debate on the Bill, the Deputy Minister for Co-operative Governance and Traditional Affairs, Obed Bapela (in Besent 2018) said "that they have been facing challenges with initiation schools since June 2012." Bapela (in Besent 2018) then continued by stating that the

> Bill will also make provisions for municipalities to strengthen their by-laws, regulatory processes. Municipalities must ensure the provision of the necessary infrastructure such as land, clean water, and sites for initiations. Traditional initiation signifies

the transformation from boyhood into adulthood. And of significance is the preparation for manhood. Leadership, respect and responsibility is a rite of passage to adulthood. Since June 2012 to date, the challenges of initiations, deaths, amputations arise mainly form the illegal … or bogus schools.

INTERGENERATIONAL TENSIONS

Historically, in almost all of Africa, tribal society has been and often still is based on the authority and ultimate manhood of the chiefs, and references to the 'big man' and rigid community and tribal hierarchies that leave young men waiting to become men. According to Lindsay and Miescher (in Barker and Ricardo 2005:11) "[t]he African 'big man' provides perhaps the most enduring image of African masculinity. Across the continent and for a long sweep of history, ambitious people (usually men) have worked to enlarge their households and use their 'wealth in people' for political and material advancement." The accumulation of power in the hands of big men and elders, or the generation of older men, continues to be a factor in Africa, contributing to ongoing power struggles between older and young men and is connected to some of the region's insurgencies. Older men in many parts of Africa – whether as fathers, chiefs or elders – determine when young men can own land, access family goods or wealth resources, and marry. This institutionalised age group stratification places junior and younger men at the service of the aged, and older men's ownership of property and women creates conflict between younger and older generations of men (Barker & Ricardo 2005:12). Throughout contemporary Africa, this intergenerational tension manifests itself in many ways. There have been tensions in South Africa, for instance, between rural elderly men and wage-earning younger men who migrate to cities for jobs. Many, if not most, of these migrant workers send income to their families, keeping their status as men even if they are not physically present. City migration and transformation have become ways for young men to usurp the elderly's strength and power. Migration to work in cities has become part of a new rite of passage in some environments. Young men escape rural power hierarchies by moving to the city, earn money that allows for some freedom and independence, as well as access to women (:12).

SEXUALITY AND MANHOOD

There are scholars and studies that say sexual experience is often associated with initiation into manhood and achievement of a culturally accepted manhood for young men in sub-Saharan Africa, as for many young men around the world. It encourages a view of sex as performance, in particular, a means of demonstrating masculine prowess. Young men, in many cultures, including Africa, are facing peer pressure to be sexually active and have multiple partners to be seen as men. Such sexual experiences can be interpreted as displays of sexual competence or achievement by peers, rather than acts of intimacy (Marsiglio 1988; WHO 2001, 2003 as referred to by Barker & Ricardo 2005:16). Sindelo (2019:n.p.), however, differs and says, as far as his knowledge goes, this does not apply to (all) Xhosa speaking people in South Africa.

INITIATION AND ANCESTORS

To connect this ritual with ancestors, is of crucial importance, especially for amaXhosa. According to David Bogopa (2010:1), lecturer in the Department of Sociology and Anthropology in the School of Governmental and Social Sciences at the Nelson Mandela University in Port Elizabeth (South Africa), "[a]ncestor worship is founded on the belief that the dead live on and are capable of influencing the lives of those who are still living." Ancestors are believed to be capable both of blessing and cursing those who still live. Therefore, their worship is motivated by "respect and fear" (:1). Hammond-Tooke (1994:2) reasons that all the different cultural groups have a special name when they refer to their ancestors. They make use of the plural form with reference to these particular and special beings as a sign of respect. Bogopa (2010:2) further argues that "[r]itual ceremonies are performed through-out the life-span [of a person], marking different stages of life, such as the birth stage and maturity stage, and even after a person has died." After the birth stage, "there must be a ritual ceremony (*ukushwana*) before the initiates can go through the *ukwaluko* process and after the initiates have graduated from the *ukwaluko* process. It is believed that performing the fore-mentioned ritual ceremonies is to thank the ancestors for protecting the initiates" (:2). In the Xhosa culture particularly, the reason for deaths during initiation is believed to be that "some parents have the tendency to not perform ritual ceremonies for their sons before sending them to *ekwalukweni*" (:3). Bogopa refers, in this regard, to the following example: "there is an important ritual ceremony known as *ukushwama*. In this ritual ceremony, a goat is slaughtered and a boy is given a right limb to eat in order to prevent misfortunes (*amashwa*) before he can be taken to an initiation school" (:3; Bogopa 2007:56). The purpose of this ritual "is to directly communicate with the ancestors so that they may look after the boy for the whole duration of the *ukwaluko* process" (Bogopa 2010:4) and to "protect the initiates from evil spirits" (:5). Bogopa then makes the very important point when he says that it

> is evident ... that, within the context of many cultures in South Africa and beyond, health and ancestors are two sides of the same coin: one cannot live a healthy life without honouring the ancestors. The process of ancestor worship takes place in the form of a life cycle, proceeding from birth to death. (:5)

IN CONCLUSION

Vincent (2008b:440) is of the opinion that "the main power of circumcision in the fear amongst the uninitiated that they might be ostracised by the community." Brunsdon (2016:268) indicates that because "circumcision is seen as a rite of passage in the journey to become fully human, the uninitiated are not regarded as human, earning them derogatory names such as 'dogs' and causing them to be excluded from certain privileges, especially in the social sphere." A boy who has not been initiated, for example, "will not be included in a family's budget for new clothing. The uninitiated will not be granted entrance to certain social gatherings either" (:268). But furthermore, they "will not be considered for sexual intercourse by females. The social perception that circumcised men are of stronger moral fibre than the uninitiated also causes African societies to lay the blame for crime or misconduct on innocent uninitiated men" (:268). This leads to the fact that "[c]andidates for initiation are thus constantly weighing the perceived dangers of initiation against the social ostracism that awaits them if they do not submit to this institution, and the fear of ostracism is clearly winning" (:268). Furthermore, "[t]raditional leaders ... discourage the use of regulated circumcision actively by labelling those who go to hospital for their circumcision ... (paper boys) or comparing them to women who gave birth in a hospital ward by plainly referring to these men as women[15]" (:268-269). With this in mind, "it should be understandable that ostracism may outweigh the risks of traditional circumcision for many young men" (:269).

With this in mind, thousands of boys are not destined to become adult men because circumcision costs them their lives. Some will not be able to have children in a normal way because their genitals are severely damaged by this practice. Mabuza (2010:2), chairperson of the CRL Commission, says in his foreword to the CRL Rights Commission's 2010-report on public hearings on male initiation schools, that the present "South African Constitution guarantees people rights that enable them to carry out their cultural practices". However, the same constitution "is not neutral on values. It challenges South African citizens to exercise their rights according to the values that are entrenched within it" (:2). These values include, according

---

15   Also see Vincent (2008a:81).

to Mabuza, "respect, human dignity and freedom. However, these rights sometimes clash and need to be discussed and negotiated" (:2). One important question that must be asked is whether certain cultural practices and traditions in a modern democracy can be more important than, for example, the right to human dignity and life. In thinking about this, we must further listen to the boys themselves and their families rather than just to the cultural elite and traditional leadership. According to Du Toit (2014), Ntombana argues that, like all cultural practices, male circumcision has always been changing and, therefore, an argument against change as such is invalid. Shaka, for example, simply abolished this practice in KwaZulu-Natal because it interfered with the training of his Zulu warriors (Van den Heever 2014). Ntombana (in Du Toit 2014) further says that this initiation practice revived with the dawn of the new political dispensation, but that the initiation in the forest is symbolically more important than the circumcision itself. He, therefore, argues for the medicalisation of circumcision and says that if it is properly incorporated in the rituals, it should not be at all subversive. He wants to see young people organise themselves and that the practice is made more voluntary.

All the different problems that relate to male initiation and circumcision give rise to an important debate, especially in a country like South Africa "that is endeavoring to heal the divisions of the past, to promote respect and tolerance of its diverse cultures, and in particular to protect those cultural practices that were marginalized, and are still threatened in the new dispensation" (CRL Rights Commission 2010:9). It is possible – as seen elsewhere in the world – to realign some cultural practices with developed and developing value systems without losing the core values and ideals that are so fundamentally important to various traditional cultural and spiritual practices and beliefs. To achieve this, however, more than legislation is required. What is needed, are partnerships between different stakeholders, such as communities, the government, and traditional leadership, especially in enforcing the necessary requirements for opening and running initiation schools, as well as providing the necessary resources and expertise in order to better contribute to the health of initiates and to support destitute families.

CHAPTER 7

RECOGNISING AND RESPONDING TO COMPLEX DILEMMAS: CHILD MARRIAGE IN SOUTH AFRICA

Elisabet le Roux

INTRODUCTION

In a June 2019 exposé on child marriage in South Africa, the investigative journalism television show *Carte Blanche* drew renewed attention to the more than 90 000 girls in South Africa who entered marriages as child brides. The show focused on a "polluted *ukuthwala*" as a major driver of child marriage, unpacking how traditional cultural practices have become warped to the extent that it leads to young girls being forced to marry older men against their will (Forced child marriages 2019). Nevertheless, South Africa remains a country with one of the lowest rates of child marriage in Africa. Compared to countries, such as Niger, where 76% of women aged 20-24 years were first married or in a union before they were 18 years old, and the Central African Republic, where it is 68% of girls, South Africa's rates are low: the last available data, collected in 2003, showed that only 6% of girls in South Africa are married before the age of 18 years (Institut National de la Statistique 2013; ICASEES 2010; Department of Health 2007).

However, these statistics paint a misleading picture of the fate of thousands of girl children[1] in South Africa. This chapter will briefly unpack the nature, drivers and consequences of child marriage, followed by a focus on South African legislation and cultural practices relevant to child marriage. This is a prelude to an in-depth discussion of three key dilemmas relating to the phenomenon, namely the inadequacy of a legislative response, the clash between the primacy of human rights versus cultural rights, and the reality of transactional intergenerational sex in relationships other than marriages. Recognition of these dilemmas leads to acknowledgement that current responses to child marriage are not merely woefully inadequate, but also fail to grasp the full scale of the problem.

---

1   While young boys can also enter into a child marriage, the overwhelming majority of children in such marriages are female. This is also the case in South Africa. Therefore, this chapter will focus on girls as victims and survivors of child marriage.

CHAPTER 7

WHAT IS CHILD MARRIAGE?

As defined in Article 1 of the United Nations Convention on the Rights of the Child, as well as Article 2 of the African Children's Charter, a child is a person – boy or girl – under the age of 18 years (Centre for Human Rights (CHR)2 2018:15). Child marriage is, therefore, where one (or both) of the parties involved in the union is (or was) a child when the marriage occurs. While both boys and girls can be involved in a child marriage, the overwhelming majority of child marriages involve a girl child marrying an older man (2018:25).

While the term 'child marriage' is often used interchangeably with 'forced marriage' or 'early marriage', these are not the same. While a child marriage may be a forced marriage, in as far as either or both parties involved in the marriage did not personally give free and full consent to the marriage, a forced marriage can also occur between adult parties. For example, this happens when a widow is forced to marry a relative of her deceased husband. Early marriage, on the other hand, is a term used to refer to marriages that occur involving an individual younger than 18 years in a country where adulthood is obtained at an age younger than 18 years or upon marriage. It can also refer to marriages where the spouses are 18 years or older, but they are not ready or able to consent to marriage, for example because of a lack of physical development (United Nations Human Rights Council 2014:3).

Child marriage rates are difficult to accurately determine, as birth registration, as well as marriage registration are lacking or inadequate in many settings. In many countries, there are no official records of child marriages, or inadequate birth registration systems make it hard to determine the age of the spouses. Nevertheless, it is clear that the prevalence of child marriages in Africa is higher than the global average and that it occurs most often in West and Central Africa (CHR 2018:19-20).

---

2   In further references to this resource, the abbreviation CHR will be used.

The various drivers of child marriage are interrelated and often mutually reinforcing, and a cause of child marriage can at the same time also be a consequence of child marriage. This is illustrated when reflecting on poverty and education as drivers of child marriage. Child marriage is linked to poverty and child marriage tends to be more common in poorer countries and in the poorest parts of a specific country (CHR 2018:30). Girls marry at a young age (or are forced to marry young by their guardians) based on the belief that the marriage will improve their and their family's material welfare (Mudarikwa, Roos & Mathibela 2018:7). However, girls that marry young often leave school early. Their lack of education can, in turn, lead to increased poverty, as they are unable to find employment. Furthermore, as education empowers girls and reduces their vulnerability to child marriage, lack of education is a driver of child marriage (CHR 2018:32).

There are seven key drivers of child marriage on the African continent (CHR 2018). The first is gender inequality, with the belief in the inferior status of women and girls present and common across the continent. Second, certain cultural and religious norms directly or indirectly promote child marriage. Poverty and lack of access to education for girls are the third and fourth major drivers of child marriage. Fifth is legal systems that allow for child marriage and this driver is usually present in countries with plural legal systems. The sixth driver is the inadequacy of the systems that ensure registration of births and marriages. It contributes to an inability to curb the practice, in as far as it allows child marriage to be performed without legal consequences. Lastly, on a continent where armed conflict is rife, the instability that results from conflict, and particularly the fear of sexual violence, act as a driver of child marriage.

The consequences of child marriage are far-reaching. Poorer health outcomes, lower levels of education, higher risk of violence and abuse, and persistent poverty are common challenges that married children face. Girls who marry young are particularly at risk for negative sexual and reproductive health consequences, linked to the common expectation that they become pregnant immediately or soon after marriage. The complications linked to pregnancy and childbirth are a major cause of death amongst 15-19 years olds in developing countries (Svanemyr et al. 2013:9). The children of mothers who marry young are (amongst other things) also at increased risk of malnutrition, stunting and death (Mudurikwa et al. 2018:10). The consequences of child marriage are not limited to those involved in the union. It impacts the broader community and country. Girls who marry young have dramatically higher fertility rates, meaning child marriage impacts population growth. This, in turn, affects the welfare of the community and country more widely. Recent studies have calculated the financial gains of ending child marriage, finding that "(g)lobally (for 106 countries) the welfare benefits that would be reaped through lower population growth from ending child marriage reach $566 billion per year in 2030" (Wodon et al. 2017:39).

Recognising the harms done by child marriage at an individual, community and national level, the international community has drafted and accepted several high-profile conventions forbidding child marriage. Two such international agreements are of particular relevance to child marriage in Africa, namely the 1989 United Nations Convention on the Rights of the Child (CRC) and the 1990 African Charter on the Rights and Welfare of the Child (ACRWC). The CRC does not explicitly refer to child marriage, although it describes several child rights that are violated by the practice. The ACRWC, however, has specific requirements on child marriage, including that all signatories have to take steps to end the practice, set the minimum age of marriage as 18 years, and make registration of all marriages compulsory (Maswikwa et al. 2015:58). In principle, the signatories, which includes South Africa, are legally bound to these agreements. In practice, however, many African countries have not abided by these stipulations. This includes South Africa, as the next section will explore.

CHILD MARRIAGE IN SOUTH AFRICA

The South African Constitution states that international law should be considered when interpreting the rights contained in the South African Bill of Rights. This would include the CRC and ACRW as discussed above, but also agreements like the Convention on the Elimination of All Forms of Discrimination against Women (CEDAW), the Universal Declaration of Human Rights, the Protocol on the Rights of Women in Africa, and the Southern African Development Community (SADC) Protocol on Gender and Development. All these agreements (to which South Africa is signatory) directly or indirectly prohibit child marriage. However, with many of these conventions there are loopholes that allow child marriage to legally continue. These loopholes are often in relation to the age of marriage. For example, the SADC Protocol on Gender and Development states that 'no person under the age of 18 shall marry, *unless otherwise specified in law...*' (emphasis added), while CEDAW states that a minimum age of marriage should be determined, but does not state what that age should be (Mudarikwa et al. 2018: 18-21).

South African legislation is unable to address child marriage, because its legislation has embraced these loopholes. Different laws set different requirements for marriages. Almost all of these laws allow those younger than 18 years to enter into marriage. For example, the Marriages Act sets different minimum ages for boys and girls: girls can be married at 15 years, while the minimum age for boys is 18 years. The Act also allows for parents, guardians, a Commissioner of Child Welfare, or a judge of the Supreme Court to provide permission should one of the spouses be younger than the required number of years (Mudarikwa et al. 2018:23-24). The Recognition of Customary Marriages Act also allows for parents, guardians, a Commissioner of Child Welfare, or a Court to provide consent for marriage, should one of the spouses be too young to provide consent. If both spouses are younger than 18 years, the Minister of Home Affairs can provide permission for the marriage to proceed (Muradikwa et al. 2018:

23-24). The Civil Unions Act, which regulates same and heterosexual unions, is actually the only South African law that sets 18 years as the minimum age of marriage for both boys and girls, and does not grant any exceptions (Mudarikwa et al. 2018:24).

Despite this lack of legislative will to eradicate child marriage, South Africa actually has relatively low child marriage rates compared to the rest of Africa. As stated earlier, an estimated 6% of girls get married while younger than 18 years, and 1% of girls while younger than 15 years (Department of Health 2007). However, these statistics arguably do not tell the real story. Various factors and practices contribute to a situation where the country's child marriage rates are arguably much higher than reported. First, there is no minimum age of marriage in the context of religious marriages, for these marriages are not recognised as valid under South African law. Only once they are registered in compliance with the Marriage Act, are they recognised. Furthermore, not all customary marriages are officially registered. The country's child marriage rates are, therefore, most likely higher than reported (Mudarikwa et al. 2018:6).

Second, two specifically South African cultural practices have been linked to child marriage, but are also not well documented, resulting in reported child marriage rates arguably being inaccurate (Mudarikwa et al. 2018:16). The first of these practices is *ukuthwala*. This practice originated with the Xhosa-speaking tribes and has expanded to other ethnic groups. *Ukuthwala* is a cultural practice of abduction, where a woman is forcibly taken by a young man to his home. This abduction is seen as a preliminary step to customary marriage. In older forms of this tradition, the practice was merely a ritual, as the girl and her abductor were of a similar age and in a consensual relationship but have not been able to secure her family's approval for their union (CHR 2018:28). However, under the banner of *ukuthwala* is now included practices, such as young girls being married to older men, a family member (of the girl) kidnapping her and taking her as wife, and abductions not being reported to the traditional authorities (Mwambene & Sloth-Nielsen 2011:2). Rarely are these practices, while resulting in underaged girls entering marriages, being recorded as child marriages.

The second practice is *ukuganisela*. With this practice, a girl's parents start marital negotiations with a boy's parents. This practice in itself violates conventions protecting the rights of the child, as marriage negotiations are done and consent is given on behalf of a child. However, the practice has metamorphosed into even more harmful forms. In modern formats, girls' parents negotiate marriages with much older men, already receiving *lobola* from him and consenting to the marriage on her behalf (Mudarikwa et al. 2018:14). While *ukuganisela* is, therefore, not an actual marriage, it can be the prelude to child marriage.

A last factor to take into account, is that South Africa is experiencing an influx of refugees, migrants and illegal immigrants from other African countries. While South Africa itself may not have high child marriage rates (although, as discussed, the validity of these statistics can be contested), there are an increasing number of people living in South Africa who come from countries where child marriage is an accepted and acceptable practice. This offers an added challenge to South Africa's attempts to eradicate the practice, for many of these individuals are undocumented and do not perform or register marriages through South African traditional or civil authorities.

DILEMMAS IN ADDRESSING CHILD MARRIAGE IN SOUTH AFRICA

The preceding overview of child marriage has already highlighted several challenges in addressing the issue globally, in Africa, and in South Africa specifically. This section will reflect on three particular dilemmas in responding to child marriage, namely the inadequacy of a legislative response, the clash between the primacy of human rights versus cultural rights, and the reality of transactional intergenerational sex in relationships other than marriages. Reflection on these dilemmas highlights the critical need for a much more comprehensive, holistic response to child marriage.

INADEQUACY OF LEGISLATIVE RESPONSE

The majority of African countries outlaw child marriage, yet the practice is still very common. Why is this? First, not all of the countries that criminalise it have the same minimum age for marriage, some have discriminatory minimum ages, or a minimum age lower than 18 years. Furthermore, the penalties for child marriage vary, ranging from small fines to 10 years' imprisonment. A number of countries, including South Africa, ban or invalidate marriages that are below the minimum age, while some prescribe a minimum age but do not criminalise or ban the practice (Svanemyr et al. 2013:12; Maswikwa et al. 2015:66). Thus, an inadequate legislative response is partly to blame for the continuation of the practice.

However, inadequate legislation is not the only challenge. The actual implementation and enforcement of existing laws are rarely adequate (CHR 2018:61). Across Africa, including South Africa, the judicial systems are weak, with a poor understanding of relevant laws and their implementation in terms of child marriage (Svanemyr et al. 2013:19). Furthermore, child marriage most often occurs under customary or religious law. While statutory law may prohibit or criminalise the practice, customary or religious laws often allow for it. It is then traditional or religious authorities that are informed of such marriages and disputes around it, not state authorities (CHR 2018:56). In such cases (CHR 2018)

> ... the authorities charged with adjudicating the case may support the practice of child marriage, and may even have been involved in deciding that the marriage at issue would take place. Even in the state justice system, judges in many jurisdictions are in support of customs that condone child marriage and so will not apply criminal sanctions if cases appear in court. (p. 57)

The result is that there are few prosecutions of child marriage perpetrators (Svanemyr et al. 2013:19). At least part of the problem is that many of those responsible for interpreting and enforcing legislation believe that child marriage is a private practice outside the purview of the law, or do not believe that child marriage is wrong. For example, a South African High Court judge has publicly argued for the validity of child marriages conducted according to the *ukuthwala* custom (CHR 2018:57, 61).

In any case, as discussed in the previous section, South Africa has a number of contradictory laws pertaining to child marriage. Criminalisation of child marriage is doomed to failure if legislation continues to allow for conditions where those younger than 18 years can marry (Maswikwa et al. 2015:58). Furthermore, as is also the case with practices like female genital mutilation/cutting, criminalising child marriage can lead not to its eradication, but to it going underground. Marriage ceremonies are then, for example, conducted at night, or marriages are only registered once the girl has reached 18 years (Svanemyr et al. 2013:20).

A major narrative present within child marriage prevention, is that the right legislation that is adequately enforced will end the practice. With such a punitive approach, the belief is that jail sentences and similar punitive measures will ensure that parents/guardians will no longer consent to such marriages, adult men will no longer marry younger girls, and traditional or religious leaders will no longer perform such marriages. Thus, many of the countries with the highest child marriage rates have prioritised passing laws that ban the practice and have put effort into strengthening and enforcing these laws. However, there is little evidence that implementation and enforcement of laws actually curb the practice. In a comparative assessment of 10 African countries, Svanemyr et al. (2013) found little correlation between the strength of child marriage legislation and prevalence or incidence trends. Where they did find declining rates, they could not ascribe it to legal reforms or mechanisms (:18). While other studies (e.g. Maswikwa et al. 2015) have found some evidence that consistent laws against child marriage can lessen child marriage prevalence, these also only argue that marriage laws of 18 years and older may prevent child marriages. It is stated by the CHR (2018) that

> (l)aws that prohibit child marriage are necessary but not sufficient to eliminate the practice in reality. In most of the countries studied, the introduction of new statutory legal sanctions and remedies determined by courts has in fact gone alongside increasing prevalence of the practice. (p. 56)

While this absence of the impact of legislation could be explained by the fact that many of these laws are recent and have not had the time to impact the practice, Svanemyr et al. (2013:19) argue that there is no reason to believe that the duration of a law will make a difference. They cite India as an example. While India was in 1929 the first country to ban child marriage, 47% of girls in India still marry before the age of 18.

This does not mean that laws and legislation around child marriage have no purpose. On the contrary, they are an important component of a holistic response. Laws let a government clarify its position, it can become a resource and motivation in communities that want to end the practice, and can be a driver and source of legitimacy for activists bent on ending the practice. Laws create an enabling environment (Svanemyr et al. 2013:19) – but they cannot be the sum total of the response to child marriage. The inability of laws to deal adequately with child marriage and ensure its eradication, highlights the importance of a holistic response to the practice. In order to end child marriage, one will have to also engage with the various drivers of the practice, including societal norms and beliefs, poverty, and lack of education.

HUMAN RIGHTS VERSUS CULTURAL RIGHTS

Much of the defence of child marriage has framed it as a culturally or religiously-mandated practice, that people of the specific culture or religion have a right to perform. This is a particularly challenging defence, due to not only the sensitivities around culture and religion, but also legal safeguards to protect cultural and religious freedom. How then, does one engage when religion or culture condones child marriage? This dilemma is exemplified in the South African controversy surrounding *ukuthwala*.

The original aim of *ukuthwala* was to enable a couple of similar age and in a consensual relationship to enter into marriage negotiations. There are different reasons for engaging in *ukuthwala*: it is a way for a couple to force the woman's father to consent to the marriage; to avoid the expense of a wedding; to speed up the marriage process if the woman is pregnant; to show the seriousness of the suitor; or to avoid immediately paying *lobola* if the suitor and his family cannot afford it. According to custom, the man must not have sex with the woman while she is kept in his home. If the man does not offer marriage, or if the offer is refused by the woman's family, a fine is paid by the man to the woman's family (Mwambene & Sloth-Nielsen 2011:3-5).

While *ukuthwala* can play an important role in communities that live according to cultural norms, the reality is that the practice has often been abused. Unmarried women or girls can be *thwala'd* without their consent, and girls can be *thwala'd* while younger than 18 years. Girls can be taken to the young man's home without her consent, and in some cases she is raped, or threatened with rape or violence, to ensure that she and her family agree to the relationship (Mwambene & Sloth-Nielsen 2011:5-7).

The South African Constitution expressly recognises the right to practice one's culture. This right allows members of the culture to engage in cultural practices without intervention from the state or other actors (Devenish 1999). Those defending the practice of *ukuthwala* thus call on this right to argue that neither the state or other actors are allowed to prohibit it or interfere with its implementation (Mwambene & Sloth-Nielsen 2011:11). However, cultural rights do not trump human rights. Both international law and South African law recognise that cultural rights should not be protected at the expense of human rights. CEDAW, the CRC, the African Children's Charter, and the African Women's Protocol, for example, all categorically state that culture and traditional practices cannot continue if it violates the basic human rights of children and women. The South African Constitution states that the exercising of cultural rights may not be inconsistent with the provisions of the South African Bill of Rights (Mwambene & Sloth-Nielsen 2011:11-12).

Based on the primacy of human rights, there are calls to outlaw practices such as *ukuthwala*, based on the argument that the practice has led to situations where girls are abducted, raped, and/or forced into marriage, thus violating their constitutional rights (Mudarikwa et al. 2018:36). However, certain commentators have asked for more circumspect navigation of the practice, for not all forms of *ukuthwala* involve child marriage and the violation of human rights. In this regard, Mwambene and Sloth-Nielsen (2011) stated:

> Thus, it may be necessary to distinguish between the practice of ukuthwala in forms which are inimical to human rights and may lead to human rights abuses, and those dimensions of the practice that advantage human rights, and promote the right to culture. (p. 13)

In arguing for the continued recognition of certain forms of *ukuthwala*, Mwambene and Sloth-Nielsen (2011) identify three original forms of *ukuthwala*. With the first, the woman is aware of the intended abduction, approves of it and has given consent. This is, in many ways, similar to an elopement and the act of abduction is only for appearances. Where the woman's father has disapproved of her suitor, *ukuthwala* can thus be an act of agency for the woman, as she is forcing her father to enter into marriage negotiations. With the second form of *ukuthwala*, the families have agreed on the union, but the woman is unaware of the agreement. *Ukuthwala* is then done as she might otherwise not agree to the marriage. Thus, the concept of the bride consenting to *ukuthwala* here is difficult to argue. The third form of *ukuthwala* is against the will of the bride and her family. There is not initial consent from either the woman or her parents, and she is taken to the home of the man by force. Rape, or the threat of rape, is used to ensure that the marriage proceeds (:6-7). While it is clear, then, that there are aspects of some of the forms of *ukuthwala* that clearly violate women's and children's rights, there are also aspects that do not do so. Mwambene and Sloth-Nielsen (2011:7) argue that the challenge is to address the objectionable aspects, without losing the culturally beneficial aspects. However, with *ukuthwala* increasingly being used to facilitate and justify highly objectionable unions, for example between much older men with young girls, or between young girls and a relative, it becomes harder to argue in its defence. Yet it is hard to legally counter such underaged forms of *ukuthwala*. First, as discussed earlier, the various relevant South African laws offer different standards by which to adjudicate what underaged marriage is. Second, *ukuthwala* is actually not a marriage, but a process of marriage negotiations. Therefore, South African laws pertaining to marriage do not apply and the practice then cannot be addressed through existing legal prohibitions on, for example, underaged marriage. In no South African law is *ukuthwala* specifically outlawed, therefore, responding to it legally will always require applying different (sometimes contradictory) laws that do not fully apply to the reality and complexity of the practice. The current legal terminology, such as that used in the South African Children's Act, is not sufficiently nuanced to either describe or regulate it (:20-22).

At the same time, as argued earlier, relying on the development of adequate and appropriate laws will arguably not be enough. Dealing with the harmful formats of *ukuthwala* that facilitate child marriage will require a much more nuanced engagement. Why, in the first place, are parents and family members forcing girls into marriages with older men? Why is this seen as acceptable behaviour by a caregiver? This again points to the need to address underlying gender and social norms, not only regarding masculinity, femininity and gender equality, but also regarding parenting and caregiving. Furthermore, with the automatic and natural defensiveness that people feel when there are attempts to change or eradicate their cultural practices, there is a genuine risk of these practices merely going underground, or even becoming more common as people see it as a way to support and strengthen their culture and cultural rights.

IS IT LESS HARMFUL IF IT IS NOT A MARRIAGE?

Cross-generational or age-disparate relationships are ones where there is a marked age difference between the two partners, in most cases the man being older than the woman. Transactional sexual relationships have been noted as an issue of concern, not only in relation to HIV & AIDS, but also gender-based violence. A number of studies have noted how such relationships, especially when linked to unequal power, play a significant role in unsafe, unequal and coercive sexual practices (Potgieter et al. 2012:193; Shefer & Strebel 2012:58). The term 'transactional sex' refers not only to traditional sex work, and is not only a result of poverty, but is also driven by societal pressures to acquire material goods and social status. Contextualised conceptions of love, gender and exchange can also play a role (Potgieter et al. 2012:193).

The literature on transactional sex has noted how the inequality within such relationships exacerbate women's vulnerability and puts them at risk (Shefer & Strebel 2012:58). This is the first dilemma to be raised here. While the vulnerability and risk of girls caught in child marriage is responded to within international, regional and national legislation and policies, as well as concerted effort by various organisations and networks bent on eradicating the practice, where is the response to *unmarried* girls in similar unequal and at-risk positions? It can be argued that in many communities and cultures a married girl at least has some recognition, status and authority as a married woman. Unmarried girls known to be in sexual relationships are, on the other hand, often stigmatised not only by the community but even by their sexual partners. See, for example, Potgieter et al.'s (2012) findings on the attitudes towards young girls who engage in sexual relationships with older mini-bus taxi-drivers in exchange for gifts and money. In this study done in the Western Cape, South Africa, the majority of the taxi drivers stigmatised the girls (:195).

Furthermore, recent research increasingly problematise the simplistic understanding of young girls *only* as victims that passively engage in such relationships out of need, and as older men *only* as perpetrators engaging actively in such relationships for sex. Men are under considerable pressure to take multiple sexual partners in order to prove their sexual prowess. There is also a very dominant narrative that successful masculinity can only be achieved through being a provider (the 'man as breadwinner' discourse). When engaging with these narratives and the cultural and social pressures it places upon men, it complicates the simplistic understanding of older men as simply (and only) perpetrators (Shefer & Strebel 2012:59-60). Also, some young girls actively seek out such relationships, as a way to acquire the popular material goods that they desire, or for the social status they receive by being in a relationship with the particular man. This introduces a broader notion of exchange, highlighting that such relationships are not automatically exploitative (Shefer & Strebel 2012:58-59). Brouard and Crewe (2012:49), by emphasising that all relationships (including marriage) "are transactional in one way or another", show that a transactional relationship is not necessarily an exploitative relationship. It is the context of the relationship that determines whether it is exploitative, and therefore, careful attention must be paid to the social and economic context.

Interrogating the simple victim/perpetrator binary of intergenerational, transactional sex allows us to identify the core beliefs underlying transactional intergenerational sex. Contextualised forms of patriarchy are creating the context in which men are privileged and materially empowered, expected and expecting to be sexually prolific and to provide materially. This patriarchal system is what is disempowering women, constructing them as materially reliant on men, and expecting material compensation for sexual activities. Brouard and Crewe (2012) make the following observation:

> What emerges is a fascinating set of ideas around gender, patriarchy and socio-economic inequality. It seems that because patriarchy allows men to be better educated, more employable and socially and culturally empowered to take charge of money

and property, and because women are expected to be dependent, reproductive and reliant on men for status and power, conditions are created for sugar daddies to emerge. In other words, if there was greater equality between men and women, and patriarchal entitlements were denied men, young girls would not need to seek out older men for affirmation and financial security, whether this was, albeit obliquely, culturally endorsed or not. (p. 53)

This discussion of unmarried, age-disparate relationships highlights added complexities on child marriage in South Africa and more generally. A simplistic focus on girls *in marriages* allow us to lose sight of the many girls in informal relationships that are facing many of the same negative consequences. It shows how patriarchal constructs of men, women and intimate relationships create the opportunity for exploitation of girls – be they married or not. Once again it emphasises the importance of engaging with the social and gender norms that underlie these harmful relationships. Engaging the way South Africans think about love, sex, relationships and gender equality is needed in order to address the root causes of not only child marriage, but other forms of intimate relationships in which girls are exploited.

CONCLUSION

Child marriage has been receiving increasing attention internationally, with many treaties, conventions, laws, movements and organisations focused on eradicating the practice. This is needed, for child marriage violates children's rights on many levels, with girl children being especially affected. However, such a rights-based approach can often fail to adequately engage with the underlying drivers of child marriage. Many countries have attempted to end the practice through legislative means but have failed to do so. In South Africa, this is also the case. Contradictory and inadequate legislation has resulted in loopholes that actually allow the practice to legally continue. Yet, even if these loopholes are addressed and uniform legislation is drafted and implemented, will it lead to an end to child marriage? As the discussion of three particular dilemmas has unpacked, this is highly unlikely. A solely punitive approach to ending child marriage is unable to address the gender and social norms that drive child marriage. People do not change their beliefs and norms because of new laws. As long as patriarchal constructions of masculinity, femininity, and intimate relationships continue unopposed, child marriage will continue. It may be hidden (for example, with marriages only formally registered once the girl turns 18 years) or take new forms (such as 'modern' *ukuthwala*), but it will not end, for leaders, parents, guardians and girls themselves will continue to believe that girl children are a commodity that can be bartered.

The complex dilemmas surrounding child marriage in South Africa point to the fact that the need is not simply to end child marriage. We need to transform how South African societies value women and girls, but also men and boys, and what is considered normal and acceptable within intimate relationships. A legislative response will, therefore, never be comprehensive enough. But neither is a simplistic focus only on child marriage. What about other practices and relationships that harm and exploit girl children but have nevertheless become 'normal' in South African society? As long as key patriarchal beliefs continue to flourish uncontested, child marriage – as well as other practices that harm and exploit girl children – will continue.

CHAPTER 8

CHILDREN AND RACISM

Henry Mbaya

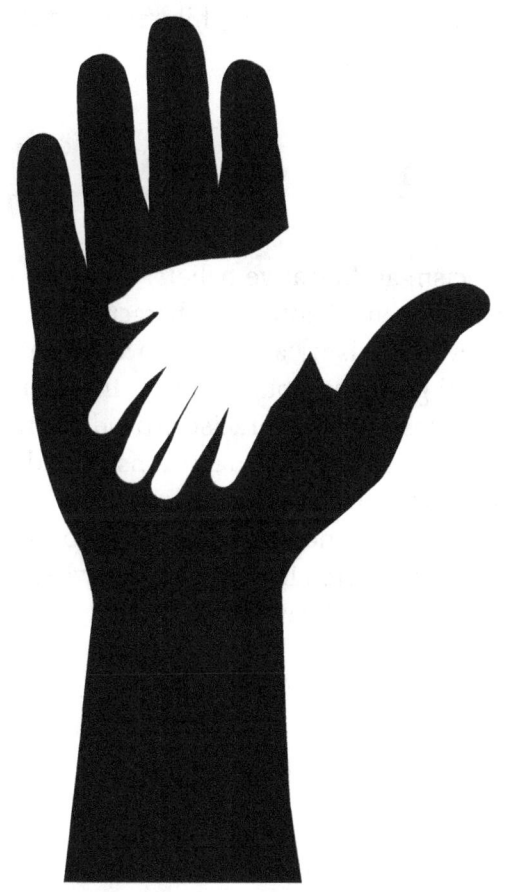

This chapter commences with defining and highlighting racism as a term and a concept; defining its nature and how it is related to identity formation, as an ethical issue with moral imperatives. Then it will give a very brief historical background of the institutionalisation of racism as apartheid in the South African educational system, followed by a discussion of racial consciousness in children by drawing on the wider global context, specifically analysing very briefly, the significance of the so-called Clark doll experiment in the USA. It then proceeds to argue that racism is a social construct determined by contextual factors, arguing that racial diversity, contrary to racism, is a 'natural' phenomenon.

From this perspective, the author then discusses responses to efforts of racial integration in schools in post-1994 South Africa. In this context, it is further argued that schools constitute critical spaces where racist attitudes and practices are formed and inculcated. Then the chapter highlights the role of literature and media in informing racist tendencies in children. Finally, it accentuates the critical role that parents, and adults play in the socialisation of children's racial attitudes.

WHAT IS RACISM?

Pachter et al. (2010:61) defined racism as "negative beliefs, attitudes, actions, or behaviours that are based on phenotypic characteristics or ethnic affiliations." In their view, "[racism] assumes an inherent superiority on the basis of perceived group attributes" (:61). In other words, perceptions of group identities engender racist attitudes. In this respect, racism can be understood as being socially constructed. It is inherent in societal norms, traditions and attitudes. In some communities, over years, wrong beliefs and attitudes have been projected to appear as 'normal' and 'acceptable'. In communities where racism is acceptable, it finds legitimation as a way of life. Pachter et al. posits that

[r]acism is often conceptualised as including beliefs and attitudes (racial prejudice) and actions and practices. It can occur on individual, internal or structural (institutional) levels, and it can either be subtle or obvious … (p. 61)

In other words, racism is holistic; it entangles one's whole personality and character. On the other hand, Davis and Gandy (1999:368) denoted that, "racial identity may be understood as an ideological position." Ideologically defined, it is "patterns of ideas, belief systems, or interpretive schemes found in a society or found amongst specific social groups" (:368). Historically in South Africa, apartheid as a race-driven ideology has defined the destinies of races and ethnicities. Racial behaviour is considered to be a determinant of social behaviour. It influences "the individual choices" we make in society (:368). Multiple factors in context and operating on different levels of our existence define our racial identity and consciousness (:369).

Qureshi et al. (2008), argue that racism is an ethical issue related to mental and psychological problems. They assert that an increasing number of research "studies link the experience of racism to a variety of health and mental problems, with stress as the most direct link" (:S4). They further assert that the understanding of racism has shifted from viewing racism as overt "associated with white supremacy to unintentional or 'aversive' racism" (:S4). In other words, according to Qureshi et al., racism is more subtle. They conclude stating that, "[r]acism in mental health care is an ethical issue for psychiatrists and psychologists because it represents a very damaging force that is associated with mental health problems, and as such requires effective response" (:S4). The negative health effects of racism suggest that it is an unnatural social practice as it estranges a victim from his or her victimiser. Because of the adverse effect it has on relationships, racism is morally untenable and reprehensible precisely because it threatens to build healthy relationships in society.

Racial identity operates on many levels and in complex layers of existence. It entails group consciousness (Davis & Gandy 1999:374), goes beyond the colour of one's skin, defines one's intellect and "operates on a symbolic level" (Kelly 2018:23-24), and a material level. The inevitable critical question that arises is: Are we born racists? Kristen Russell (2017), citing Jason Marsh, answers that

> [no], we aren't necessarily born racist … But we are born with a certain predisposition to fear that which we deem to be unlike us somehow. We are born with a predisposition to group people into categories. (n.p.)

Russell (2017:n.p.), citing Jason Marsh (2010:n.p.) continued stating that racism is about categorising people into racially different and inferior groups, where they are stereotyped and considered as the opposite to us. In short, racism is about an individual or group's assertion of power and identity. However, it goes beyond group categorisation. It is also rooted in systems and structures, it is institutional. As Constantine (in Small-Glover et al. (2013:49) puts it succinctly, "[r]acism is an institutional pattern of power and social control that attempts to oppress people based on their ethnic or racial group membership."

Jones (in Small-Glover et al. 2013:49.) categorised racism into three components: individual, institutional, and cultural. In Jones' view, individual racism entails subjecting a person to discriminatory practices on account of their ethnic or racial "group and seeks to deprive them of access to opportunities" (:49). Fundamentally, it is about disempowering others by denying them access to resources, and by extension, power. Thus, this chapter will argue that children's racism operates not only on a morphological level but entails symbolic order and consciousness as well.

CHAPTER 8

INSTITUTIONALISATION OF RACISM IN THE SOUTH AFRICAN EDUCATIONAL SYSTEM

In South Africa, while the foundation of racism was laid long before, it was institutionalised from 1948 onwards. The *Bantu Education Act* of 1953, as it especially affected Black children in schools, laid a firm foundation of school racism as it continues to be experienced until today (Levy 2015:n.p.). The then Minister, Hendrik Verwoerd introduced *Bantu Education* to parliament, which was designed "to prepare African children for the lower echelons of the labour market" (:n.p.). Education in this new system would effectively be run by the Native Affairs Department (NAD) where Verwoerd (as minister) could more effectively control it.

Verwoerd's attempts to sanitise the implementation of Bantu Education as beneficial for the "'spiritual virtues of the Bantu' community and his senseless rationale for Bantu Education could not change the perceptions of African parents that this was a measure for the intellectual enslavement of their children" (Levy 2015:n.p.). Facilities and support structures and systems were heavily skewed against Black children to favour White children, with under-qualified teachers. "Each African pupil received only 14% of the amount spent on a white pupil and just over half the sum spent on an Indian or Coloured student" (:n.p.).

Feldman (2018) noted that Bantu Education affected White children on psychological level and through propaganda. Using propaganda and operating on the level of mind-forming, young white children were socialised into believing that apartheid was not wrong. White children knew little or nothing at all about the life of Black people. In other words, in schools to some extent, the racist ideology of apartheid operated on the level of ideology. It made a subtle impression on the malleable minds of young white children.

RACIAL CONSCIOUSNESS IN CHILDREN – CLARK'S DOLL EXPERIMENT IN THE USA

The question as to at what age children begin to acquire racist attitudes has exercised academic debate for a long time (Katz 1976:2). Katz (:2) noted that the "evidence available suggests that by three or four years of age many children make differential responses to skin colour and other racial cues." While there seems to be a consensus that ethnic attitudes start developing early in the nursery school years, the question of children's early preferences, however, still remain unresolved. Katz (:62) further stated that, "many theorists argue that the development of ethnic attitudes is tied to the processes of self-development in a child's identity." It is assumed that part of the self-discovery processes of children, entails learning which group they belong to or not. In other words, the development of self-consciousness in early child development is a critical phase in the forming of racial identity consciousness.

An experiment was performed in the 1940s by psychologists, Kenneth Bancroft Clark and his wife, Mamie Phipps Clark, to attempt to understand the indicators of racial bias in Black children (1947:169). Kenneth Clark experimented with Black children of ages from six to nine, with two dolls, one white and the other one, black. He posed questions to them such as, "Show me the doll that you like to play with … show me the doll that's a nice doll … show me the doll that's a bad doll" (:169). It was noted that, "[t]he black children who attended segregated schools had an even higher instance of choosing the black doll as bad and preferring the white doll to play with – over 70%" (:169). When Clark asked those boys and girls, "[n]ow show me the doll that's most like you", some became "emotionally upset at having to identify with the doll that they had rejected" (:169). Some even stormed out of the room. As Clark recalled, he and his wife concluded that "color in a racist society was a very disturbing and traumatic component of an individual's sense of his own self-esteem and worth" (:169). The Clark's experiment showed that Black children experienced racial segregation as traumatic. It is clear from the experiment that the racial ordering in society made them to believe and understand that to be Black was inferior, and, therefore, being less than human. It estranged them; it undermined their dignity. American Society had socialised them to believe that Whites were superior to Blacks; that being Black was ugly. According to Oelofsen (2015:135), a similar study conducted in South Africa in 2011, showed that in spite of efforts to bridge racial gaps, "South African children still show[ed] sensitivity to 'race'." Oelofsen (2015) states that,

> [s]imilar studies conducted in other parts of the world seemed to confirm the perception that white children show[ed] a high own-race preference, which is not present in black or mixed 'race' children. (p.135)

Oelofsen (2015:135) asserted that, "the symbolic order in which white is seen as good and pure, while black is seen as the opposite, namely evil and tainted, is one which still permeates the global discourse." Global order fosters perceptions that define whiteness as 'right' and 'might' and blackness as its opposite. Oelofsen (2015:135) went on to conclude that, "[t]hese stereotypes, [are] ... embedded deep within many of our collective psyches". In other words, for Oelofsen, racism is a global challenge that is driven by more or less established perceptions and attitudes of White people's racial superiority over Black people that operate along binary and symbolic language, stereotyping racial superiority versus inferiority. From this perspective, we can conclude that racism exists to undermine the dignity of Black people.

RACISM AS A SOCIAL CONSTRUCT

Wipfler (2019:n.p.) argued that "[c]hildren are not, by nature, racist. Nor are they born with damaging assumptions about people in any definable group." They are socially conditioned to be racially biased.

Hewitt (2018) noted that racial-ethnic socialisation entails four components: "(1) instilling cultural pride; (2) preparation for bias; (3) promotion of mistrust; and (4) egalitarianism." In her view "[t]he goal of racial socialization is to provide children with a healthy sense of themselves while giving them tools to actively cope with varying forms of oppression" (Hewitt 2018). She further opined that

> [b]lack children and adolescents who learn that others may have negative attitudes towards them but who have these messages mediated by parents, peers, and other important adults are less likely to have negative outcomes and more likely to be resilient in adverse conditions.

Racism is contrary to the natural ordering of society where diversity is normative. As Claire McCarthy (2019) verbalised it:

> Biologically we are truly just one race, sharing 99.9% of our genes no matter what the color of our skin or what part of the world we come from. But historically we have found ways to not just identify differences, but to oppress people because of them. (p. 1)

McCarthy (2019:1) further expressed that "irrespective of the fact that biologically we are the same as humans, nonetheless, people still perceive differences, they assume racial superiority, racism still persists as a 'socially transmitted disease'." It is a social malady because it rests on false premises that one racial group of people is inherently superior to the other. It dehumanises people and arrogates power to one group over the other. Racism influences our attitudes and actions to people when we have stereotyped them according to race categories on the basis of their appearance and our perceptions of them (:1). Thus, it determines how we order our relations in society. It is ideological and determined by assumptions of superiority over the other group. It is socially constructed and determined and thus, it is a mask. It is a mask that people invent and wear to hide their inner fears and insecurities. It is a coping mechanism. Therefore, Oelofsen (2015:135) has argued that the white superiority complex is socially structured in a manner that it relates to black identity, which itself, is specifically created for that purpose. In particular, it exists and functions in terms of a symbolic order of existence and meaning. William Gumede (2016:n.p.) has argued that even though racism was abolished by legislation in South Africa, it still manifests itself in very sophisticated and subtle ways in daily lives and institutions. He asserted that

> [r]acism is proscribed in South Africa so day to day racism is now more subtle. The difficulty therefore is that racism, because it is so ingrained, is often unconscious. Just as the police, for example, may put less effort into investigating crimes against ordinary blacks, newsrooms may put fewer resources into covering them. But blacks often also perpetuate racism. Shouting 'racism' to sideline rivals, for self-enrichment at the expense of the public good, or to deflect attention from our own foibles, undermines the fight against racism. (:n.p.)

Gumede (2016) makes crucial points such as that racism is so entrenched in the mind-set of South Africans that sometimes it comes out unwittingly, and that Blacks also perpetuate racism in various subtle practices and attitudes. It lurks behind racial solidarity and "to support often very morally flawed, corrupt and dishonest leaders and undemocratic practices, also undermines the battle against racism" (:n.p.). These practices, according to Gumede, "only reinforces deeply held racial stereotypes of black" and he concludes asserting that "better governance is crucial in slaying the racism dragon" (:n.p.). Thus, Gumede has raised a moral and ethical dimension of racism, namely, negligence in reporting wrongdoing, and sometimes demonising one's rivals as racist in an attempt to silence them for the wrongdoing.

RACISM IS UNNATURAL AS DIVERSITY AND INCLUSIVITY IS NATURAL

Racism has psychological effects. It is an issue that entails emotions. Swart et al. (2010) conducted a study exploring the effects of interracial, interactive contacts in relation to racial prejudice in South Africa, with specific "attention to the mediational role of intergroup anxiety" (:310). In the study, the psychological dimension of race came to the fore, for example the factor of intergroup anxiety. According to Swart et al., the study demonstrated that close racial interaction by race reduces anxiety. In their argument, they concluded that racial interaction, rather than exclusion, has been associated with "reduced intergroup anxiety, increased affective empathy, positive outgroup attitudes, greater perceived outgroup variability, and reduced negative action tendencies" (:326). They add: "These findings suggest that crossgroup friendships may indeed be important in bringing about improved intergroup relations and intergroup understanding within the South African context, and highlight the central importance of intergroup emotions in the contact–prejudice relationship" (:326).

POST-1994 RACIAL INTEGRATION IN SCHOOLS

Citing Chisholm (2005:215), Meier & Hartell (2009:184) concluded that just as racial separation constituted the characteristic feature of schools in the apartheid era, racial integration became a characteristic feature in the post-apartheid era. Thus, in the 1990s a significant amount of Government-commissioned research focused on the challenges faced in addressing racism and integration in schools. Notably, the *South African School Act* (1996) laid down the principle of restructuring schools in the image of non-racialism and outlawed all forms of discrimination.

Meier and Hartell (2009:181) observed that schools have responded in diverse ways to policies and legislation to desegregate, put in place after 1994. The assimilationist approach, adopted in most schools, requires learners from previously advantaged backgrounds to adapt to the curriculum, cultures and ethos designed for a different racial group (:181). Therefore, this leaves the status quo intact as the learners merely have to assimilate into a different educational system.

With regard to the 'colour blind' approach, educators claim to see the learner and not the colour but in fact educators gloss over or suppress their racist attitudes, consequently, nothing changes (Meier & Hartell 2009:181). Educators who follow this approach are not willing to change as they believe that to do so would be lowering the standards of the White schools. The contributionist approach, which seeks to change the institutional culture of the school, is not helpful either (:181). Occasional observation of Indian or Zulu cultural days in the yearly calendar of the school pays only token recognition to the cultural contributions of learners from previously disadvantaged schools. It does not transform the institutional race culture of the school (:181). The problem is that the schools do not go beneath the surface to transform the ethos and ideological learnings of the curriculum and open access to equal opportunities. In fact, these efforts fall short of addressing racist attitudes and practices embedded in the age-old traditions, and ethos of schools, some of which are not so obvious.

Zungu (2017:n.p.) expressed the opinion that "[o]ur schools are the breeding ground of racism in South Africa." Zungu went on to note that

> [i]t's no longer individuals that are racist per se; it's institutions like schools that perpetuate white supremacy in more surreptitious ways ... [It] has become institutionalised ... children are uniquely exposed and vulnerable to the racial prejudices of friends and teachers. (n.p.)

Zungu's opinions raise the critical issue of the relationship between school space and the power of racism and ideology on the one hand, and on the other how these factors shape the interactions of learners in designated spaces of schools.

SCHOOLS AS SPACES OF SOCIALISATION OF RACISM

Space embodies and configures power. It influences how people relate to it, and vice versa. Doreen Massey (2009) puts it as follows:

> The way in which space is conceptualised, in intellectual work, in social life, and in political practice, matters. It has effects, intellectual, social and political... [It entails] three characteristics: First: that space is the product of relations (including the absence of relations). Space is a complexity of networks, links, exchanges, connections, from the intimate level of our daily lives (think of spatial relations within the home for example) to the global level of financial corporations, for instance, or of counter-hegemonic political activists. (p. 16)

Humans relate to space, as it relates to them. It shapes and moulds them as they shape and mould it. Thus, space entails identity and meaning for people. As Massey (2009) states further:

> [S]pace is a «product»: it is produced through the establishment or refusal of relations. It also implies, as a logical consequence, that space is in its very nature «social» (where social is taken to mean «more than individual», rather than simply «human»). (p. 17)

Space configures multiple dimensions of power relationships in social networks. It defines the possibilities and limitations of those networks; it can liberate, as well as constrain relationships. As Massey (2009) puts it:

> If there is to be a relation (or, indeed, a non-relation) there needs to be at least more than one thing to do the relating, or not.

This leads to the second proposition about the characteristics of space. This is indeed that space is the dimension of multiplicity. (p. 17)

In this regard, Massey (2009) concludes:

Without space as a dimension it would not be possible for there to be multiplicity (in the sense of the simultaneous coexistence of more than one thing). Equally, and as the mirror image of this, without multiplicity space itself could not exist (space is the product of relations within multiplicity). Space and multiplicity are mutually constitutive. (p. 17)

Space embodies power which configures multiple dimensions of relationships. In turn, these relationships give meaning to space. Hence, interactions in designated spaces shape perceptions and reality. Schools entail special spaces of social interaction. As designated places for imparting knowledge, they are structures where ideological assumptions, ideals and practices of the ruling elite are inculcated. Child racism is one of such issues. It is transmitted through cultural practices of the dominant which may masquerade as 'discipline' or as the acceptable conduct or behaviour code of the school. For instance, on 15 July 2019, Mbobo (2019:n.p.) reported that a high school in Pretoria imposed Western hairstyles on African children. The story roused rage from Black parents nationwide. "Parents from other races wondered why Africans were being dramatic about hair, but this serves as an example of policies that were created without considering Africans" (:n.p.). This incident shows that schools constitute critical spaces for the socialisation of children into racism. In this respect, space configured the power to include or exclude, to integrate or segregate.

Racism is an issue of power; the power to assert oneself over the other. As Jerome Joorst (2019) argued:

> Racism is also closely linked to structures of power. Teachers, for example, often hold more power – either directly inscribed in policies or codes or indirectly exercised through education practices – than learners in a classroom setting. The way the teacher uses that power can determine the extent to which a learner, especially one who is of a different race group to the teachers, can speak back to that power ... (n.p.)

In other words, issues of power in the school are intricately interwoven in race relationships. These dimensions of power are deep-seated and sometimes almost silent. Thus, they cannot easily be identified. They lurk behind the traditions, structures and ethos of school life. As Joorst (2019) observed:

> Racism, meanwhile, includes beliefs, thoughts and actions based on the idea that one race is innately superior to another. Many of the events that play out in South African schools can be classified as implicit racism. That's because racism in schools very often emanates from broader structural and institutional racism. This is less easy to recognise from the outside than instances of racist language or behaviour. (n.p.)

Zungu (2017) has been highly critical of institutional racism in schools and has noted the subtle manner in which racism plays out in schools. In his view "[i]t is perpetuated almost unknowingly." Believing that apartheid is over and that racial diversity is a reality, these children are often unable to notice racist attitudes and actions. The system operates in such a way that Black children do not often notice racist practices operating in the system. Black children tend to be treated as subordinates to their White counterparts (Zungu 2017).

In other words, racism operates on the level of consciousness and ideology. These practices run counter to principles of justice and natural order. Wipfler (2019) is of the opinion that (c)ontrary to popular belief, children have a keen inborn sense of justice. They are built to protest loudly when they or someone else is being treated badly. This sense of justice runs deep ... We don't have to teach children respect for people of other races and abilities. We simply need to preserve their trust in themselves and others, and their inborn sense of justice. (n.p.)

Anderson and Dougé (2019), offered more insights into the processes of learning bias in children by stating that

[t]he process of learning racial bias is a lot like learning a new language ... As early as 6 months, a baby's brain can notice race-based differences. By ages 2 to 4, children can internalize racial bias. By age 12, many children become set in their beliefs – giving parents a decade to mould the learning process, so that it decreases racial bias and improves cultural understanding. But like language immersion, children exposed to society will gain fluency in racial bias even if their parents do nothing. (n.p.)

In other words, racial bias is acquired through a fine process of cultural internalisation and consciousness. Children pick up racial attitudes from their parents and teachers or other adults in society through a complex process of socialisation.

THE ROLE OF LITERATURE IN RACIAL SOCIALISATION

In this socialisation process, literature plays a significant role in perpetuating racist perceptions and attitudes in children in South Africa. Klein (1985), for example, noted that

[m]any adults and children believe that books can be racist ... [It is] a book that imprints a racist image on the reader's mind ...

> The racist view is that presented by the dominant (here, white) group of all other groups as being in some way inferior. (p.4)

The standards by which the dominant group measures all others are also themselves determined by the dominant group, and so are inevitably distorted. Racism in books can have many causes, from the unthinking and insensitive passing on of prevailing attitudes, to the conscious strategy of rendering the "'other' as 'lesser', in order to attack or exploit them..." (Klein 1985:14). These books "instil in children the attitudes and the values of the author which form the 'residue' in the child's mind" (:14). Children become victims of racist ideology.

To some extent, the legacy of apartheid on children's literature continues to impact South Africa today. For instance, MacCann and Maddy (2001) noted that

> South African children's novels (for ages eight to eighteen) have not portrayed Blacks as ready for equal opportunities. Nor have they shown Africans capable of taking their destiny into their own hands. (p. xiii)

In contrast, "they have typically depicted them as entirely unfit for civic responsibility ..." (MacCann &d Maddy 2001:xiii). In their view, therefore, "[c]hildren's literature is an indicator that points to the tenacity of such calculated racial bias" (:xiii).

THE ROLE OF THE MEDIA IN RACIAL SOCIALISATION

Davis and Gandy (1999) noted that

> [m]edia representations play an important role in informing the ways in which we understand social, cultural, ethnic, and racial

differences. Racial identity may play an especially powerful role in shaping our responses to mass media. (p. 36)

For instance, Hewitt (2018:n.p.), speaking from an American context, asserts that, "Black Panther, besides living up to the hype of its potential success, it also counters many popular depictions of what it means to be Black and African." As a movie, with all its positive elements, as well as its limitations, it opens opportunities for parents and caregivers to talk with their children about race. The film brings about "important dynamics of what it means to be African versus African American to the strength and determination of Black women" (:n.p.).

In South Africa, the role of the media in socialising children into racism has come under scrutiny by the government. In August 2000, the South African Human Rights Commission produced a report entitled 'Faultlines: An Inquiry into Racism in the Media: South African government'. The report expressed the view that in South Africa, child racism is historically deeply rooted in the national psyche of the nation. In particular, it highlighted the deep hegemonic character of racism. A part of the report (South African Human Rights Commission 2000) declared that

> (t)he historic ideology of a meritocracy based on race is passed down through the generations at the level of truism. It is not questioned at the time it is conveyed – by society to child – because the information is offered uncontroversially. It is also justified by what the child sees in the world of reality. Any later questioning of truism is difficult when it has been accepted in early childhood when values are formed. (p. 58)

In other words, society has so much 'naturalised' racism that it has been easily accepted as a way of life that cannot be changed. It operates on the level of the taken-for-granted and all races have accepted more or less the status quo. The South African Human Rights Commission Report (2000) went on to state that

> [m]ost importantly, racist ideology is absorbed in the same way by both races. The national culture is essentially the culture of the dominant 'race', but because it is national everyone within that culture absorbs it. In South Africa Black children are given the same essential messages as White children – to the effect that White people are superior to Black people. Like White children they receive the information as fact. It is justified by everything they see around them in terms of successful access to resources and opportunities and worldly achievement. (p. 58)

Racism as a social construct, so entrenched in the attitudes, habits and life-style, is re-enforced by systems and structures which allow and deny access to resources in society on racial grounds. In other words, perceptions and attitudes of racism are buttressed by material conditions on the ground. The report (South African Human Rights Commission 2000:58) continued to assert that accommodation to the ideology by both sides is the fundamental challenge facing the society. This report further stated

> [t]his is a defining characteristic of racism: both sides believe the ideology to some degree. This is different from mutually hostile groups who are roughly equal in strength: neither of them internalises the stigmatising stereotypes of the 'other'. (p. 58)

The report shows the extent to which the media plays a critical role in entrenching racist tendencies in children in South Africa. However, the media is merely one important pillar of society that inculcates racist attitudes and lifestyle. The role of parents or adults in influencing children is equally critical.

In 2018, *Eye-Witness News* reported that the Retail giant shop H & M was compelled to apologise for using a Black child to promote a sweatshirt with the slogan "coolest monkey in the jungle". The company withdrew the ad from its "website after hundreds of social media users accused it of being racist. However, it continues to sell the hooded top online" (:n.p.). The use of the ad with this slogan, raises the ethical issue as to the image of the boy used.

In 2006, the *Media Monitoring Project* (MMP), conducted a research project to determine how media represented children, the Empowering Children & Media project (ECM) 29. The study dealt with various topics that affected children, one of which was race. The MMP's (Mtwana & Bird 2006:17) study found that racial issues affecting children "were not generally discussed in the media unless it was in a report dealing specifically with a racial/racist incident." Such reporting, however, did not give a background and an in-depth analysis to the issues "around human rights and discrimination." One example related to two Black children who were told by a White farmer to paint themselves with white paint. This incident was not reported as racist even though it had a strong racial dimension to it.

As a comparative case, the MMP (Mtwana & Bird 2006) cited an incident that involved the coverage of the Happy Sindane case, the 16 year old from Bronkhorstpruit. The media reported that "he was in search of his 'White' parents claiming that he was kidnapped by a 'Black' domestic worker and she brought him to the township as her child" (:17). While the media clearly identified the incident as racial, "it had little analysis of the racial issues at stake" (:17). There are two issues here regarding journalism. It is possible that the reporters lacked the skills of journalism, or there was a deliberate negligence, or oversight on reporting on such crucial issues. This kind of reporting gives the impression that the issues were not very important. However, more importantly, in either case, it would seem to suggest that the media was complicit in ignoring the issues of human rights and justice that underlay the racial incidents. It would seem to me that the under-reporting may also have some ethical implications with regard to the manner of reporting of these incidents.

THE ROLE OF PARENTS IN RACIAL SOCIALISATION

The role of parents in racial socialisation plays a critical role in moulding racial identity in children. Lee (2019:n.p.) observed that grade-schoolers are impressionable from a very early age. They are at a stage when they can form opinions about themselves, as well as of others around them. "This is when their natural curiosity about differences in appearance and cultural backgrounds really begin to come into play." (:n.p.). Lee further states that:

> [m]ost are born with a natural sense of justice and fairness. Unless they are taught to be hurtful and cruel, children know that it's wrong to attack others either physically or with words. All we have to do is nurture this natural love of people and get out of their way. (:n.p.)

Similarly, as Kang (2017) observed,

> [c]hildren form biases early, and can quickly pick up cues from adults as well as peers ... Kids may be exposed to prejudiced attitudes at home, as well as at school. These learned biases can have a significant impact on how they perceive and treat others. (:n.p.)

From the American context, Wipfler (2019) stated how a child relates and responds to racist situations and contexts. She pronounced that

> [w]hen any child witnesses racism, it frightens [him and her]. The racism fastens onto fears that have cracked a child's confidence in himself and others, like a secondary infection invades an open wound. [He/she] doesn't feel good enough or strong enough to reject racist mistreatment and protest it. So

the words, tones, and attitudes are imprinted in his mind, along with a fresh helping of fear. (:n.p.)

If he is a black child, according to Wipfler (2019),

[h]is fears have propped the door open for the racist tones, words, and stereotypes to enter his mind and become part of how he thinks about himself and his people. When he feels upset, separate, afraid, or angry, he will believe the racist content. (:n.p.)

A black child "who is feeling upset may also act out the oppressor role of racism, targeting either himself or other children of color" (Wipfler 2019:n.p.). About white children, Wipfler stated:

[a] white child's fears also make [him or her] vulnerable to adopting racist tones, words, and stereotypes. When a white child feels separate, scared, or disconnected, he tries to escape these feelings by playing out the oppressor role he has been frightened by. The intensity of his actions will reflect the depth of the fears that the child carried before the racism he witnessed gave those fears a racial twist. (:n.p.)

In a report by the National Academies of Sciences, Engineering, and Medicine (2016) it is pointed out that

[c]hild outcomes are interconnected within and across diverse domains of development. They result from and are enhanced by early positive and supportive interactions with parents and other caregivers. These early interactions can have a long-lasting ripple effect on development across the life course. (:46)

Wipfler (2019:n.p.) makes a similar point by stating that the parents' influence in winning trust can be critical to the life-long development of a wholesome character in a child. In her view, it is crucial that parents endeavour to develop a very close relationship with the child; showing the child lots of affection and set 'sensible limits' for the child. Grown-ups who do not attack the child, will make the child feel at home and relaxed with others. In this kind of environment, the child grows up to trust people (:n.p.).

Wipfler's argument is crucial. Sooner or later, the child will start projecting in the wider community attitudes and habits picked up in the family. Socialisation of a child on this level will have long-term consequences for the wider society. According to McAdoo (1999:7), studies done in the USA concluded that it was more difficult to raise children to have pride in their group identity in an environment where their group was perceived negatively by the wider community. McAdoo (:7) further noted that the "difference may exist between a child's self-concept and his or her ethnic or racial identity. These are two distinct variables, and they are often at odds with each other."

On the other hand, according to Pachter et al. (2010:n.p.), "[r]acism can be conceptualised as a toxic stressor that may affect health and well-being." McCarthy (2019) noted that racism can be seen as a disease.

> Racism and its effects can lead to chronic stress for children. And chronic stress leads to actual changes in hormones that cause inflammation in the body, a marker of chronic disease. Stress that a mother experiences during pregnancy can affect children even before they are born. (p. 1)

POSITIVE PARENTING: PARENT-CHILD RELATIONSHIPS

Racial socialisation can also have positive dimensions. Klein (1985:23) gave an example of parents' positive influence on children's ability to confront racial bias. She refers to the seven-year-old Maria who was able to point to racism and sexism in a book. Burt, Kit Lei and

CHAPTER 8

Simons (2017:418) declared that "[s]cholarship suggests that racial socialization practices may promote resilience to racial discrimination in part by fostering positive racial identities." They argue that

> [a]mong Black Americans, racial identity is defined as "the significance and qualitative meaning that individuals attribute to being Black in their conceptualizations of self"... (p. 419)

For parents to achieve this, Anderson and Douge (2019:n.p.) suggest that they must first come to terms with their own racial attitudes before they can correct attitudes of racial and ethnic intolerance in children. Lee (2019:n.p.) expresses the same view stating that "[p]arents must first face up to their racial prejudices before they deal with racial messages they impart on their children." To be a role model for their children, parents must first deal with their racially influenced thoughts, feelings and actions. Lee (:n.p.) opined that to foster a "culture of inclusiveness, we must face up to and acknowledge our own racial biases, so that we can deal with those that are unfair or cause harm to others." Anderson and Douge (2019) went further saying that "[i]f you want your children to believe what you preach, you have to exhibit those behaviors as well", and they added to this that

> [c]hildren learn racial bias through everyday comments and actions from adults. It entails the process of socialisation; that take place on deeper levels, of thinking, internalization of thoughts, which influence perceptions. Your everyday comments and actions will say more than anything else. Have a wide, culturally diverse social network. Encourage your children to have diverse circles of friends, as well. This lends itself to engagement in multicultural activities and experiences. (:n.p.)

But parents should also call out racism and discuss it with their children (Russell 2017:n.p.). Lee (2019:n.p.) emphasised that "[t]alking about different cultures and customs and races and answering any questions they have taught your child that it's okay to notice differences, and more importantly, it teaches him that it's good to talk about them." It is much better to discuss children's questions about physical and cultural differences, than ignoring it and not helping them to understand and accept these differences.

Lee (2019:n.p.) also made the point that understanding the feelings and behaviour of people in other communities can not only open possibilities for healing after a tragedy has occurred but can also prevent future ones. In conclusion, Kang (2017:n.p.) stated that by learning to deal with the situation with forthrightness, and frankly sharing with friends, 'authority figures' will make children feel empowered, and positive to deal with negative situations.

CONCLUSION

This chapter started by defining and highlighting racism as a societal problem. Specifically, it argued that racism is a social construct, conditioned by societal attitudes and lifestyles. It demonstrated that racism is unnatural, as it runs counter to natural principles of human equality. It also argued that racist attitudes in children derive from the processes of socialisation in society in four areas: the school, literature, the media and the home. It was emphasised that schools and the educational system play a most critical role in socialising children in racist attitudes and practices. The critical role that parents play in fostering racist attitudes and habits in children was discussed and some perspectives on positive parenting were stressed.

CHAPTER 9

REFLECTIONS ON THE EFFECTIVENESS OF CHILD SUPPORT GRANTS

Krige Siebrits

INTRODUCTION

South Africa's unusually large social assistance system annually transfers some 3% of the country's gross domestic product (GDP) to the poor as cash grants.[1] The child support grant (CSG) programme is one of the cornerstones of this system. Government spending on this programme exceeds 1% of South Africa's GDP, and, in March 2019, nearly 70% of the 17.8 million grants disbursed in South Africa were CSGs (South African Social Security Agency 2019:18).

The premise of this chapter is that a humane society should maintain safety net schemes to meet the basic needs of children and other vulnerable persons. Given the extent of poverty in South Africa and its severe effects on large numbers of children, this premise implies that measures, such as the CSG programme, are essential. Yet the same factors that make such interventions essential also underscore the necessity of ensuring their effectiveness. An appropriate criterion for assessing the effectiveness of the CSG programme is the degree to which its benefits to children are maximised. The design and implementation of the programme, as well as the usage of the funds by households, all influence its efficacy. In turn, the choices that manifest in these aspects of the programme reflect the beliefs of society about its obligations to poor children, those of policymakers about the requisites and agency of the poor, and those of caregivers about the needs of children and the role of grant money within household budgets. The salience of choices rooted in beliefs imparts a strong ethical slant to attempts to assess the effectiveness of the CSG programme.

The chapter proceeds with an overview of economic and social influences on the living conditions of South African children. This section highlights the high incidence of poverty in South Africa and its severe effects on children. Next, the chapter sketches the history

---

[1] According to the World Bank (2018:16), government spending on social assistance programmes in developing countries averages about 1.5% of GDP.

CHAPTER 9

of the CSG programme and outlines its main characteristics. A review of empirical research into the effectiveness of CSGs follows. This section also identifies limitations of the programme. Against this backdrop, the final section offers broad suggestions for improving the CSG programme itself and for enhancing its effectiveness by means of changes to other policies that affect the living conditions and future prospects of children.

THE LIVING CONDITIONS OF SOUTH AFRICAN CHILDREN

Table 1, which shows data from the Living Conditions Survey (LCS) 2014/15, confirms that poverty is rife in South Africa. In 2015, 13.8 million South Africans (that is, 25.2% of the population) earned less than the equivalent of R6 456 in April 2019 prices – the minimum amount needed to purchase enough food to remain in adequate health. The incomes of fully 21.9 million persons (40.0% of the South African population) fell short of the equivalent of R9 468 in April 2019 prices, which meant that they had to sacrifice food to purchase essential non-food items. Well over half of the population – a total of 30.4 million persons – earned less than the equivalent of R14 520 in April 2019 prices. These South Africans could not purchase adequate volumes of essential food and non-food items.

Table 1: Measures of income poverty in South Africa (2015)

Poverty lines (Rands per person per annum)#	Millions of persons	Per cent of population
Food poverty line (R6 456)##	13.8	25.2
Lower-bound poverty line (R9 468)##	21.9	40.0
Upper-bound poverty line (R14 520)##	30.4	55.5

Source: Statistics South Africa (2017a:14).

Notes:
\# The poverty line amounts in the Statistics South Africa report were adjusted to April 2019 values using Table B.1 and B.2 in Statistics South Africa (2019a:5).

\## Statistics South Africa (2017:7a) described the three poverty lines as follows: "Stats SA employed an internationally recognised approach – the cost-of-basic-needs approach – to produce three poverty lines, namely the food poverty line (FPL), the lower-bound poverty line (LBPL), and the upper-bound poverty line (UBPL) ... The FPL is the rand value below which individuals are unable to purchase or consume enough food to supply them with the minimum per-capita-per-day energy requirement for adequate health. The LBPL and UBPL are derived using the FPL as a base, but also include a non-food component. Individuals at the LBPL do not have command over enough resources to purchase or consume both adequate food and non-food items and are, therefore, forced to sacrifice food to obtain essential non-food items. Meanwhile, individuals at the UBPL can purchase both adequate levels of food and non-food items."

It is well known that South Africa has one of the most unequal distributions of income of all countries. The summary of the South African income distribution in Table 2 underscores the extent of poverty. The figures in this table are also based on the findings of the LCS 2014/15; as such, they reflect the situation in 2015, but all amounts are inflated to April 2019 values.

Table 2: The distribution of income in South Africa (2015)

Income decile	Average annual income (Rand)#	Per cent of total income
1 (Poorest)	7 661	0.6
2	19 818	1.1
3	30 219	1.5
4	42 832	2.1
5	57 152	2.9
6	79 216	4.1
7	114 393	6.0
8	177 953	9.7
9	315 278	18.1
10 (Richest)	841 419	53.9

Sources: Statistics South Africa (2017b:208; 2019:164).

Note: # This column contains average household incomes adjusted to April 2019 values using Table B.1 and B.2 in Statistics South Africa (2019b:5).

It transpires from Table 2 that only households in the four richest deciles had average incomes of R100 000 or more per annum in April 2019 prices. In fact, the average annual income of the richest decile of households was almost 110 times that of households in the poorest decile, 42 times that of households in decile 2 and almost 28 times that of households in decile 3. Whereas 53.9% of total household income accrued to the richest 10% of households, the income share of the poorest 50% of households was a mere 8.2%.

Figure 1 shows that the high incidence of poverty severely affects South African children: The LCS 2014/15 revealed that the portions of children living in poverty were higher than those of adults irrespective of the choice of poverty line.[2] It is alarming to note that two-thirds of all children in South Africa then lived in households that were unable

---

2 Statistics South Africa (2018:28) classify everyone aged 0-17 years as children.

to afford adequate volumes of essential food and non-food items. In fact, the households in which fully one-third of children lived in 2015 could not even purchase enough food to remain in adequate health.

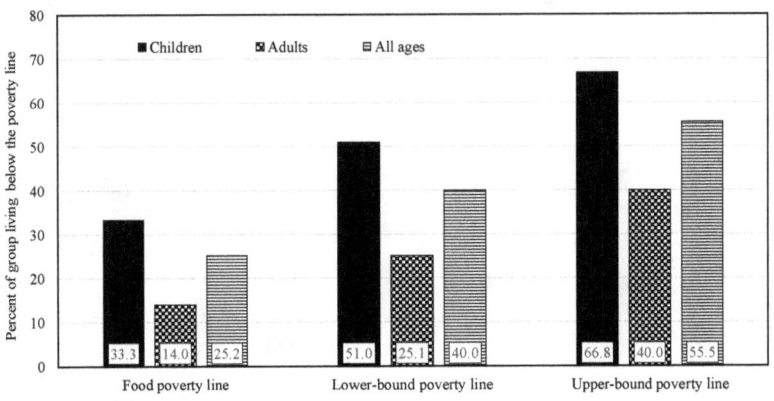

Source: Statistics South Africa (2018:31).

Figure 1–The incidence of poverty among South African children (2015)

The high incidence of poverty among children reflects their status as non-economically active dependents, as well as characteristics of the households in which they live. The majority of South African children live in large households with too few employed persons to generate enough income to escape poverty. In 2015, fully 71.4% of children lived in households with five or more members (Statistics South Africa 2018:29). Only 35.9% of the households with children had two employed persons, while 33.7% had one and 30.4% had none (Statistics South Africa 2018:29). The effect of large dependency burdens was clearly visible in child poverty figures for 2015: Whereas 23.1% of children in households with fewer than three members lived below the lower-bound poverty line, fully 70.4% of children in households with seven or more members lived below the LBP (Statistics South Africa

2018:36). The link between the extent of poverty and household size is similar for the food poverty line and the upper-bound poverty line.[3]

Poor labour market outcomes, as well as the erosion of family structures, contribute to high dependency burdens and inadequate incomes to escape poverty. While total employment increased from 9.5 million in 1995 to 16.4 million in September 2019 (Festus et al. 2016:587; Statistics South Africa 2019c:1), the labour force expanded much faster. Hence, the number of unemployed individuals increased over the same period from 2 million (17.6% of the labour force) to 6.7 million (29.1% of the labour force) (Festus et al. 2016:587; Statistics South Africa 2019c:1). As pointed out by Blaauw (2017:350), many workers in informal employment also struggle to support their dependents because they earn low or irregular incomes. Turning to family structures, only 32.9% of South African children lived with both their biological parents in 2015, while 41.4% lived with their biological mothers and 3.8% with their biological fathers (Statistics South Africa 2018:44). The remaining 21.9% of children lived in households in which neither of their biological parents were present. This rupturing of traditional family structures is one of the main reasons why so few children live in households with two or more income earners.

Table 3 shows the proportions of South African children who lack access to important facilities and public services. The South African Government has markedly expanded access to most of these facilities and services since the political transition in 1994 (see South Africa 2019). Nonetheless, it is clear from the table that the deprivation suffered by many South African children extends beyond inadequate financial resources.

---

[3] It should not be inferred from this connection that a preference for many children is a major cause of household poverty in South Africa. Many large households are not made up of nuclear families; instead, they consist of members of extended families who live together to share resources (including social assistance grants) and reduce some living expenses.

Table 3: South African children's access to facilities and public services (2015)

Facility or service	Percent without full access
Formal housing	22.1
Electricity for lighting	7.9
Piped water in dwelling	24.1
Flush toilet in the dwelling or the yard	49.7
Refuse removal	50.5
Medical aid	87.6
Medical clinic within 2 km of dwelling	49.6
Early childhood development programme	61.6
Safe play areas	65.1

Source: Statistics South Africa (2018:36-47).

The statistics presented in this section emphasise the importance of policy interventions that can improve the living conditions of South African children by providing them with financial resources, facilities and other public services. This reality is a vital aspect of the context within which the effectiveness of the CSG programme should be assessed.

HISTORY AND EVOLUTION OF THE CHILD SUPPORT GRANT

The CSG programme was introduced in April 1998 to replace the State Maintenance Grant (SMG), which had been in existence since the 1930s. The SMG dated from a time when the social security system was designed around the needs of whites and was based on a household structure model of nuclear families with formal marriage in which fathers were breadwinners and mothers primarily homemakers and child-rearers (Lund 2007:22). Hence, the SMG was targeted at a well-defined group of vulnerable persons. Woolard, Harttgen and Klasen (2011) state:

> The State Maintenance Grant was intended for a parent or guardian living with a child under 18 if the applicant was unmarried, widowed or separated; had been deserted by their spouse for more than 6 months; had a spouse who received a social grant; or had a spouse who had been in prison, a drug treatment centre or a similar institution for more than 6 months. Applicants had to prove that they had made efforts to apply for private maintenance from the other parent but had been unsuccessful in doing so. There were limitations not only on non-parent receipt of the grant, but also on eligibility with regard to children born outside of marriage. (p. 362)

The SMG was means-tested and had two components: A parent allowance and a child allowance. The grant was relatively generous (Lund 2007:15). In July 1995, for example, the parent allowance amounted to R410 per month at current prices and the child allowance to R127 (R537 in July 1995 prices was the equivalent of R2 075 in April 2019 prices). Hence, the total value of a SMG exceeded the R410 of the grants to elderly and disabled persons, which were the two biggest social assistance programmes at the time. The coverage of the programme was limited, though: According to Lund (:16), some 200 000 women and a similar number of children received SMGs or the equivalent grants disbursed in the so-called homelands in the early 1990s (:16). Only one out of every 1 000 white children then received an SMG, largely because the means test excluded most white families from eligibility (:16). Access was much more widespread among coloureds and Indians – in the early 1990s, roughly 50 out of every 1 000 coloured children and 40 out of every 1 000 Indian children received such grants – but the underdeveloped nature of similar programmes in the homelands and feeble enrolment efforts elsewhere in South Africa limited access among African children to 14 out of every 1 000 (:16).

When the various welfare administrations were merged and apartheid-era discrimination in access to social assistance was eliminated, it transpired that expansion to all eligible children probably would have raised the cost of the SMG programme twenty-fold (Woolard et al. 2011:362). Such a large increase would not have been affordable. It was against this backdrop that the Government appointed the Lund Committee in 1995 to assess the prevailing system and to recommend other options to assist needy children and families. The Committee's 1996 report recommended the creation of a child-focused programme with much wider coverage but smaller grant amounts. This proposal was the basis for the introduction of the CSG.

At the time of its introduction, the CSG amounted to R100 per month – the equivalent of R319 in April 2019 prices. Since the inception of the programme, the grant has been disbursed to the qualifying child's primary caregiver, who must be a South African citizen, permanent resident or refugee. The CSG initially was available only to children younger than seven years, and eligibility was determined by a means test based on total household income, presentation of various documents and demonstration of efforts to secure other forms of funds.[4] The onerous nature of these requirements contributed to the slow initial take-up rate depicted in Figure 2. In response to this, the Government abolished some requirements that still linked eligibility for the CSG to family structure and relaxed the means test by linking it to the income of the primary caregiver and his or her spouse (instead of that of the beneficiary's entire household) (Lund 2007:74-75; Woolard et al. 2011:363). In addition, eligibility was expanded in a step-wise manner to children under the ages of nine (2003), 11 (2004), 14 (2003-2005), 15 (2009) and 18 (2010-2012) (Williams 2007:8; Patel & Plagerson 2016:40). The expansion to children under the age of 18 was accompanied by a further relaxation of the means test. The

---

4   For the purposes of the means test, caregivers had to submit wage certificates for themselves and their spouses, proof of receipt of private pensions, proof (in the form of bank statements) of cash investments, and affidavits with proof of household income. In addition, they had to present identification documents and photos, confirmation of the biological parents' consent to applicant's status as primary caregivers, and birth certificates and clinic cards of the child beneficiaries. Lund (2007:72-78) provided a detailed discussion of these requirements and their effects.

outcome of these measures was a sharp increase in the take-up of the CSG from almost 1.3 million in 2002 to almost 9.6 million in 2010 (see Figure 2). Although the rate of growth has slowed notably since then, disbursements reached 12.2 million in 2018. This implied that about 62% of South African children under the age of 18 received a CSG.[5]

The Government has regularly increased the amount of the CSG to compensate for the eroding effect of inflation. At the time of writing this (February 2020), the grant amounts to R425 per month. Hence, the increase from the initial amount of R100 per month represented real growth in its buying power: If the CSG merely had increased with the consumer price index, it would have amounted to R324 in November 2019. In combination, these adjustments to the amount of the grant and growth in the number of beneficiaries caused a marked increase in government expenditure on CSGs (see Figure 3). Such spending grew from R1.4 billion in 2001 to R55.8 billion in 2018. This represented an increase from 0.14% of GDP to 1.18%, with a marked slowdown from 2010 onwards. Several economists have argued that the CSG programme (and, indeed the social grant system as a whole) is affordable in its current form, but have added that further expansion would be unwise from a fiscal sustainability point of view (Leibbrandt & Woolard 2010:28-29; Van der Berg & Siebrits 2010:8-13; Woolard et al. 2011:372-374).

---

5   This ratio is based on the 2018 child population figure of 19 741 000 in Hall (2019:216).

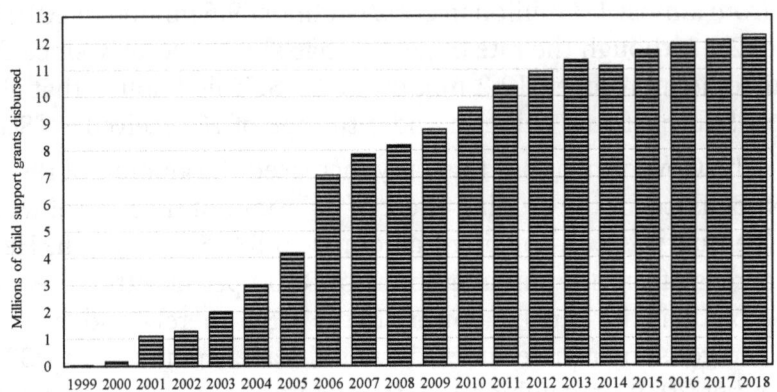

Sources: South African Social Security Agency (2009:20; 2018:21).

Figure 2: Growth in the disbursement of child support grants (1999-2018)

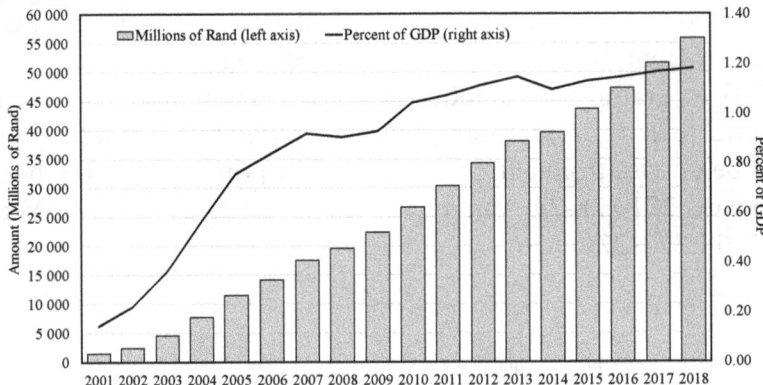

Sources: Spending on CSGs – National Treasury (2001:62, 65; 2004:73; 2005:55; 2007:333; 2008:319; 2009:352; 2010:362; 2011:403; 2012:421; 2013:439; 2014:424; 2015:301; 2016:299; 2017:324; 2018:348; 2019:351). GDP–SA Reserve Bank electronic database (South African Reserve Bank n.d.).

Figure 3: Government spending on child support grants (2001-2018)

As was stated earlier, the means test formula that determines eligibility for the CSG was changed soon after the inception of the programme and again in 2010. In addition, the cut-off amount has been adjusted regularly to compensate for inflation. In the 2019/20 fiscal year, disbursement of CSGs was restricted to single caregivers who earned less than R50 400 per annum and married caregivers who earned less than R100 800 per annum (National Treasury 2019:351). Although the eligibility requirements have been relaxed, caregivers must still provide identity documents and proof of their caregiver status and income, as well as birth certificates for the child beneficiaries. In 2010, the Government introduced the further requirement that caregivers should annually submit school attendance certificates for child beneficiaries between the ages of seven and 18. However, it was clear from the outset that disbursement of the grant would not be jeopardised if children fail to attend school or if the caregivers do not submit such certificates. The absence of a mechanism to force caregivers to ensure that children regularly attend school has rendered the condition weak.

THE EFFECTIVENESS AND LIMITATIONS OF THE CSG PROGRAMME

The previous section of this chapter stated that the CSG programme disbursed R55.8 billion – the equivalent of 1.18% of South Africa's GDP – in 2018. Fiscal incidence studies have established that all the grant programmes are well targeted at poor households: The means tests are effective at preventing large-scale leakage of grant money to higher-income groups (Maboshe & Woolard 2018:10-12). The purpose of this section is to discuss the effectiveness of the CSG programme, which has to do with the extent to which it benefits children in poor households, the forms such benefits take, and its limitations. To this end, the section surveys the large body of empirical research into these issues.

The extent to which children benefit from cash transfers depends on the choices of the adults who receive and spend the money on their behalf. Caregivers could spend CSG money on the needs of children or use it for their own ends, which might range from luxuries and 'sin goods' (such as alcoholic beverages, tobacco products and lottery tickets) to the transport costs of job-search activities. Several studies (Bengtsson 2012; d'Agostino, Scarlato & Napolitano 2017; Delany et al. 2008; Goldblatt 2006; Khosa & Kaseke 2017; Patel et al. 2011; Samson et al. 2004; Vorster & De Waal 2008; Williams 2007) have analysed the self-reported spending patterns of households that receive CSGs. None has reported evidence of large-scale squandering of grant money. The recurring finding of these studies has been that households pool the funds with other sources of income (e.g. wages, old-age grants and remittances) and mainly buy food, clothing, transportation services, heating and other basic items needed by children and adults.[6] To be sure, such income pooling implies that the grants are not spent solely on the needs of children. Very poor households, however, literally cannot afford not to share their few steady sources of income, such as monthly grants.

At least some caregivers are likely to underreport the extent to which they use CSG money to buy luxuries, 'sin goods' and entertainment. This likelihood raises doubts about the reliability of survey findings regarding the spending of grant money. The credibility of these findings is enhanced by other research findings, though. For one thing, the consumption patterns reported by CSG-receiving households are very similar to those for all lower-income households in official publications of Statistics South Africa. Table 4, which contains statistics from the LCS 2014/15, confirms this: households in the four poorest deciles reported that four categories of spending (food and non-alcoholic beverages; housing, water, electricity, gas and other fuels; transport services; and clothing and footwear) accounted for more than 75% of their total consumption expenditure.[7] The

---

[6] Research on the usage of the old-age grant in South Africa (e.g. Case & Deaton 1998) and various cash transfers available in other countries (e.g. Evans & Popova 2017) has yielded similar findings.

[7] The table also shows the more varied average consumption pattern of the richer households in the ninth decile.

expenditure share of alcoholic beverages, tobacco and narcotics by households in these deciles was about 2%.

Table 4: The composition of spending by selected groups of South African households (2013/14)

Expenditure category	Percentages of total expenditure				
	Decile 1	Decile 2	Decile 3	Decile 4	Decile 9
Food and non-alcoholic beverages	31.1	32.4	31.9	31.1	10.5
Clothing and footwear	8.0	8.5	8.7	8.9	4.6
Housing, water, electricity, gas and other fuels	29.0	26.2	24.7	24.2	33.9
Transport	11.8	10.7	10.7	11.3	15.1
Alcoholic beverages, tobacco and narcotics	2.2	1.9	1.9	1.9	0.9
Furnishings, household equipment and routine house maintenance	3.0	3.8	4.1	4.1	4.9
Health	0.9	0.8	0.9	0.8	0.8
Communication	5.0	4.8	4.6	4.5	3.6
Recreation and culture	1.4	1.7	2.2	2.3	4.3
Education	0.3	0.4	0.5	0.7	3.0
Restaurants and hotels	1.6	2.0	2.2	2.2	1.9
Miscellaneous goods and services	5.7	6.8	7.6	7.9	16.3
Other unclassified expenses	0.0	0.0	0.0	0.1	0.1
Total	100.0	100.0	100.0	100.0	100.0
Subtotal (first four categories)	79.9	77.8	76.0	75.5	64.1

Source: Statistics South Africa (2017b:106).

This evidence is not compelling, however, because it may be the case that poorer households routinely misreport their spending patterns, irrespective of whether surveys focus on their use of CSG money or other income sources. This makes it important to obtain direct evidence of the effects of CSGs on children. Hence, several studies have tried to establish whether receipt of CSGs improves the nutrition, health and educational outcomes of children. The very high take-up rate of the CSG in poor households have precluded quasi-experimental comparisons of recipients and non-recipients. Hence, most of these studies have compared children of similar ages that had been receiving CSGs for different periods of time.[8] Agüero, Carter and Woolard (2007), d'Agostino et al. (2017) and Patel et al. (2018) found that longer receipt of CSGs improved food security in poor households, as well as the nutrition of resident children. Moreover, height-for-age scores suggested that the physical development of children was enhanced by these and other benefits of longer-term access to CSG money (Coetzee 2013; Delany et al. 2008).[9] Enrolment in the CSG programme at a very young age also has been linked positively to regular school attendance, better grades and a stronger likelihood of attaining higher levels of schooling (Coetzee 2013; Eyal & Woolard 2013; Patel et al. 2018).

Misuse of cash transfer programmes can also take the form of undesirable behavioural changes to become or remain eligible for payments. On this score, many South Africans have expressed concern about the possibility that large numbers of female caregivers (including adolescents) may have been having babies for the sole purpose of obtaining grant money (Makiwane 2010:201). While empirical research into this question remains scant, the available evidence is inconsistent with widespread behaviour of this nature. The declines in the total fertility rates of adult and adolescent South African women that had started in the 1980s and 1990s, respectively, did not stop

---

8   Such differences came about because some caregivers applied for grants sooner than others did when the CSG was introduced and whenever the eligibility age was raised.

9   The other benefits include reduced susceptibility to illness (see Heinrich et al. 2012).

or reverse after the introduction of the CSG (Branson, Ardington & Leibbrandt 2013:8-11; Makiwane 2010:195, 200).[10]

By international standards, however, the fertility rate among adolescent South African women remains high (Branson et al. 2013:21). Hence, it is notable that some studies have suggested that the CSG may be a mitigating factor. Rosenberg et al (2015), for example, reported that caregivers who receive CSGs were less likely than non-recipient mothers to have a second child soon after the first. In addition, Heinrich et al. (2012:93-101) found that female adolescents who lived in households receiving CSGs or who received such grants from a very young age were less likely to engage in sexual activity (especially with multiple partners) and to fall pregnant than their peers who no longer received CSGs or started receiving them later in their childhood years. By contrast, Cluver et al. (2013) did not find an association between receipt of a CSG and the likelihood of multiple sex partners. However, their survey in urban and rural areas of Mpumalanga and the Western Cape showed that female adolescents who live in CSG-receiving households were only half as likely to engage in transactional sex and one-third less likely to have sexual relationships with markedly older men than their peers living in non-recipient households. Grinspun (2016:48) offered an important possible explanation for these findings: "It appears that the grant reduces the economic pressure that can drive teenage girls to take risks regarding partner selection or limit their power to negotiate sex."

Studies of South Africa's old-age pension scheme (e.g. Duflo 2003) and transfer programmes in other countries (e.g. Evans & Popova 2017) have suggested that women generally are more likely to spend cash benefits on the needs of children than men are. Although the rules of the CSG programme are gender-neutral, the vast majority of recipient caregivers are women (Patel, Knijn & Van Wel 2015:380).[11]

---

10 Makiwane (2010:195) defines the total fertility rate as the "the number of children a hypothetical woman would have during her lifetime if she conforms to the current fertility rates of women in different reproductive age groups." This implies that the teenage fertility rate is the "the number of births per 1 000 women aged 15-19 in a specified period of time" (Makiwane 2010:195).

11 A nationwide survey by Vorster and De Waal (2008), for example, found that 96% of the caregivers of CSG recipients were women.

This may well be one of the reasons for the positive outcomes discussed thus far in this section. Research has shown that the CSG has also contributed to the empowerment of female caregivers by lessening the indignity of extreme poverty, reducing their financial dependence on others (most notably their partners), strengthening their roles in decision making about the use of household resources and enabling them to be more involved in the day-to-care care of their children (see Granlund & Hochfeld 2020; Khosa & Kaseke 2017; Patel, 2012; Patel & Hochfeld 2011; Patel et al. 2015; Wright et al. 2015; Zembe-Mkabilea et al. 2015). These benefits are particularly important in a society characterised by high levels of gender inequality and gender-based violence.

In sum, a credible body of evidence suggests that the CSG programme is highly effective. The programme provides large amounts of cash to poor households with children and avoids extensive leakage to the affluent. Furthermore, caregivers generally use the money to the benefit of children and the programme has not given rise to substantial perverse behavioural responses. Instead, it has contributed to the empowerment of many female caregivers. These conclusions do not imply that no caregivers waste CSG money or that no one engages in undesirable behaviour to access grants. Such problems, however, do not seem serious enough to negate the positive effects of CSGs or to warrant a fundamental reconsideration of the programme. Having said this, it should be added that the CSG programme is not without limitations. The remainder of this section identifies some of these limitations, and the next section suggests some remedial reforms.

Perhaps the most obvious and serious limitation of the CSG programme is the small size of the grant. As was explained earlier, policymakers chose to make relatively small grants available to the largest possible number of children in poor households. The Government accepted the recommendation of the Lund Committee to base the amount of the grant on the cost of food for a child under the age of seven years, and drew on independent research to set its initial value at R100 per month (the equivalent of R319 per month in April 2019 prices) (Budlender 2018:95). According to Budlender (:95),

"Government acknowledged that food was not the only child-related cost but argued that the CSG should be regarded as part of a larger package of services." While the grant has been increased regularly and has grown in real terms since its introduction, the basis of its determination was not changed as eligibility was expanded in steps to qualifying children up to the age of 18. Hence, it no longer suffices to cover even the food needs of many beneficiaries. In April 2017, for example, the CSG amounted to R380 per month – the equivalent of R415 per month or R4 974 per annum in April 2019 prices. Thus, it was markedly lower than April 2017 value of the food poverty line, which amounted to R6 951 per annum in April 2019 prices. The upper-bound poverty line, which probably was a more accurate yardstick of the cost of meeting all basic needs of adolescent CSG beneficiaries, then amounted to no less than R14 896 per annum.

In addition, a number of studies have identified other factors that undermine the effectiveness of the CSG programme. These factors are not directly related to the design of the programme, but influence its efficacy via the milieu within which the grants are used and by shaping the decisions of caregivers and children. Research has shown, for example, that the knowledge and skills of caregivers influence the effects of the grants on children. Heinrich et al. (2012:47-50) found that the positive effects of the CSGs on the height-for-age scores of children and the likelihood that they attend a pre-school were significantly higher if the mothers had eight or more years of schooling. They argued that this probably reflected the ability of better-educated mothers to make more effective use of cash grants. More recently, an analysis of data from the fourth and fifth waves of the National Income Dynamics Study (NIDS) suggested that receipt of the CSG does not enhance the physical growth of recipient children if the caregivers "... do not command the necessary financial knowledge to manage it for the benefit of children" (Von Fintel, Von Fintel & Buthelezi, 2019:12).[12] Although their analysis could not identify

---

12 The NIDS questionnaire contained five questions that have been used in many countries to gauge the financial literacy of survey respondents. The following is an example of these questions: "Suppose you put money in the bank for two years and the bank agrees to add 15 percent per year to your account. Will the

specific mechanisms that link the financial literacy of caregivers to children's physical development, Von Fintel et al. (2019:18) argued that it may have to do with the quality of diets: Financially literate mothers did not spend larger portions of their incomes on food that their non-financially literate peers did, which suggested that the improved child development outcomes probably reflected purchases of more nutritious fare.

Torkelson (2020) identified two further adverse consequences of the limited money management skills of some caregivers, namely a proclivity to fall prey to unscrupulous moneylenders and peddlers of other financial products. In 2012, the South African Government followed a trend in developing countries by linking cash transfers to measures to promote integration of the poor into the formal financial sector. To this end, it contracted a private company, Cash Paymaster Services (CPS, a subsidiary of Net1) to handle the disbursement of all social grants. CPS opened accounts for millions of grant recipients at Grindrod Bank, and issued them with smartcards that gave the company access to their full account histories. Using proprietary technology and its control over the bank accounts, CPS exploited caregivers' unfamiliarity with electronic transactions and limited financial skills to establish lucrative subsidiaries that extended microloans, made various payments, and sold insurance and prepaid utility services (:5-9). The ability to deduct loan repayments and insurance premiums from recipients' bank accounts made these businesses virtually risk-free to CPS. However, many caregivers became heavily indebted to the CPS subsidiaries and were forced to borrow more from other moneylenders that charged exorbitant interest rates and used abusive practices to ensure repayment. As Torkelson put it:

> People effectively used their future social grant payments for present needs through credit, diminishing the value of their grant in upcoming months, and causing further consumption crises. The grant meant to be given to the most vulnerable people

bank add more money to your account the second year than it did the first year, or will it add the same amount of money in both years?"

for basic needs was transferred instead to a private corporation through the repayment of debts.[13] (p. 9)

Aspects of this dispensation ended when the contract between the South African Social Security Agency and CPS expired in 2017. Yet many grant-receiving households remain heavily burdened by debts to formal and informal lenders (Torkelson 2020:9). Such indebtedness largely reflects the inability of their members to secure steady jobs in an economy experiencing very high levels of unemployment, but often is exacerbated by inadequate understanding of the consequences of excessive borrowing.

Research has suggested that non-programme factors also stymie some of the benefits of CSGs to children. Cluver et al. (2014) studied determinants of the HIV infection risk of South African adolescents. They found that the risk fell from 40% among teenagers who received neither CSGs nor psychosocial support in the previous year to about 25% among those who received a grant or school feeding. The incidence of risky behaviour dropped further to about 17% among boys and girls who received grants, school feeding and positive parenting. In a related study, Cluver et al. (2016) reported further benefits from adding school-based care by counsellors and teachers to the package of measures supporting cash grants. The reported incidence of risky sex among boys exposed to the full package of measures – which the authors describe as "cash, care and classroom" – was 6%, compared to 22% among those with no such exposure. The corresponding figures for girls were 7% and 15%, respectively. Only 2% of girls who received CSGs and free schooling reported engaging in sex for economic reasons, compared to 10% of their peers who did not.

As was mentioned earlier, the environments within which caregivers and children live further undermine the effectiveness of CSGs. Combinations of material deprivation, poor living conditions, family disruption (reflecting factors, such as declining marriage rates,

---

13 While James (2014) showed that many low-income households in South Africa were heavily indebted to formal and informal lenders even before CPS assumed responsibility for the disbursement of social grants, Fanta et al. (2017) confirmed that their uptake of funeral insurance and credit products had increased markedly from 2012 onwards.

migrant labour and HIV/Aids-related deaths, among others), family and neighbourhood violence, and deficient parenting skills often characterise these environments (see Hall & Richter 2018:29-30).

SUGGESTIONS FOR IMPROVING THE CSG PROGRAMME

The foregoing suggested two reforms that should make the CSG programme more effective: A significant increase in the size of the grants, and the introduction of other interventions that would increase the benefits to children by improving their living environments, their lifestyle choices, and the spending choices of caregivers. The first option seems unaffordable now in view of the scale of the programme and the precarious state of the public finances (see Burger & Calitz 2019). Indeed, its longer-term affordability would remain questionable even if the fiscal situation improves markedly – as was pointed out earlier, a threefold increase would be needed merely to raise the value of the CSG to the upper-bound poverty line.

Affordability considerations aside, the feasibility of the second option also would be inhibited by the limited capacity of the government to implement and administer such complementary programmes. However, it would be possible to introduce such programmes on a limited scale and expand them in line with the growth in budgetary resources and administrative capacity. It transpired in the previous section that programmes to improve the financial literacy and parenting skills of caregivers, as well as ones to provide psychosocial care to children should be core elements of such endeavours. When designing and implementing such interventions, policymakers should incorporate lessons from other programmes with similar objectives. The Sihleng'imizi programme (a family strengthening intervention for CSG beneficiaries and their families piloted in Johannesburg in 2017 by the University of Johannesburg's Centre for Social Development in Africa) is an example of such an initiative (see Patel et al. 2019).

CHAPTER 9

Thoughtful affluent persons know that it is inadequate to restrict efforts to help the less fortunate to small cash gifts. Such gifts enable poor persons to meet some of their short-term consumption needs, but cannot break the enduring shackles of poverty. This chapter has shown that the CSG programme effectively boosts the consumption spending of poor households, and at the same time improves the longer-term prospects of some children via positive effects on their learning abilities and health. The complementary programmes proposed in this section have the potential to significantly strengthen these benefits of CSGs. Ultimately, however, children living in poor households cannot attain comfortable standards of living unless they secure good jobs in a flourishing economy. Hence, it is deeply worrying that South Africa has an exceptionally poor education system (see Spaull 2015) and a badly underperforming economy characterised by one of the highest unemployment rates in the world. These realities prevent realisation of the rich potential of the CSG programme; in fact, they constrain many recipients' prospects of securing decent livelihoods to such an extent that their grants assume the much diminished role of palliative handouts. Discussions of the poor performance of the South African education system and economy fall outside the scope of the chapter. Yet no one interested in improving the circumstances and prospects of South African children can afford to ignore the effects of these problems nor to deny the urgency of resolving them.

CHAPTER 10

PROTECTING CHILDREN IN THE DIGITAL SOCIETY

Louis Fourie

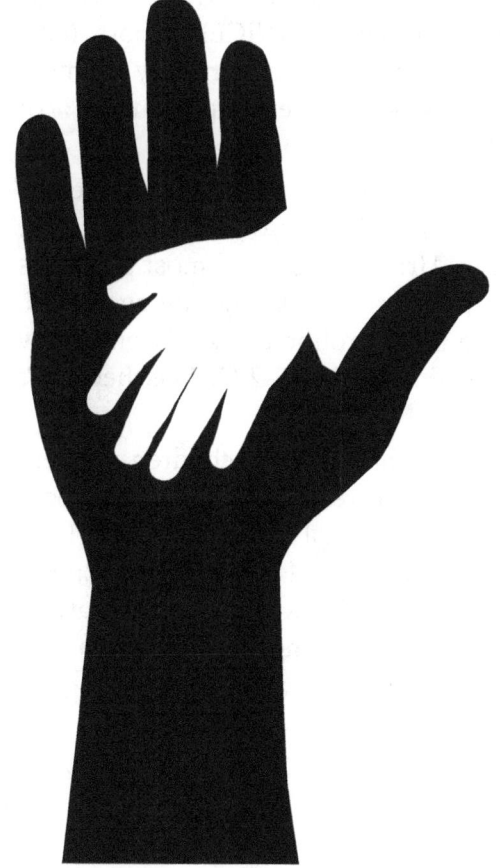

INTRODUCTION AND BACKGROUND

All over the world glowing computer, tablet or mobile phone screens are illuminating the faces of children who are often so immersed in what the technology offers that they are unaware of the world around them (Third et al. 2017:9). Information and Communication Technology (ICT) has become pervasive in almost all spheres of daily life. And with the general adoption of ICT, children increasingly have access at home and school to computers or personal smart phones (Rizza & Pereira 2013:9).

At about 4.54 billion active users worldwide (58.2% of the population), each spending an average 6.5 hours online each day, the internet plays a major role worldwide in changing the methods and speed of communication (Minić & Spalević 2014:417; Lin 2019; Clement 2020). Since about one third of internet users in the world are children, it is understandable that the internet has a significant effect on their lives (Livingstone, Carr & Byrne 2015:6; Byrne & Burton 2017:39-40). According to a recent UNICEF report (eds. Keeley & Little 2017:1), the youth of ages 15-24 are currently the most connected age group, with a 71% presence online compared to 48% of the total population of the world.

Social media has become ubiquitous and the preferred instruments of interpersonal communication, as well as educational, political and business exchange. In Africa, the second most populous continent, where about half the population is below the age of 15, children and young people are the most prolific users of trendy new technology and social media (Ephraim 2013:275-277; Mascheroni & Ólafsson 2018:15).

The predominant use of mobile technologies by children to access the internet (Byrne & Burton 2017:44) has resulted in a new 'bedroom culture' where online access becomes personal and private with little or no supervision by the parents (Wojniak & Majorek 2016:132; eds. Keeley & Little 2017:1). Children all over the world are also starting to use the internet at an increasingly younger age and are often able to use a mobile phone or tablet before they learn to talk, leaving many online policies lacking since they predominantly focus on children above 12 years (OECD 2016:100-103; Byrne & Burton 2017:44).

Due to the importance of social networking such as Facebook, WhatsApp, Snapchat and Instagram to cultivate and sustain interpersonal relationships, 86.3% of children in South Africa have a social networking account. The most popular are WhatsApp (94.2%) and Facebook (68.5%). However, only one in three children has set their social networking profiles to private. The remaining two-thirds of children are exposed to high risk (Phyfer, Burton & Leoschut 2016:31, 35; Graafland 2018:16; cf. DQ Institute 2018).

Children use the internet more than any other medium to communicate and socialise. Technology, such as chat applications, e-mail, instant messaging, online virtual worlds, multiplayer online games, and social networking made it possible for children to communicate and socialise far beyond the safety of their homes. Digital technology has become a normal part of life and is merely a nonorganic extension of their bodies, while social media is perceived as a 'real' world and not a virtual world (Minić & Spalević 2014:426). However, it is the ubiquity, the easy accessibility and anonymity of this technology that create new risks of abuse irrespective of the geographic location of children (Mishna, McLukie & Saini 2009:107; Rizza & Pereira 2013:9, 39; Wojniak & Majorek 2016:132). New technology often coincides with new ways of misuse or abuse of that technology (Hachiya 2017:177).

The DQ Impact Report (DQ Institute 2018) indicated that 56% of 8-12 year old children are exposed to cyber-risks, such as cyberbullying, video game addiction, online grooming and online sexual behaviour, while 64% of South African children engage in cyber risks. In South Africa, 34.5% of children have been exposed to hate speech and 51.2% to inappropriate sexual images (Phyfer et al. 2016:39, 50, 66). The high percentages can possibly be attributed to insufficient social structures to deal with cyber risks, such as a lower public awareness about cyber-risks; ineffective online protection policies; a lack of preparation of children, and a low involvement of parents (DQ Institute 2018).

The DQ Institute (2018) study further found that the combination of a mobile phone and social media increases the risk of the child to 70% due to longer screen time (32 hours or more per week) and less supervision (50% of 8-12 year olds access the internet via mobile phone) (cf. Rideout 2015:16, 40). It is estimated that by the end of 2020, about 390 million 8-12 year old children will be at risk. This problem is exacerbated by the exponential growth of constant connectivity (720 million of 8-12 year olds online by the end of 2020) and a general lack of protection. A total of 90% of the 720 million child users worldwide are from emerging ICT countries where the cyber risk for children is significantly higher.

Just like urbanisation and globalisation during previous eras, digital technology has changed the world immensely. The digitalisation of our world is an inescapable force that impacts almost every sphere of our lives – shaping our economies, societies and cultures. And as increasingly more children gain access to the online world, it is also changing childhood forever. Children are, from their birth, imbued with a constant stream of digital technology shaping their life experiences, perceptions, ideas and worldviews and are at the epicentre of ICT changes (Valentine & Holloway 2001:71-72; eds. Keeley & Little 2017:1, 8-9).

DEFINING THE PROBLEM

Unfortunately, as is the case with all new technology, digital technology does not come without significant risks to the safety, privacy and well-being of children (Grant 2010:4-5; Minić & Spalević 2014:417). Digital technology can easily amplify existing offline threats and misuse, as well as expand opportunities for taking advantage of children's often poorly managed privacy, thus increasing the vulnerability of susceptible children. The result is that children often encounter cyberbullying, harassment, unwanted sexual solicitation, and improper advertising and marketing driven by algorithms (Byrne & Burton

2017:40). These challenges will only intensify in future as the digital revolution progresses and the lives of children are touched by artificial intelligence, robotics, machine learning, deep learning, the Internet of Things (IoT) with its ubiquitous sensors and monitoring, and an increasing number of digital devices and online platforms (eds. Keeley & Little 2017:1, 8-9).

Children's rapid adoption of the internet and other online technologies, together with an increase in time spent online, and the constantly changing media landscape (e.g. more apps and tailored sites, more individualised media use, and more mobile internet), expose children to digital risks and harmful content, as well as threaten their privacy and safety (Livingstone et al. 2014:272, 275, 279-280; see Paniagua and Istance 2018:62-65).

Digital technology is not only intensifying some well-known childhood risks, such as bullying, but also encouraging new forms of the exploitation of children, such as 'made-to-order' child pornography and live streaming of explicit sexual abuse of children. Due to the internet, it is now easier than ever for predators to contact unsuspecting children through anonymous and poorly protected social media profiles and even game forums. Innovative new technologies, such as crypto currencies are unfortunately powering the Dark Web with its harmful child content and streaming of child sexual abuse, while making it increasingly difficult for law enforcement to stay abreast (eds. Keeley & Little 2017:2).

Strangely enough, 92% of all child sexual abuse websites identified by the Internet Watch Foundation are hosted in only five countries, namely the Netherlands, United States, Canada, France and the Russian Federation (eds. Keeley & Little 2017:2). Until now, efforts to address this problem has had relatively little impact.

This chapter will touch on the abovementioned ethical issues that affect children who are immersed in technology while growing up in the digital era. Various digital risks that children are exposed to will be covered, the ethical challenges involved, as well as the role of the different stakeholders in assisting children to build resilience. Although there are several views about the intrinsic dangers of the digital world in comparison to offline dangers, the aim of the chapter is to point out the digital risks without being alarmist or selective as is sometimes the case with the popular media.

A TYPOLOGY OF ICT-RELATED RISKS

Various classifications of ICT-related risks exist, but the taxonomy developed by EU Kids Online is particularly valuable in the understanding of the concerns. EU Kids Online groups the concerns into three categories, namely content, contact and conduct risks as displayed in Table 1. Content risks are those where the child is the receiver of mass-produced content, while contact risks refers to the risks where the child is an active participant in an adult-initiated activity. Conduct risks entails peer-to-peer risks where the child is a perpetrator, actor or creator of risky content or contact (Livingstone & Haddon 2009:7-8).

The category of conduct risks goes against the popular myth of the harmless or innocent 'victim-child' that limits the child to the role of a passive recipient of content or abuse and thus ignores the active role or online conduct of children against other children (Barbovschi & Dreier 2013:60).

Table 1: Classification of ICT-related risks

	Content Child as receiver (Mostly mass productions)	Contact Child as participant (Adult-initiated activity)	Conduct Child as actor (Child as perpetrator or creator of risky content or contact)
Aggression and violence	• Websites encouraging unhealthy or dangerous behaviours, such as self-harm, self-abuse, self-mutilation, suicide, bulimia, anorexia, bomb-making, or drugs preparation • Hate speech and hateful content • Exposure to extremist, violent, or gruesome images and content • Exaggerated information	• Harassment, stalking • Radicalisation • Persuasion to take part in harmful or perilous behaviours • Hate speech	• Cyberbullying, stalking and harassment • Digital violence • Digital humiliation of others • Hostile and violent peer activity • Hateful materials about other children

Sexual abuse	• Unwanted or harmful exposure to inappropriate, sexual or pornographic images or content • Unethical behaviour • Hyper-sexualisation • Vulgarism	• Participation in unsafe communication, e.g. an adult seeking inappropriate contact • Seduction and luring into meeting strangers in the real world • Sexual harassment • Sexual solicitation • Sexual grooming • Cyber stalking • Child exploitation • Sexual extortion	• Production, posting, distribution and consumption of child abuse or sexual material • Child sexual abuse • Child-produced indecent images • Sexting
Values	• Racist or discriminatory material • Biased information or advice (e.g. drugs; promiscuity) • Exposure to inaccurate or misleading information • Ascribing infallibility to a machine • Internet addiction	• Ideological persuasion • Wrongful persuasion (e.g. self-harm)	• Potentially harmful user-generated content • Provoking racism • Encouraging suicide, anorexia • Narcissism

CHAPTER 10

| Commercial exploitation | • Embedded advertising and marketing
• Spam
• Sponsorship | • Tracking and harvesting of personal information
• AI & algorithms pressuring children, e.g. nudging
• Violation and misuse of personal data
• Hacking
• Fraud and theft | • Online gambling
• Illegal downloading and copyright infringement
• Hacking
• Live streaming of child sexual abuse
• Trafficking for the purpose of sexual exploitation
• Sexual exploitation of children in travel and tourism |

Sources: Livingstone and Haddon (2009:7-8), Keeley and Little (eds. 2017:68, 72-73) and Matyjas (2008:207-208).

The EU Kids Online II survey of 2009 to 2010 provided a unique and valuable insight into a range of activities undertaken by children online, the various risks that accompany them, as well as the parental strategies to reduce these risks. Although the survey focused on Europe, it collected valuable qualitative data from nearly 10 000 children and clearly illustrated the correlation between online opportunities and risks (Livingstone et al. 2011:142).

The study found that the biggest concern for children is around content risks, such as pornography and violent images (58%), followed by contact and conduct risks (42%). Younger children are more concerned with content-related risks, with a growing concern regarding pornographic content during their teen years. As they grow older, the concern around conduct and contact-related risks increases. It is significant that some of the risks that are very prominent in the media and on the public agenda, such as sharing personal information online, or talking to and meeting strangers, were rarely mentioned. The highest risk was attributed to video-sharing sites (e.g. YouTube)

(32%), followed by websites (29%), social networking sites (13%) and games (10%) (Livingstone et al. 2014:1-7; Wojniak & Majorek 2016:132-133).

What makes the situation more complex is that it is much more difficult for children to judge behaviour as right or wrong in the virtual world (Vesnaj & Niveditha 2012:2) due to a "sense of disorientation and isolation leading to the disregard of reality" and a blending of reality and virtual reality (Minić & Spalević 2014:418-419).

ICT-RELATED RISKS

Although the digital world did not create the unethical behaviour of sexual abuse and exploitation of children, it does facilitate existing forms and also creates totally new forms.

CONTENT RISKS

EXPOSURE TO INAPPROPRIATE CONTENT

Perhaps the most widely known danger is the easy access of children to a superfluity of anti-social content, such as pornography, destructive religious sectarianism, fascism, child abuse, and many more (Matyjas 2008:203). Of the content-related offences, exposure to abusive child pornography tends to be dominant (Mishna et al. 2009:113; Minić & Spalević 2014:421). The exposure takes place through immoral websites, vulgar expressions in chat rooms, profane language and sacrilege (Aslani et al. 2013:215), as well the production and dissemination of graphic sexual content via mobile devices (Mishna et al. 2009:108). The widespread use of mobile technology and easy access to broadband internet has increased the vulnerability of children, especially those without the necessary protection. Research indicated that as high as 53% of exposure victims were under ten years old (eds. Keeley & Little 2017:77-79).

A further contributor to inappropriate content is hateful websites that propagate violent behaviour amongst children through violent murder videos and other acts of violence (Aslani et al. 2013:215).

Children's unrestrained and easy access to pornography and inappropriate content on the internet is partly due to parents' inability to exercise control or to implement an 'appropriate-use' policy. Interestingly, it seems that parents' concerns are less about protecting the innocence of the child but rather about the knowledge about alternative sexual traditions and models of sexuality that could invade the perceived sanctity of the home (Valentine & Holloway 2001:72).

VIOLENT GAMES

Unfortunately, some games that are meant for child entertainment are full of brutality and violence and have a negative influence on the development and behaviour of children. Certain games are known to cultivate aggression, a feeling of unlimited power over others, narcissism, a disregard for rules, extreme competitiveness and submission of others, impetuosity, and emotional apathy. Games often allow children protection against the real world and allow them to fulfil their dreams and desires. This escape from the real to an illusionary world – often to fill a void or escape rejection – is the very reason why games become psychologically addictive (Matyjas 2008:202, 205-206). It is for this reason that parents should be aware of the dangers presented by games, as well as the underlying problems (:206-207).

Children easily believe in the infallibility of the computer with the result that "the nihilism of modern technology destroys sensibility, solidarity, and critical thinking" as summarised by Minić and Spalević (2014:427). The revival of known magic and religious rituals by the techno-culture, and especially games, often takes the soul of the child as victim and shakes the very foundation of humanity (:427).

DIGITAL ADDICTION

Although technology provides access to an overabundance of digital content, entertainment and social connectivity, premature and unrestrained use of digital technology can lead to digital and screen addiction (eds. Keeley & Little 2017:9). Children often use the internet as a substitute reality to escape daily routine, obligations and real life problems. Children who spend an exorbitant amount of time in the virtual world experience deterioration in traditional social interactions. They neglect their studies and even basic physiological needs, such as sleeping and eating (Matyjas 2008:203-204).

CONTACT RISKS

SEXUAL ABUSE AND EXPLOITATION

The internet is increasingly being used by children to meet people and make friends since children find it easier to be themselves in a virtual world. This is further promoted by social networks that aim to promote homophily by bringing like-minded people together, based on their user profiles (Graafland 2018:17).

Although social media provides a platform for children to meet and befriend people, it does entail several risks because children are less careful whom they socialise with on the internet and would often share personal information, engage in undesirable exchanges or meet strangers in person (Graafland 2018:17-18). This behaviour increases the probability of sexual harassment, grooming, and sexual abuse by adults (Lupton & Williamson 2017:782). The proliferation of mobile devices and broadband access has made children more accessible than ever before.

Technological advances exacerbate the above problem by allowing perpetrators to remain anonymous, operate under fake identities, mask their digital tracks, simultaneously pursue multiple victims, and track them across websites and platforms, (eds. Keeley & Little 2017:77-79). Cryptocurrencies used as anonymous payment systems and end-to-end encrypted platforms used for the sharing of abusive media, make the tracking by law enforcement exceptionally difficult and thus contributed to an increase in the live streaming and distribution of child exploitation material. This situation is further complicated through the distribution of child sexual abuse material through Peer-to-Peer (P2P) network file sharing, the Deep Web and the Dark Web. The Dark Web conceals content and uses anonymity granting web browsers and is known for numerous illegal markets and online child abuse circles (eds. Keeley & Little 2017:79-80).

Contact risks can take several forms:

- *Internet paedophilia:* Internet paedophilia is one of the most prominent forms of computer crime in many countries. Paedophiles increasingly use technology to search the internet for potential child victims and are often part of organised crime. Many paedophiles have made the internet their playground and, under the guise of anonymity, constantly subject children to inappropriate sexual messages that have an effect on their psychological development. The typical modus operandi is to falsely present themselves as a peer to gain the trust of the child, which is then used to start a sexual discussion, exchange explicit sexual photos or meet in person (Minić & Spalević 2014:419, 421-425).

- *Cyber stalking:* Cyber stalking involves the use of the internet to pursue, harass, or contact children in an unsolicited fashion ranging from irritating e-mails to death threats. Often the aim is to identify, 'groom', and entice individuals to perform sexual acts on or offline. Cyber stalkers are skilful at siphoning personal information about a child through communications with a child's online friendship group. Some of the children are so distraught by fear that the stalker would harm them that they engage in self-harming behaviour (Mishna et al. 2009:108-109, 111-112).

- *Grooming*: The internet with its wealth of social networking sites, e-mail, instant messaging and chat rooms creates endless opportunities for online predators to groom their victims by gaining the child's attention or trust and befriending them before moving the communication to video- and photo-sharing platforms, which can lead to content-driven or financially driven extortion or personal offline meetings (UNICEF 2012:15; eds. Keeley & Little 2017:77-79). Since much of the grooming or the befriending of children online for sexual abuse is happening across borders it poses exceptional challenges to law enforcement agencies (Livingstone et al. 2015:12).

- *Cyber solicitation:* The solicitation of teenagers to engage in online sexual acts, 'cybering' (explicit sexual dialogue) or 'flashing' (displaying nudity via webcams) is endemic and usually comes from an older unknown or known person, some of whom are in positions of power and trust. They usually get the child to give in through constant pressure, by offering rewards, and even threats. Quite often the nudity is reposted all over social networking sites without consent, leading to remorse, regret, shame and self-harm amongst victims, who fear that it may resurface anytime since it has an infinite existence. The volume of online child abuse images has grown to such an extent that law enforcement units are not able to cope (Livingstone et al. 2015:12). The online cyber-sexual encounters sometimes progress to actual meetings with all the fear and dangers involved (Mishna et al. 2009:112-113; cf. Third et al. 2017:16).

- *Online dating:* For many children, the internet is an integral component of their romantic and sexual discovery.

Numerous children as young as 13 years old are involved in passionate online romantic and sexual relationships (Mishna et al. 2009:109). These encounters range from cybering and flashing to long-term relationships that often progress to meetings in the real world (:109-110).

COMMERCIAL HARVESTING AND MISUSE OF DATA

Technologists had an idealistic dream of a connected world where everyone could communicate and share their knowledge. Unfortunately, the digital footprints of people (and children) on the web are being thoroughly mined into a trillions-of-rand-a-year industry. The face, voice, body functions and private lives of individuals are being tracked and closely monitored by marketing companies. With the propagation of the Internet of Things (IoT), most devices are now connected to the internet and sensors are increasingly embedded in objects. Large technology companies are collecting every post, click, like, website visited, and purchase in real-time through 'Push Pages' (sharing of user's profile identifiers between companies) and 'fingerprinting' (an incredibly accurate method of identifying people). If the newer 'canvas' method of fingerprinting is used, entailing embedded coding in the HTML5 code of a website, users could be identified precisely without the use of cookies. And unlike cookies, nothing that is saved on the computer can be deleted (Fourie 2020).

Face- and voice-recognition algorithms are employed to track and create a lifelong digital record of all movements, conversations and actions in public. This gathered data is so extensive that it is possible to determine a child's medical history and religiosity (Regan & Jesse 2019:171).

Over time, organisations can form a very accurate picture of a child's emotional pulse – what they like, what gets their attention, what they fear, what their boundaries are, and what it would take to cross those boundaries. The data collection techniques have grown so sophisticated that marketers, advertisers, and politicians are becoming increasingly proficient to predict the preferences of people and children even before they have considered the choices by themselves. Companies are known to target children as young as four in an attempt to manipulate their consumption patterns. This exploitation of the identity and privacy rights of children may lead to the development of materialistic values and an identity through the purchase of certain consumer goods. Children thus become more susceptible to the persuasion of the current consumer culture, without fully understanding the impact (Lennie 2013:55-57). Human beings, including children, have now become a very valuable commodity.

The gathering of personal data of children through the internet and social media profiles is a growing concern, especially where privacy settings and online security are not well managed. Unfortunately, children often reveal valuable information to marketers, such as personal (e.g. name and e-mail) and profile data (e.g. preferences, hobbies, favourite brands and shops) because of the 'privacy paradox' or perceived benefits to data disclosure. Privacy remains a fuzzy concept for children due to the blurring of the borders between private and public in the online world (Rizza & Pereira 2013:24-25).

If this data is combined with internet tracking data, it places their online privacy at considerable risk and even allows companies to manipulate children's online behaviour and decisions through behavioural targeting and marketing (eds. Keeley & Little 2017:91-92). Google was fined $170 million in September 2019 for illegally collecting personal information from children and using it to target them with advertisements (Fourie 2020).

All this personal information is used to feed people a constant stream of 'personalised' content (cf. Whittlestone et al. 2019:20). This targeted marketing is aimed at changing the behaviour of people. However, in truth, the presented reality is a very filtered reality. The role of the now defunct Cambridge Analytica in the pro-Brexit campaign before the referendum, as well as the 2016 USA election, is infamous. By gathering 5 000 data points on each USA voter through the scraping of their Facebook and other social media accounts, they were able to connect the dots and very accurately profile each voter and predict their personality. Since personality drives behaviour and behaviour influences people's decisions and how they vote, Cambridge Analytica in support of the Republican Party used this psychological data to embark on a major influencing campaign of voters via social media by inter alia appealing to their fears and hate (*The Guardian* n.d.).

The power of big data, personal profiling and psychographics through the use of artificial intelligence and deep learning will increasingly impact our lives. It is calculated that when a child becomes eighteen, thousands of data points would exist on the web due to the interaction of the child. Disinformation and fake news will increasingly be used, which makes the web dangerous for uninformed children to use. And we currently have little control and little leverage with regard to this dangerous psychological manipulation and exposure of minors to inappropriate commercial advertising where the choices of the child are predetermined.

In the physical world, the extent of advertising and selling of products and services to children are well regulated. Unfortunately, this is not the case in the virtual world, where the extensive mining of personal data, viral marketing, advert games, and in-app purchases place enormous commercial and peer pressure on children and their privacy (Lennie 2013:54; Livingstone et al. 2015:12). Unfortunately, legal frameworks governing this extensive data collection are also still lacking (Regan & Jesse 2019:171).

CONDUCT RISKS

Public dialogue often focuses on the exposure of children to *content* risks (e.g. pornography) and *contact* risks (e.g. online grooming by paedophiles). However, research found that children's own *conduct* is increasingly causing harm to themselves and/or to other children (Livingstone et al. 2014:278, 280). Cyberbullying, youth-produced sexual imagery, sexting, sextortion, and abuses of the privacy of children are emergent concerns all over the world (Bulger et al. 2017:753).

Unfortunately, the response worldwide to the above risks has mostly been to restrict access to harmful or age-inappropriate content, rather than focusing on the underlying needs as indicated by the youth themselves: finding reliable sources of information, finding support for relationship challenges and dealing with peers (Bulger et al. 2017:753).

It seems that peer-to-peer threats are already entrenched in social media interactions. Conflict between children, often applauded by peers, can easily result in harm, as well as identity and reputational damage (Livingstone et al. 2014:280; Mascheroni & Ólafsson 2018: 25-27).

THE CHILD AS ACTOR

Children participate in a variety of online activities, such as texting, chatting, blogging, vlogging, and the exchange of pictures. Although these activities allow children to exercise their right to expression, it also involves some serious risks (Middaugh, Clark & Ballard 2017:128). Unfortunately, many of these risks go unnoticed since children are considered only as victims (Livingstone et al. 2015:12).

The borders between private and public are very vague to a child of the digital age. Many children, therefore, engage in online sexual exchanges with strangers and would easily send or download online sexual content (DQ Institute 2018). Especially older children would send or post suggestive messages and nude or semi-nude pictures of themselves (Kosenko, Luurs and Binder 2017:142). This behaviour could harm the privacy and endanger children as sexually explicit pictures rapidly spread online and also remain on the internet indefinitely (Livingstone et al. 2015:12). Several cases of revenge pornography by children – the spreading of compromising pictures online of former partners without their consent – have also been documented (OECD 2016:106). These pictures are also often used in blackmail, which has, in certain instances, led to suicide (eds. Keeley & Little 2017:74)

CHILD-PRODUCED SEXUAL CONTENT

According to research, a significant number of young people engage in the production and distribution of sexual content, for example online streaming for payment (eds. Keeley & Little 2017:77-79; cf. Lennie 2013:3), making them liable for prosecution (cf. Cranmer, Selwyn & Potter 2009:128). In some instances, countries make provision for consensual activities between minors as a normal discovery of sexuality (Bulger et al. 2017:756-757). In South Africa, sexting is chargeable under sections 18, 19 and 20 of the *Criminal Law (Sexual Offences and Related Matters) Amendment Act* (RSA, Act No. 5 of 2015), but consensual sex between children is no longer a crime if the children are between 12 and 16 years old.

As the internet and social networking sites become the normal place to socialise, it is logical that as children grow older and enter puberty, their sexual discourse will also migrate to the online space. Legislation will have to be more sensitive to the complexities of dealing with immature and often innocent children acting with intention and agency. Although current policy and legal frameworks aim to protect children online, substantial development is needed to balance it with the rights of children to participation and engagement. The 'innocence' view of children in need of protection does not hold in all cases (Bulger et al. 2017:759).

CYBERBULLYING

Cyberbullying feeds off the neglect of privacy principles by children, such as the sharing of personal information or images with perceived trusted others (Rizza & Pereira 2013:24-25). A strategy to curb cyberbullying will have to start with the respect of privacy and the limiting of disclosure to others.

Cyberbullying is when children use digital media to wilfully and repeatedly torment, harass, intimidate, embarrass, humiliate, denigrate, or demean other children through hurtful, cruel or threatening messages; flaming; disclosing of secrets; posting of embarrassing, obscene or slanderous information or pictures; impersonation of the victim; cyber stalking; deliberate exclusion of someone from a group; purposefully unfriending (outing or social exclusion) someone or pretending to befriend someone (Popovac & Leoschut 2012:1; Ephraim 2013:209; Lennie 2013:3; Rizza & Pereira 2013:12; eds. Keeley & Little 2017:74-76).

Research found that South Africa has one of the highest prevalence of cyber aggression and cyberbullying among children. Social media is the most common platform for cyberbullying and the most common perpetrator in South Africa is a classmate. However, the bullying is also done by strangers and known adults. The majority of people feel that current anti-bullying measures are insufficient (Popovac & Leoschut 2012:3; Lennie 2013:49; Newall 2018:3-9).

Two features make cyberbullying significantly different from traditional bullying, namely anonymity and accessibility. Online anonymity minimises the perpetrator's fear of punishment, strengthens the power imbalance between the perpetrator and the victim and, therefore, stimulates more violent and castigatory behaviour (Rizza & Pereira 2013:12; Graafland 2018:24). Virtual spaces allow attacks at any time and place, while mobile phones make the escape from abuse and harassment nearly impossible (Rizza & Pereira 2013:12-13; Minić & Spalević 2014:426; eds. Keeley & Little 2017:74-76). Smart phones added a new dimension since cyberbullying can now go beyond the power of words to include pictures and videos. The lack of visual and auditory feedback regarding the consequences of the actions of the perpetrator reduces the feeling of empathy and leads to a greater tendency to engage in aggressive behaviour in online spaces (Lennie 2013:51-53).

According to research, cyberbullying and violence is often fuelled by violent video games and gossip, which has become quite natural and acceptable in today's life (the naturalistic fallacy) (Lennie 2013:8).

Social media is the ideal tool for gossip. Since it is often accompanied by images and screen captures, it is much harder to defuse due to the perceived truthfulness of images. Social networks are also used by some children for self-promotion, narcissism, and self-gossip (Rizza & Pereira 2013:24, 40; cf. Third et al. 2017:9).

From a legal viewpoint, cyberbullies can find themselves in contravention of the law in some countries. For example, threats of violence, criminal coercion, stalking, and hate crimes are all criminal acts (Ephraim 2013:279; Rizza & Pereira 2013:24).

Cyberbullying can have a negative effect on the psychological and emotional well-being of children, such as higher anxiety, depression, confusion, guilt, shame, lower self-esteem, suicidal thoughts and attempts, self-harm, as well as higher rates of illness, higher absenteeism, lower academic achievement, and withdrawal from peers and family (Mishna et al. 2009:111; Popovac & Leoschut 2012:5; Lennie 2013:50; Rizza & Pereira 2013:15).

Although there is substantial research on cyberbullying as is evident from the above, relatively little is known about cyber-bystanders witnessing the bullying online (cf. Mascheroni & Ólafsson 2018:28-30).

SEXTING

The practise of 'sexting' (the transmitting of sexually explicit images through text messages) to other children has gained in popularity in the last few years. Sexting is the creation, sending, receiving, or forwarding of sexually explicit messages, images or photographs between mobile phones and carries tremendous risk. Quite often, these images are widely disseminated, even if not maliciously intended. It is almost impossible to remove the images from people's phones although it may have been deleted from social media. Some proponents believe sexting is just a normal and healthy mode of sexual expression and the forming of relationships by children. However, evidence exists that highlights the negative consequences although the association between sexting and risky sexual behaviour seems to be weak (Hachiya 2017:181-183; Kosenko et al. 2017:141-143, 153-154).

Many cases have been documented where a child has sent sexually explicit images in confidence to a romantic partner just to later find that it has been circulated throughout the school. Some of these cases led to the suicide of the child. Texting involves complicated ethical issues that have a fundamental influence on the welfare of children (Lennie 2013:3)

Although sexting by children may be consensual, it remains illegal in many countries to re-transmit the image, to use it as revenge porn, or to blackmail a child by threatening to forward the image. Since child pornography laws were composed long before sexting became commonplace, some countries consider the sending of sexual images by a child (even of themselves) as a criminal act under the child-pornography laws, which can result in them being placed on the sexual offenders list – a lifelong sentence (Hachiya 2017:177, 180-182).

It has also been proven that children engaged in sexting are more likely to be involved in sexual activity, often with multiple partners (Hachiya 2017:181).

ETHICAL CHALLENGES

In the past, technology has often been seen from an instrumental perspective as a tool that fulfils a specific purpose, but more recently, there is a growing understanding of the ethical nature of ICT since it impacts the well-being of people (Lennie 2013:33).

Technological improvements are often motivated under the pretext of efficiency. This has unfortunately led to 'a moral vacuum' where current principles are just not efficient enough to deal with the new moral challenges created by digital technology. Digital technology can easily exacerbate prevailing ethical problems, such as the proliferation of highly sexualised content or cyberbullying; or create new ethical problems exclusive to the digital sphere, such as sexting (Lennie 2013:35, 42).

Although there has been some growth in scholarship with regard to ethical challenges to children, there is limited analysis of how ICT-based issues that are ethical in nature, directly affect children. And when ethical challenges are discussed, the challenges are often very superficial as in the case of Grant (2010:12) and his students. A deeper understanding of the challenges and their inherent connection to the social and human nature of digital communication are of importance to prepare children for future participation in the digital world (Lennie 2013:5, 11).

Eventually the transformative nature of technology reshapes children's self-perceptions, their relationships with other children, their perceptions of time and speed, and their way of thinking (Lennie 2013:13-14, 23-24). The cyberculture and internet, together with all the inherent dangers, can generate fear, hyper-agitation, and desensitisation amongst children (Matyjas 2008:195-196). Research indicates that the digital media pose dangers to the physical, emotional, intellectual, and behavioural development of children, as well as the functioning of the family. Excessive online activities often have a detrimental influence on the psychological development of children, often limiting physical interpersonal relationships (Matyjas 2008:196, 201).

The ethical challenge is that as our adoption of ICT increases, society increasingly submits to the sovereignty of technology, which could have an undue impact on the daily lives of children as cyberspace becomes their playground for social interaction (Lennie 2013:1; Löfberg 2003:142). For these children, information technology provides a disembodied way of living through Virtual Reality, anonymous interaction and the use of pseudonyms in chat rooms (Sando 2003:171). Dreyfus (2001:106-107) warns against this disembodied lifestyle and behaviour experienced by people (and children) in cyberspace that is partly based on a Christian-Platonic foundation:

> ... when we enter cyberspace and leave behind our animal-shaped, emotional, intuitive, situated, vulnerable, embodied selves, and

thereby gain a remarkable new freedom never before available to human beings, we might, at the same time, necessarily lose some of our crucial capacities: our ability to make sense of things so as to distinguish the relevant from the irrelevant, our sense of the seriousness of success and failure that is necessary for learning, and our need to get a maximum grip on the world that gives us our sense of the reality of things. … Indeed … I hope to show that, if our body goes, so does relevance, skill, reality, and meaning. (pp. 6-7)

Embodiment is a guard against false fantasies about power, invulnerability and immortality. Embodiment ensures fragility, vulnerability, the possibility of touching, empathy, and dependence on others and the material environment (Sando 2003:184).

It was Kendall (1999:60) that noted that the word 'cyberspace' has a science fiction tone and thus reflects the propensity amongst people to view the online world as an independent reality, totally independent from the real world where human beings are vulnerable. Although she believes that there is no disconnect between the real and online worlds and that people move happily between the worlds since they "perceive their identities and selves as integral and continuous" (Kendall 1999:60), it is not necessarily true of children. The body is an important ethical sensor, which helps us to be aware of the needs and vulnerability of our fellow human beings.

Therefore, any technology which proposes to overcome embodiment and vulnerability, is ethically dangerous because it does away with an important reminder of the essence of being human. What may be acquired in invulnerability and disembodiment may be lost in indifference and aggression against other people. The ethical challenge is that if embodiment is important in the formation of a child's character and online ethical behaviour, then excessive time spent in cyberspace by children seems to be problematic (Sando 2003:185-186).

Although digital technologies have many benefits (eds. Keeley & Little 2017:2), the lack of ethical values has greatly contributed to the abuse of children, amongst others, sexual exploitation, promotion of immoral ideas and behaviours, misuse of private data, and identity theft (Aslani et al. 2013:214).

Since the start of the millennium, AI and algorithm-based information technology has grown exponentially and has improved the understanding of business operations and the quality of decision making tremendously. Unfortunately, there is also a deleterious side to the use of algorithms, which raises serious ethical concerns (Adams et al. 2018:213; Yang 2019:4-5).

The first challenge comes with the irrational belief that technology is morally neutral and that algorithms are unbiased. Although technology may have no sense of good or evil, algorithms always 'bear the fingerprints of its creator(s)', which certainly influences the models of rational analysis and decision making of the user and, therefore, creates some contentious ethical challenges. Technology often changes our relationships with one another and forms our moral and institutional values (Ephraim 2013:280). It does happen that organisational leaders interfere with developers and influence prejudice and preferences of the system (Yang 2019:4-6). The widely publicised use of big data and algorithms by Cambridge Analytica to influence public opinion, manipulate referenda and elections, is a good example of misuse. Such use is an erosion of social justice and, in essence, threatens democracy, especially when used on children (*The Guardian* n.d.; Yang 2019:6).

A second challenge is the use of nudging theory. Nudging is widely used by online companies such as Takealot's 'You might also like …' and Netflix's 'Because you have seen …' and can assist decision makers to make better decisions by limiting the number of choices. Unfortunately, nudging is also used to influence the decision of buyers and often steer them to more expensive services and products, which often leads to the exploitation of unsuspecting children (Yang 2019: 18-20).

Although some progress has been made, a third ethical challenge is that algorithms are not yet very successful in judging human values, which could lead to a sacrifice of fairness and justice due to an inability to distinguish between good and evil. It is thus possible that in the self-development of algorithms they become destructive (Young 2019: 24-25).

A fourth ethical challenge is the Search Engine Manipulation Effect (SEME) that entails the manipulation of search engine results by search engine providers, as well as the 'echo chamber' effect on social media, which can easily limit the critical thinking and freedom of choice of children (Epstein & Robertson 2015:E4512-E4513, E4518-E4520; Krasodomski-Jones 2016:6, 33-35; Bergen 2017).

Industry and government will have to ensure that better values and models based on current ethical guidelines are built into algorithms even if it puts fairness ahead of profit (O'Neil 2016:202; Yang 2019:26). IBM, in 2019, published the *Everyday Ethics for Artificial Intelligence* where they state: "Ethics must be embedded into the design and development process from the very beginning of AI creation" (IBM 2019:8). Due to the rapid evolution of AI technology in terms of capabilities and impact on especially children, AI systems' designers and developers must understand the ethical concerns involved in their work (Yang 2019:40). The ethics around AI and algorithms need serious consideration and should guide all AI and algorithm design and development (Adams et al. 2018:216).

Current practices in the use of AI, big data and algorithms have many major ethical and societal implications, with particular reference to children. Although many of the other online challenges have been addressed to some extent, little agreement currently exists on core ethical issues and frameworks underpinning the ethical approach to the development and deployment of these technologies. Often the algorithms are based on such complex internal logic or have developed via deep learning that even developers do not fully understand the logic (Whittlestone et al. 2019:1-2, 20).

Rizza and Pereira (2013:22) refer to social media as dwellings where children act out their lives, construct and negotiate cultural meanings and develop their identities. But it is exactly here that ethical challenges arise. Ethical values, such as autonomy, identity, integrity, responsibility, privacy, freedom, informed consent and justice are contested by the current development and use of ICT. ICT tools are changing normative ethics and ethical behaviour.

In many national legal systems, every person's right to a personal identity has been entrenched. However, in the digital world, identity has become fluid, dynamic and flexible making it possible for children to be who they wish to be. In the online world, it is possible for a child to have multiple identities. Cyberbullying, for instance, precisely challenges this identity of the child (Rizza & Pereira 2013:23-24). Unfortunately, current regulations are not focusing on addressing violations of a child's identity and reputation and tend to rather focus on privacy.

Since social media do not adhere to the traditional protection against excesses, such as respect for other children, to be careful of strangers and to adhere to certain limits with regard to relationships. Ephraim (2013:280-281) suggests a culture-centred approach that maintains cultural and ethical values and standards, which inter alia include the qualities of compassion, respect for human dignity, and the right to privacy.

COUNTER MEASURES

A SHARED RESPONSIBILITY

The task of ensuring the safety of children online is so complex that a concerted multi-stakeholder collaborative approach between parents, peers, teachers, children, communities, schools, civil society, industry, government, NGOs, international organisations and law enforcement is needed to ensure effective protection of children in the digital domain. Increasing the awareness among children, families, religious communities, the ICT sector, media and government will break the ignorance around child sexual abuse (O'Neill 2013a:258; eds. Keeley & Little 2017:89). In particular, collaboration between the technology industry and law enforcement is essential to limit online child abuse and exploitation (eds. Keeley & Little 2017:6, 9, 11).

PARENTAL RESPONSIBILITY

In order to protect children from the dangers of the digital world, parents should teach their children to use the internet in a focused manner. But perhaps the most important point is a genuine interest in their children's experiences in the complex digital world and open discussions and guidance around the challenges they experience (Matyjas 2008:204; eds. Keeley & Little 2017:69). Parents need to pay attention to the online activities and make time to be with their children while they are online. They should watch for signs of meanness and act immediately by blocking and reporting the bullying or exploitation of their child (Ephraim 2013:283; eds. Keeley & Little 2017:89).

The exponential development of technology, and, in particular, the lack of a proper distinction between the real and the virtual worlds, has affected the essence of families. Cyber space became a fundamental part of the living space of families and with it came the many challenges of abuse, manipulation and exploitation (ITU & UNICEF 2015:9-10, 13; Minić & Spalević 2014:424-425, 427-428). However, parents often feel overwhelmed due to a lack of awareness, digital knowledge and competence, which makes it difficult for them to take control of their children's digital lives or to effectively protect them online (O'Neill 2013a:257; Livingstone et al. 2015:13; Livingstone et al. 2017:83, 99). Since parents are gateways to child online safety, cyber training to improve their digital understanding and skills is important in the detection and handling of online dangers (eds. Keeley & Little 2017:88-89; Livingstone et al. 2017:100-101).

Since children are often unaware of the importance of privacy settings and its possible consequences, parents must ensure that the default privacy settings are set for the maximum protection of the privacy of their children (EC 2012:10-11). Parents could also consider the use of parental controls and teach their children to keep profiles private by setting it to only allow viewing by friends and family (eds.

Keeley & Little 2017:89). Verifiable parental consent could be used for children under a certain age (EC 2012:10-11). However, parents should not use technical tools to escape their obligation of talking to their children about inappropriate and dangerous online sexual behaviour (Staksrud & Kirksæther 2013:32).

In a study undertaken in South Africa, 43.6% of children stated that they would almost never speak to their parents about what they do on the internet and only 8.6% very often or often talk to their parents about disconcerting online issues. A large number of children can also use a webcam (42.1%), download music or films (71.9%) or visit a social networking site (65.3%) without parental supervision (Phyfer et al. 2016:117-118). Although parenting may be different in different parts of the world, parents will have to become engaged in their children's internet activities.

Just as parents establish temporal and geographic restrictions with regard to physical spaces in order to protect their children from harm, they should set clear time and space limits with regard to the internet and should be informed what their children are doing or whom they are visiting (Valentine & Holloway 2001:76-77). Parental responsibility changes according to the age and development level of the child. Just as parents will not let a young and inexperienced child cycle unaccompanied on a busy road or without a helmet, similarly equivalent precautions should be taken before a young child is allowed onto the highway of the internet (O'Neill 2013a:259).

THE VALUE OF PEER SUPPORT AND COMMUNITIES

According to research, children should be encouraged to show empathy and support each other when abused. If possible, they should become 'upstanders' against abuse and cyberbullying (eds. Keely & Little 2017:108). Experience has proved that one of the best ways to address the dynamic phenomenon of cyberbullying and other exploitation of children, is to increase awareness through the use of children and to give compelling support to the process. This should be followed up by the creation of safe spaces where children could discuss the challenges they experience online (Rizza & Pereira 2013:8).

The appointment of cyber mentors or virtual peer support has proved valuable. The online mentoring by peers is anonymous and protected by a software filter, while being monitored by senior cyber mentors (Mishna et al. 2009:107).

THE ROLE OF THE SCHOOL

Digital and media literacy should be taught in all schools from the very early years to keep children informed and safe online and should go beyond technical skills (EC 2012:8). It should include how children could protect themselves from online dangers, such as cyberbullying and sexual abuse by not sharing photos or filling out personal details on online forms. They should understand the risk of creating and sharing content and that every post online (text, photo or video) is no longer private and possibly cannot be erased. Especially self-generated content, such as sexually explicit material exposes them to the risk of cyberbullying or extortion and may be distributed all over the internet. Children should understand how important it is to protect their personal information (eds. Keeley & Little 2017:128-129).

Research indicates that although children are aware of online risks and dangers, they mostly describe their risks in terms of operational user problems or media-hyped fears. Schools should, therefore, systematically educate children regarding online dangers, risks and e-safety to ensure that they become responsible digital citizens (Cranmer et al. 2009:127; Mishna et al. 2009:107; DQ Institute 2018). They should be enabled to take responsibility for their online behaviour; to practice safety; to protect their data and devices; to establish healthy social relationships with others; and to use digital technology and media in a disciplined way (eds. Keeley & Little 2017:3; DQ Institute 2018).

Teachers, trained in the use of appropriate monitoring and filtering software, could be assigned as internet safety coordinators (Cranmer et al. 2009:129). Since cyberbullying often emerges within the school environment, schools can play a substantial role in addressing the phenomenon through social and emotional learning (Rizza & Pereira 2013:20; Wojniak & Majorek 2016:133).

LEVERAGE THE POWER OF THE PRIVATE SECTOR

Since the private sector plays a key role in the digital revolution, businesses have become integrated into the lives of children and should, due to their power and influence, play a much greater role in protecting children by removing unsuitable content (eds. Keeley & Little 2017:129). Especially internet service providers (ISPs) and content providers play a significant role in respect to corporate responsibility practices to ensure the safety of children through the promotion of ethical standards on data and privacy (Ephraim 2013:283; Ságvári & Máder 2013:155-156; eds. Keeley & Little 2017:3, 11). Companies should integrate child rights into all corporate policies and management processes (ITU & UNICEF 2015:12).

The presence of large numbers of underage children on services (and websites) originally intended for adult audiences creates a huge embarrassment for many digital companies. Although companies, such as Facebook, would not readily admit to the problem, they apparently delete about 20 000 accounts of children under 13 years per day that provided false information about their age (O'Neill 2013a:255). Social media networks, therefore, should assist in child safety by providing 'report abuse' buttons, enforcing strict age limits for new user accounts, using filtering technologies, creating child safety zones on the internet and thorough age and identity verification (Graafland 2018:39).

Based on the legal principle of the 'duty of care', companies must do much more to take reasonable care so as not to harm the children who use their online services even if not legitimately registered (O'Neill 2013a:255). It is just not enough for companies, such as Facebook, to state that they cannot guarantee that the platform is safe and that people use it at their own risk. Even if there is no legal obligation on online companies, such as Facebook, to accept responsibility for underage child users, there is unquestionably an ethical obligation under common law to exercise a due standard of care and ensure the safety of their service given the high prevalence of underage users. Verification of age should not only rely on technical methods, but also involve the parents and undertake awareness campaigns (O'Neill 2013a:256). Technology companies could also, in collaboration with government, create a system of content classification and corresponding age rating for all services, and integrate it with parental controls (EC 2012:12). Unfortunately, many parents allow their underage children to create social networking accounts. It thus seems futile to state that parents should have the final say if their child could open a social networking account (O'Neill 2013a:254).

Service providers could make their platforms more suitable for underage children by limiting the visibility of profiles through a default private setting (O'Neill 2013a:255). Companies should adjust technology according to current ethics (Rizza & Pereira 2013:8). A good example of how technology can be customised to assist with intentionality is the decision of a German state to prohibit the Facebook 'Like' button because it allows illegal profiling and violates privacy laws (Mack 2011).

As a major driving force of the Fourth Industrial Revolution, the ICT industry is ethically bounded by the obligation to place the protection of children at the very heart of all technological innovation and to develop industry standards to ensure the safety of children accordingly (ITU & UNICEF 2015:12; eds. Keeley & Little 2017:69). Industry should create a safe online environment for children by implementing age appropriate privacy settings (Wojniak & Majorek 2016:134-35; eds. Keeley & Little 2017:89). Technology companies should also share their knowledge, expertise and digital tools with law enforcement agencies to improve the protection of children online. Parents could be assisted with tools, such as filtering, blocking and age verification (eds. Keeley & Little 2017:126-127, 130).

CHAPTER 10

ETHICAL DESIGN AND PRIVACY

It is well known that technologies are often purposely designed to exploit human or child weaknesses, psychological biases or vulnerabilities, such as the need for social acceptance or the fear of rejection. Technology companies will have to reconsider their designs to ensure that they are ethical and not only focused on the exploitation of children for financial gain. They should embrace the principle of safety-by-design that incorporates security, safety and privacy features into their products (O'Neill 2013a:259; Rizza & Pereira 2013:28-29; eds. Keely & Little 2017:108, 129-130). Ethics must thus "be embedded in the design and development process" (IBM 2019:8).

Privacy is of the utmost importance where children are involved. Proper protection of the privacy of children necessitates an alignment between technology and regulation. For instance, social media will have to consider simple functionalities, such as the giving of consent to others to publish information, as well as undo and redundancy functions (Rizza & Pereira 2013:26).

The large technology and advertising companies will have to balance their use of personal data to improve the quality and efficiency of services versus respecting the privacy and autonomy of individuals; automation for convenience versus self-actualisation and dignity; as well as ensure that the algorithms are not biased and treat all children fairly and equally (Whittlestone et al. 2019:2).

One of the major concerns with regard to AI, big data and algorithms is that it is fairly easy to change the original purpose for which it was created, essentially modifying their ethical valence. Although supposed to be domain-neutral, the information acquisition and processing, and decision-making techniques of AI, as well as big data and algorithm technologies, can become progressively pervasive in the lives of children. There is indeed a need for regulation in this regard to protect vulnerable children (Whittlestone et al. 2019:8, 11).

TECHNOLOGY TOOLS

Several technology tools could be used to monitor children's activities and to filter prohibited connections and websites (Valentine & Holloway 2001:77-78; cf. Grant 2010:9). New forensic tools using AI can also assist in curbing the sexual abuse of children. Systems are available that can monitor peer-to-peer (P2P) network activity and will furnish the identity of sharers of child sexual abuse material, as well as their geolocation. Profiling and semantic recognition can be used to detect abusive content, behaviour and cyberbullying (Rizza & Pereira 2013:21-22).

Since Microsoft donated its PhotoDNA technology to the International Centre for Missing and Exploited Children and it was integrated with INTERPOL's International Child Sexual Exploitation (ICSE) database, it is possible to search for the unique signature or digital fingerprint of any online image (eds. Keeley & Little 2017: 88-89).

In Europe, the tool iCOP has been developed to detect new or previously unknown child sexual abuse material that is shared on P2P networks. iCOP performs live forensic analysis through the use of AI and machine learning to compare hundreds of thousands of files to detect recent or on-going child abuse (eds. Keeley & Little 2017: 88-89).

THE ROLE OF GOVERNMENT

To enable children to effectively deal with online risks of sexual abuse, it is important that the state should establish adequate mechanisms for the reporting of abusive content and contacts (EC 2012:9). As part of their Safer Internet Action, the European Union and Canada established national hotlines to allow children to anonymously report content that is believed to be illegal (Mishna et al. 2009:107). Although hotlines play an important role as a reporting mechanism, it can never be the sole solution. Alternatively, many countries filtered, and blocked sites containing sexual abuse material of children and use software detection tools and upload filters at the level of internet service providers (O'Neill 2013b:39, 41-45, 48, 51-52; Wojniak & Majorek 2016:134).

The state should also scale up awareness amongst all children, parents, and teachers to make them cyber-aware and ensure that peer education amongst children is promoted (eds. Keeley & Little 2017:89). In Europe, awareness centres, promoting safe and responsible internet and cell phone use, are used with great success (Rizza & Pereira 2013:11; eds. Keely & Little 2017:108).

Government law enforcement could also build profiles of potential perpetrators, their signature moves, and aggressive terminology and patterns of dominance in online conversations to make it more difficult for them to hide behind multiple digital personas.

Although some policy makers worldwide are addressing the online risks that are endangering children, countries in Africa and South Africa are unfortunately often lacking behind with the formulation of policy frameworks and national strategies regarding the online safety of children. South Africa needs a common ICT strategy and a standardised and integrated approach to uphold children's rights and preserve child safety online.

LEGAL PROTECTION

In June 2016, internet access was recognised as one of the basic human rights (Human Rights Council 2016:4, 53-55). However, due to the exponential growth in ICT and high rate of internet adoption, the policy, governance and legislative frameworks, determining online access and use, could not keep up and are mostly territorial (Bulger et al. 2017:751).

Children's right to protection when they go online is an internationally entrenched principle in laws that protect children from online exploitation and maltreatment (Bulger et al. 2017:751). These laws mostly build on the decisions of the United Nations (UN) Convention on the Rights of the Child (UN 1989) in the digital age and include inter alia their rights to freedom of expression of views, thoughts, beliefs and opinion (UN 1989 articles 12-14); freedom of association and participation (Article 15); the right to privacy and protection against unlawful attacks on their honour and reputation (Article 16) and the right to protection "from all forms of physical or mental violence, injury or abuse, neglect or negligent treatment, maltreatment or exploitation, including sexual abuse" (Article 19) (UN 1989). It is the responsibility of government to develop legal and policy frameworks to protect the child as legitimate rights-holder with full human rights (Livingstone et al. 2015:9; Bulger et al. 2017: 751-752).

Often, countries included special provisions within existing laws and regulations to fulfil the above-mentioned obligation and to protect children from online exploitation and abuse. Most countries, therefore, criminalised the creation, dissemination and consumption of Child Sexual Abuse Material (CSAM or child pornography) and the online solicitation and grooming of children. Access to certain harmful content is also restricted, such as gambling and 'adult' pornography (Bulger et al. 2017:751-752).

Graafland (2020:39) is of the opinion that "the majority of risks that exist both online and offline, existing laws and regulation apply and no additional laws are needed." However, it is not enough to merely adapt current laws to make what is illegal offline also illegal online. What is needed is to think anew from the traditional elements of the crime, such as activity, intention, unlawfulness, knowledge of unlawfulness and prejudice, to create new offences based on the inherent features of cyber characteristics. From the very essence of cyber-activities, it is important to anticipate criminal activity and, therefore, to create offences based on the early phases of criminal activity. Especially with regard to the protection of children, it is important that a new offence is created by penalising the introduction to a crime as opposed to a completed crime where the consequences are irreversible. By approaching crime on this basis, criminality is created on the basis of the anticipation of a crime as opposed to a traditionally completed offence, which is judged by the consequences of such crimes. The intention of this pre-emptive approach is to strengthen the deterrent and preventative feature of crime as opposed to the penal feature (Fourie, Heath & Fourie 2011).

Some countries do make an effort to think innovatively, such as France, that made the filming and online distribution of violent acts ('happy slapping') a crime. Japan made it illegal to arrange dates with minors who have been met on dating websites. Australia, Ireland, Norway, France, the UK, New Zealand and Japan promulgated legislation with regard to cyber-grooming (Graafland 2018:39). But although children comprise a third of internet users in the world, most national policies focus on the adult user, while broader national policies focusing on the child do not adequately address the challenges accompanying digital technologies. It is important that children be included in all ICT regulation, policies and acts (ITU & UNICEF 2015:6-7; eds. Keeley & Little 2017:130).

Government needs to enact laws criminalising all forms of sexual abuse and exploitation of children, with particular reference to online abuse (eds. Keeley & Little 2017:88-89). Unfortunately, the transnational nature of internet services and providers limits the power of governments to fully address the challenges experienced by children online (Livingstone et al. 2015:13). Due to the exponential development of technologies, especially in the fourth industrial era, technological developments often outpace ethical frameworks and legal definitions. It would, therefore, be more appropriate for countries to adopt tech-neutral policies and definitions (Graafland 2018:39).

In South Africa, legislation focuses only on the general protection of children, together with some civil and criminal legislation basically relevant to ICTs. Unfortunately, the environment for children's rights and protection in the digital era is seriously wanting in South Africa. Legislation with regard to the online safety of children is at best limited, fragmented and sometimes even contradictory (Bulger et al. 2017:754). The South African Law Reform Commission (2015:24-47) expressed serious concerns regarding the creation, distribution and exposure of children to child abuse material, as well as sexting by children and the online grooming of children by adults. The commission, therefore, initiated a discussion on law reform in this regard and pointed out several important gaps regarding the protection of children in current South African Law, such as the inadequacy of some definitions, the lack of criminalising of certain online activities, the fragmentation of the protection of children, and the inadequate protection of children with regard to online abuse (:55-137).

The *Children's Act* (RSA, Act No. 38 of 2005) has been revised after public consultation in *The Children's Amendment Bill* of 2019 (RSA 2019b) and did attempt to align the *Children's Act* with the *Criminal Law (Sexual Offences and Related Matters), Amendment Act*, 2008, for example with regard to a child's right to privacy (RSA, Act No 5 of 2015:15). However, with regard to the protection of children against exploitation and abuse, the amended bill is at best insufficient and does not really address or cross-reference cyber dangers.

The protection of children from online sexual abuse received worldwide attention and led to several initiatives, such as the United Nations Convention on the Rights of the Child (UN CRC) and the resultant Optional Protocol on the Sale of Children, Child Prostitution and Child Pornography; the Council of Europe's Convention on Cybercrime; and the Global Alliance Against Child Sexual Abuse encompassing 52 countries. Together, these initiatives have made the distribution of inappropriate child abuse materials illegal. Although South Africa aligned itself with these international principles (Bulger et al. 2017:755), much of the practical implementation must still be seen.

In the USA, child pornography is defined as any visual depiction of sexually explicit conduct involving a person less than 18 years of age. "Misleading domain names" and "misleading words or images on the internet" that may cause children to unintentionally view explicit child abuse material online are prohibited (US Department of Justice 2015). The European Union also includes 'virtual child pornography' and 'grooming' in their 2011 directive to member states (Bulger et al. 2017:755–756).

In South Africa, legislation addressing child pornography was promulgated in 1996 as the *Film and Publications Board Act* (RSA, Act

No. 65 of 1996) and amended in 2019 in the *Film and Publications Board Amendment Act* (RSA, Act No. 11 of 2019) to align the definition of child pornography with the Criminal Law Act. The definition of the "distribution" of online material was expanded to include content streaming and that of "harmful" to include "emotional, psychological and moral distress." The term "hate speech" referring to "any speech, gesture, conduct, writing, display or publication, made using the internet ..., which propagates, advocates or communicates words against any person or identifiable group ... to incite harm and promote or propagate hatred..." has been included. Amendments to the *Film and Publications Board Act* in 2019 provided much more extensive definitions of sexual abuse images of children, as well as the inclusion of revenge pornography (RSA, Act No. 11 of 2019). Unfortunately, current definitions in South African legislation do not include the downloading of an image on any digital device (Bulger et al. 2017:756).

South Africa has further criminalised the exposure of children to pornography and acts of sexual grooming of children under the *Criminal Law (Sexual Offences and Related Matters) Amendment Act* (RSA, Act No. 5 of 2015), which included online sexual offences. The Justice Alliance of South Africa (JASA) has been working without much success on an Internet and Cell Phone Pornography Bill that endeavours to totally ban pornography from the country by ensuring that it is filtered out at Tier One service providers (South African Law Reform Commission 2015:138-139, 148).

However, the online behaviour of children and in particular youth-produced and shared sexual content, bring several new challenges in the protection of children and overlaps with the legal definition of adults involved in offensive practices (Bulger et al. 2017:756). Legislative frameworks are often too narrow in their approach to properly address the complexities of children's online experiences and usually depart from children as vulnerable victims, thus disregarding their agency and participation (Livingstone et al. 2015:5). Sexting or the distribution of nude images among children is, for example, considered a criminal offence in some countries and can lead to prosecution, punishment and listing as sex-offenders of adolescents (UNICEF 2012:54, 79–80; Byrne, Albright & Kardefelt-Winther 2016:6).

In Europe, the child online safety emphasis has shifted from a focus on protection and restriction to a greater focus on awareness and the empowerment of children and parents (Mascheroni et al. 2013:218). Instead of trying to provide a safer internet for children, the aim is shifting to a better internet service for children (EC 2012:2-17). Other regions, and in particular Africa, still need to make this change in focus from a safer to a better internet. The complexity of the challenge calls for a holistic approach to child rights based on evidence (reliable data) and not on the traditional approach of combating child sexual abuse often based on sensational incidents and media reports (UNICEF 2012:11; Livingstone 2013:103-106; Livingstone et al. 2015:16-17). The Centre for Justice and Crime Prevention in South Africa has done excellent evidence-based work regarding the barriers, opportunities and risks experienced by South African children (Phyfer et al. 2016:1-129).

Children are not only a vulnerable group, but also active participants, agents and creators of online content. Policy makers will have to tend to rigorous investigation and much more detailed and credible data about the use of digital technology by children, as well as their real-life circumstances and social norms (Byrne & Burton 2017:41-43).

Unfortunately, South Africa lacks an overarching policy on ICT and children. Policies are currently scattered over a number of sectors, for example education, cybersecurity, child welfare and protection, and are often handled by different departments and ministries, while the impact is rarely measured (Byrne & Burton 2017:47-48). Existing South African legislation is at best ineffective to combat online child abuse. South Africa is in need of a new law that specifically deals with the "creation, possession and distribution of child abuse material" (South African Law Reform Commission 2015:146-147).

CYBERBULLYING

Cyberbullying is often incorrectly framed as a privacy issue, but should rather be seen as an identity-related ethical issue. If it is seen as a privacy issue, policy strategies focus on data protection. While the right to privacy entails the suppression of private aspects of children from public knowledge, the right to identity entails the dissemination of information of children to the public sphere without authorisation and in ways that cannot be reconciled with their identity or public image. Government would thus do better by focusing their policies on the identity rights of children (Rizza & Pereira 2013:26, 31).

In order to combat cyberbullying, a multi-dimensional strategy and holistic approach should be followed since cyberbullying is never just online. Parents, the school, peer groups, social services and the media could play an important preventative role to change the values, beliefs and behaviour around cyberbullying (Rizza & Pereira 2013:15-16, 18, 21).

HARVESTING OF DATA

The widespread gathering of personal data by the large technological and advertising companies inter alia through tracking, facial and voice recognition raises many concerns and will have to be addressed. Privacy is a human right and not a commercial concession. However, views on privacy rights differ between the USA, UK, Continental Europe, Asia, Africa, Latin America, as well as between political structures.

Threats to privacy are constantly arising – especially from the commercial and security sectors, and social networks (Stückelberger 2014:22) leading to the following concerns that need to be addressed:

- Any collection of information about an individual or child should only take place with the knowledge and consent of the individual or parent. It is an open question if the Fair Information Practice Principles (FIPPs) found in current privacy policies are effective at all (Regan & Jesse 2019:175).

- Children have the right to remain anonymous and unidentified. This right is often protected in law by a clause on 'personally identifiable information' or information directly related to a specific individual. However, with multiple data points per person, big data, artificial intelligence algorithms and data analytics, it is almost impossible to remain anonymous (Regan & Jesse 2019:177-179). Legislation will need to be adapted accordingly. Although the *Protection of Personal Information Act* (RSA, Act No. 4 of 2013) of South Africa, promulgated in 2013, does provide significant protection with regard to the collecting, storing, processing and sharing of personal information, little has yet been done regarding its implementation since government has failed to appoint a regulator.

- Analytics powered by big data increasingly challenge individual autonomy. Algorithms, for instance, lead and nudge children to buy specific items and use specific routes or restaurants. The danger is that children are subjected to a continuous loop without freedom to make their own decisions. The danger with nudges is that they manipulate children (Regan & Jesse 2019:179-180).

- Big data uses algorithms and AI to make predictions about individuals. But research has shown that algorithms can be biased and can thus discriminate on the basis of race, gender, age or other personal traits (Regan & Jesse 2019:180-181, 188-189). Companies will have to ensure that their algorithms are free of bias and treats all people fairly and equally.

Data generated through digital tracking and the use of social media is often used for profiling of children and inappropriate marketing and advertising. Several new electronic toys are also connected to the internet and transmit data about the thoughts and feelings of children to toy manufacturers. It is important to establish safeguards, such as data anonymisation, encryption, secure data storage, and the prohibition of the use of data without consent, to protect the privacy of children. The privacy settings of children should by default be set to maximum. Technology and advertising companies should not monetise the information of children and should protect data, such as the child's location and browsing habits (eds. Keeley and Little 2017:127-128).

CONCLUSION

We live in a time, where the confluence of real and virtual worlds creates new contexts and ontologies that we are continuously struggling to fully comprehend. Our ethical values, according to which we act and use technology, are constantly put to the test. The problem is that we have often left this debate to the corporates and their developers who largely have profit as their main goal (Rizza & Pereira 2013:29).

The ethical debate cannot be left to the corporates to decide according to which values children should live (Rizza & Pereira 2013:30). The internet and social media have an impact on the social development of the child and the broader society. A multi-stakeholder approach is, therefore, necessary to protect the child in this volatile and often pervasive and dangerous virtual world of dangers and uncertainties and to ensure that it rather becomes an important source of opportunity and empowerment where children can become the authors of their own future (Third et al. 2017:3). This approach entails an essential role by the parents, as well as the support of industry, school, NGOs and government.

Although the internet and social media were originally designed for adults, children are increasingly using it. Digital laws, policies, practices, guidelines and technology products should in future better reflect children's need and ensure their safety (Third et al. 2017:18). Many safety issues around content, contact and conduct on the internet need to be addressed – in particular the issue of the unauthorised use of social media by underage children (Neill 2013a:260).

The growing use of data collection and algorithms by large marketing and advertising firms to influence children in a vulnerable period of their lives is of great concern. Wide legal protection against commercial data collection is afforded to children in many countries, but enforcement is markedly poor. Authorities and industry will have to pay greater attention to software design aspects of the services rendered to children. Minimum safety standards underpinned by ethics and ethical accountability should be enforced to reduce the risks to children (Neill 2013a:260).

If stakeholders do not take the harming of children through technology at least as serious as offline risks, it has the ability to spiral out of control and even mobilise violence on a massive scale. This sadly transpired recently in Myanmar when a social media campaign resulted in horrendous violence against members of the Rohingya ethic minority, which led to the killing and mutilation of many children and hundreds of thousands of refugees (eds. Keeley & Little 2017:vi).

REFERENCES

CHAPTER I

Archard, D. 2004. *Children rights and childhood*. 2nd ed. Routledge, London and New York.

Bankoff G., Frerks, G. & Hilhorst D. (eds.). 2004. *Mapping vulnerability: Disasters, development, and people*, Earthscan, London.

Bosch, D.J. 2011. *Transforming mission. Paradigm shifts in theology of mission*. Twentieth anniversary edn. Orbis Books, New York.

Brown, B. 2015. *Rising strong*, Vermilion, London. Kindle Edn.

Brown, C.E. 2013. The concept of vulnerability and its use in the care and control of young people. PhD thesis. School of Sociology and Social Policy, The University of Leeds, Leeds.

Brown, K. 2014. Questioning the vulnerability zeitgeist: Care and control practices with 'vulnerable' young people. *Social Policy & Society*, 13(3): 371-387.

Brown, K. 2015. *Vulnerability and young people. Care and social control in policy and practice*. Policy Press, Bristol.

Brown, K., Ecclestone, K. & Emmel, N. 2017. The many faces of vulnerability. *Social Policy & Society*, 16(3):497-510. https://doi.org/10.1017/S1474746416000610.

Brueggemann, W. 1994. Remembering Rachel's children: an urban agenda for people who notice. *Word & World* 14(4):377-383.

Butler, D. 2004. *Precarious life. The powers of mourning and violence*. Verso, London/New York.

Castells, M. 2010a. *The information age: Economy, society and culture. Vol. 1: The rise of the network society*. 2nd edn. Wiley-Blackwell, West Sussex.

Castells, M. 2010b. *The information age: Economy, society and culture. Vol. 2: The power of identity*. 2nd edn. Wiley-Blackwell, West Sussex.

Castells, M. 2010c. *The information age: Economy, society and culture. Vol. 3: End of millennium*. 2nd edn. Wiley-Blackwell, West Sussex.

Collins, J. 2014. The contours of "vulnerability", 54-96. In: J. Wallbank & J. Herring (eds.). *Vulnerabilities, care and family law*. Routledge, New York.

Fineman, M.A. 2011. The vulnerable subject: Anchoring equality in the human condition, 161-175. In: M.A. Fineman (ed.). *Transcending the boundaries of law. Generations of feminism and legal theory*. Routledge, New York.

Formosa, P. 2014. The role of vulnerability in Kantian ethics, 88-109. In: C. Mackenzie, W. Rogers & S. Dodds (eds.). *Vulnerability. New essays in ethics and feminist philosophy*. Oxford University Press, Oxford.

Goodin, R.E. 1985. *Protecting the vulnerable. A reanalysis of our social responsibilities*. The University of Chicago Press, Chicago.

Grobbelaar, J. 2012. *Child Theology and the African context*. Child Theology Movement, London.

Hall, K. 2019a. Demography of South Africa's children, 216-220. In: M. Shung-King, L. Lake, D. Sanders & M. Hendricks (eds.). *South African Child Gauge* 2019. Children's Institute, University of Cape Town, Cape Town.

Hall, K. 2019b. Demography – Children in South Africa. Viewed 23 January 2020, from http://www.childrencount.uct.ac.za./indicator.php?domain=1&indicator=1.

Herring, J. 2018. *Vulnerability, childhood and the law*. Springer International Publishing, Cham.

REFERENCES

James, A. & A., 2012. *Key concepts in Childhood Studies*. SAGE Publications, London.

Jensen, D.H. 2005. *Graced vulnerability. A Theology of Childhood*. The Pilgrim Press, Cleveland.

Johnson, D.J., Agbenjiga, D.L. & Bahemuka J.M. 2013. Vulnerable childhood in a global context: Embracing the sacred trust, 12-22. In: D.J. Johnson, D.L. Agbenjiga & R.K. Hitchcock (eds.). *Vulnerable children. Global challenges in education, health, well-being and child's rights*. Springer Science & Business Media, New York.

Käll, L.F. 2016. Vulnerable bodies and embodied boundaries, 1-12. In: L.F. Käll (ed.). *Bodies, boundaries and vulnerabilities interrogating social, cultural and political aspects of embodiment*. Springer, Cham.

Koopman, N. 2008. Vulnerable Church in a Vulnerable World? Towards an Ecclesiology of Vulnerability. *Journal of Reformed Theology*, 2:240-254.

Koopman, N. 2013. Hope, vulnerability and disability? A theological perspective, 43-54. In: J. Claassens, L. Swartz & L. Hansen (eds.). *Searching for dignity – Conversations on human dignity, theology and disability*. Stellenbosch: African Sun Media.

Koopman, N. 2016. Public theology and the plight of children in Africa, 193-209. In: J. Grobbelaar & G. Breed (eds.). *Welcoming Africa's children – Theological and ministry perspectives*. AOSIS, Cape Town. http://www.dx.doi.org/10.4102/aosis.2016.waccs13.06.

Levine, C., Faden, R., Grady, C., Hammerschmidt D., Eckenwiler, L. & Sugarman, J. 2004. The limitations of "vulnerability" as a protection for human research participants. *The American Journal of Bioethics*, 4(3): 44-49. DOI: 10.1080/15265160490497083.

Luna, 2019. Identifying and evaluating layers of vulnerability – a way forward. *Developing World Bioethics*, 19:86-95.

MacIntyre, A.C. 1999. *Dependent rational animals: Why human beings need the virtues*. Open Court Publishing, Chicago and La Salle.

Mackenzie, C., Rogers, W. & Dodds, S. 2014. Introduction: What is vulnerability, and why does it matter for moral theory?, 1-29. In: C. Mackenzie, W. Rogers & S. Dodds (eds.). *Vulnerability. New essays in ethics and feminist philosophy*. Oxford University Press, Oxford.

McCarthy, M.C. 2005. An ecclesiology of groaning: Augustine, the Psalms, and the making of church. *Theological Studies*, 66:23-48.

Nifosi-Sutton, I. 2017. *The protection of vulnerable groups under international human rights*, Routledge, New York.

Office of Theology and Worship of the Presbyterian Church (USA). (n.d.). *Confession of Belhar September 1986*. Viewed 9 April 2020, from http://www.pcusa.org/media/uploads/theologyandworship/pdfs/belhar.pdf.

Placher, W.C. 1994. *Narratives of a vulnerable God: Christ, Theology, and Scripture*. Westminster John Knox Press, Louisville.

Placher, W.C. 2010. *Mark. Belief. A Theological commentary on the Bible*. Westminster John Knox Press, Louisville. Kindle edn.

Qvortrup, J. 2005. A voice for children in statistical and social accounting: A plea for children's right to be heard, 83-103. In: A. James & A. Prout (eds.). *Constructing and reconstructing childhood: Contemporary issues in the sociological study of childhood*. 2nd ed. Falmer Press, London/Washington, DC.

Reynolds, T.E. 2008. *Vulnerable communion. A theology of disability and hospitality*. Brazos Press, Grand Rapids.

Schweiger, G. 2019. Ethics, poverty and children's vulnerability. *Ethics and Social Welfare*, 13(3):288-301. https://doi.org/10.1080/17496535.2019.1593480.

Shung-King, M., Lake, L., Sanders, D. & Hendricks, M. (eds.). 2019. *South African Child Gauge 2019 – Child and adolescent health. Leave no one behind*. Children's Institute, University of Cape Town, Cape Town.

Sloane, A. 2012. Justifying advocacy A Biblical and Theological rationale for speaking the truth to power on behalf of the vulnerable. *Evangelical Review of Theology* 36(2):176-186.

Smit, D.J. 1984 ... op 'n besondere wyse die God van die noodlydende, die arme en die veronregte ... (... in a special way the God of the destitute, poor and wronged ...), 60-73. In: G.D. Cloete & D.J. Smit (eds.). *'n Oomblik van Waarheid (A moment of truth)*. Tafelberg Uitgewers, Kaapstad.

Smit, D.J. 2016. Welcoming children? – On building cultures of trust?, 1-41. In: J. Grobbelaar & G. Breed (eds.). *Welcoming Africa's children – Theological and ministry perspectives*. AOSIS, Cape Town. http://www.dx.doi.org/10.4102/aosis.2016.waccs13.01.

Stats SA. 2018. *Demographic profile of adolescents in South Africa*, Report 03-00-10. Statistics South Africa, Pretoria.

Stats SA. 2019. *Mid-year population estimates 2019*. Statistical Release P0302. Statistics South Africa, Pretoria.

Turner, B.S. 2006. *Vulnerability and human rights*. The Pennsylvania State University Press, University Park.

Wall, J. 2010. *Ethics in light of childhood*. Georgetown University Press, Washington, DC.

Wallbank, J. & Herring, J. 2014. Introduction: vulnerabilities, care and family law, 12-53. In: J. Wallbank & J. Herring (eds.). *Vulnerabilities, care and family law*. Routledge, New York.

Wright, T. 2004. *Paul for everyone: Romans part 1: Chapters 1-8*. Society for Promoting Christian Knowledge, London.

CHAPTER 2

African Child Policy Forum (ACPF). 2019. *Sexual exploitation of children in Africa: A silent emergency*. Oak Foundation, Mozambique.

Arigatou International & Global Network of Religions for Children. 2017. GNRC *5th Forum ending violence against children: Faith communities in action*. Panama City, Panama.

Baptist Union, 2016. Response to the South African Human Rights Commission's proposal to outlaw spanking. Viewed 5 April 2018, from http://www.baptistunion.org.za/index.php/press-release/.

Burton, P., Ward, C.L., Artz, L. & Leoschut, L. 2016. *The Optimus study on child abuse, violence and neglect in South Africa*. Research Report, South Africa: Centre for Justice and Crime Prevention at University of Cape Town, Cape Town.

Chames, C., & Lemovsky, D. 2014. Towards effective child protection. Adopting a systems approach, 43-50. In: S. Mathews, L. Jamieson, L. Lake & C Smith (eds). *The South African Child Gauge 2014*. Children's Institute, University of Cape Town, Cape Town.

Child Rights International Network (CRIN). 2014. *Child sexual abuse and the Holy See: The need for justice, accountability and reform*. Child Rights International Network, London.

Churches' Network for Non-violence (CNNV). 2015. *Faith-based support for prohibition and elimination of corporal punishment of children – a global overview*. London.

Economist Intelligence Unit. 2018. *Out of the shadows: Shining light on the response to child abuse and exploitation*. Viewed 25 Nov 2019, from https://outoftheshadows.eiu.com/.

Eyber, C. & Palm, S. 2019. A mixed blessing: roles of faith communities in ending violence against children. Briefing paper: Joint Learning Initiative on Faith and Local Communities Ending Violence Against Children Hub. Washington, DC.

Fang, X., Fry, D.A., Ganz, G., Casey, T., & Ward, C.L. 2016. *The economic burden of violence against children in South Africa*. Save the Children South Africa, Georgia State University and Universities of Cape Town and Edinburgh.

REFERENCES

Fulu, E., McCook, S. & Falb, K. 2017. *What works evidence review: Intersections of violence against women and violence against children.* Viewed 5 April 2018, from https://prevention-collaborative.org/wp-content/uploads/2018/11/VAC-VAW-Evidence-Brief_new_crop1.pdfa/.

Girls Not Brides, 2017. *South Africa: child marriage statistics.* Viewed 20 November 2019, from https://www.girlsnotbrides.org/child-marriage/south-africa/.

Hsiao, C., Fry, D., Ward, C.L., Ganz, G., Casey, T., Zheng, X. & Fang, X. 2018. Violence against children in South Africa: The cost of inaction to society and the economy. *British Medical Journal Global Health*, 3(1): 1-7.

Jamieson, L., Mathews, S., & Röhrs, S. 2018. Stopping family violence: Integrated approaches to address violence against women and children, 81-92. In: K. Hall, L. Richter, Z. Mokkomane & L. Lake (eds.). *The South African Child Gauge 2018.* Children's Institute, University of Cape Town, Cape Town.

Jensen, D.H. 2005. *Graced vulnerability: A theology of childhood.* Pilgrim Press, Cleveland.

Jewkes, R.K., Dunkle, K., Ndunad, M., Jamaa, P.N. & Purene, A. 2010. Associations between childhood adversity and depression, substance abuse and HIV & HSV2 incident infections in rural South African youth. *Child Abuse & Neglect*, 34(11):833-841.

Mandela, N. 2002. Foreword, ix. In: E. Krug, L.L. Dahlberg, J.A. Mercy, A.B. Zw & R. Lozano (eds.). *World report on violence and health.* World Health Organization, Geneva.

Matthews, S. 2018. The link between violence against women and children matters. Here's why. *The Conversation*, 22 November 2018. Viewed 5 October 2019, from https://theconversation.com/the-link-between-violence-against-women-and-children-matters-heres-why-106942/.

Mathews, S. & Benvenuti, P. 2014. Violence against children in South Africa: Developing a prevention agenda, 26-34. In: S. Mathews, L. Jamieson, L. Lake & C. Smith (eds). *The South African Child Gauge 2014*. Children's Institute, University of Cape Town, Cape Town.

Mathews, S. & Martin, L. 2016. Developing an understanding of fatal child abuse and neglect: Results from the South African child death review pilot study. *South African Medical Journal,* 106(12):1160-1163.

Meinck, F., Cluver, L.D., Boyes, M.E. & Loening-Voysey, H. 2016. Physical, emotional and sexual adolescent abuse victimisation in South Africa: Prevalence, incidence, perpetrators and locations. *Journal of Epidemiology and Community Health,* 70(9):910-916.

Miller, S. 2019. Corporal punishment of children fuels gender-based violence. *Daily Maverick Citizen,* 26 November 2019, n.p.

Moore, E. & Himonga, C. 2018. Living customary law and families in South Africa, 61-69. In: S. Mathews, L. Jamieson, L. Lake, L. & C. Smith (eds.). *The South African Child Gauge 2018*. Children's Institute, University of Cape Town, Cape Town.

Naidoo. E. 2019. Deception intensifies as SA gov't defends sexual indoctrination! 19 November 2019. *Family Policy Institute*. Viewed 20 November 2019, from https://joynews.co.za/deception-intensifies-as-sa-govt-defends-sexual-indoctrination/.

Nessan, C.L. 2018. Child liberation theology. *Currents in Theology & Mission,* 45(3):6-13.

Niekirk, J. & Makaoe, M. 2014. The prevention of violence against children: Creating a common understanding, 35-42. In: S. Mathews, L. Jamieson, L. Lake & C. Smith (eds.). *The South African Child Gauge 2014*. Children's Institute, University of Cape Town, Cape Town.

Nolan, A. 1995. Church and state in a changing context, 151-156. In: B. Pityana & C. Villa-Vicencio (eds.). *Being the church in South Africa today*. South Africa Council of Churches, Johannesburg.

REFERENCES

Pais, M. 2014. Introduction, 7-8. In: S. Mathews, L. Jamieson, L. Lake & C. Smith (eds.). *The South African Child Gauge 2014.* Children's Institute, University of Cape Town, Cape Town.

Pais, J. 1971. *Suffer the children: A theology of liberation by a victim of child abuse.* Paulist Press, Mahwah.

Palm. S. 2018. Church outrage against smacking aids violence against South Africa's children. *The Conversation,* 14 January 2018, n.p.

Palm, S. 2019a. "Scoping study on faith actors" involvement in the prevention, elimination and perpetuation of violence against children. Expert Consultation Report. JLI EVAC Hub. Viewed 20 Nov 2019, from https://jliflc.com/resources/evac-literature-review/.

Palm, S. 2019b. Building bridges or walls? Human rights & religious freedom – A South African history, 175-198. In: D. Forster, E. Gerle & G. Gunther (eds.). *Many modernities: Freedom of religion in different settings.* Wipf and Stock Publishers, Eugene.

Palm, S. & Eyber, C. 2019. *Why faith? Engaging faith mechanisms to end violence against children.* Briefing paper: Joint Learning Initiative on Faith and Local Communities Ending Violence Against Children Hub, Washington, DC.

Religions for Peace & UNICEF. 2006. Kyoto Declaration: Declaration on violence against children – A multi-religious commitment to confront violence against children. *Religions for Peace VIII World Assembly,* Kyoto, Japan, 2006.

Richter, L.M., Mathews, S., Kagura, J. & Nonterah, E. 2018a. A longitudinal perspective on violence in the lives of South African children from the birth to twenty plus cohort study in Johannesburg-Soweto. *South African Medical Journal,* 108(3):181-186.

Richter L.M, Mathews, S., Nonterah, E. & Masilela, L. 2018b. A longitudinal perspective on boys as victims of childhood sexual abuse in South Africa: Consequences for adult mental health. *Child Abuse & Neglect,* 84:1-10.

Robinson, M. & Hanmer, S. 2014. Engaging religious communities to protect children from abuse, neglect, and exploitation. *Child Abuse & Neglect* 38(4):600-611.

Röhrs, S. 2017. Shifting attitudes and behaviours underpinning physical punishment of children. Briefing paper. Children's Institute, University of Cape Town, Cape Town.

Rule, S. & Mncwango, B. 2010. Christianity in South Africa: Theory and practice, 185-198. In: B. Roberts, M. Kivilu & Y.L. Davies (eds.). *South African social attitudes: 2nd report. Reflections on the age of hope.* Human Sciences Research Council, Cape Town.

Rutledge, K. & Eyber, C. 2019. "Scoping study on faith actors" involvement in the prevention, elimination and perpetuation of violence against children: Literature review. EVAC Hub, Washington DC. Viewed 5 October 2019, from https://jliflc.com/resources/evac-literature-review/.

Stoller, R. 2017. Towards a child liberation theology. Viewed 15 November 2019, from http://www.patheos.com/blogs/unfundamentalistparenting/2016/04/towards-a-child-liberation-theology/.

Swain, M., & Palm S. 2019. Faith and corporal punishment of children, TV Interview on *The Women Show* 10 Nov 2019, Cape Town TV, South Africa. Viewed 15 Nov 2019, from https://www.youtube.com/watch?v=UfbtSSuiA30/.

Trofgruben, T. 2018. Toxic theology: A pastoral response to Bible passages often used to justify the abuse of children or prevent them from seeking care. *Currents in Theology and Mission,* 45(3):56-60.

Tutu, D. 2006. *Ending legalised violence against children: Global report 2006.* Global Initiative to End All Corporal Punishment of Children. Viewed 5 October 2018, from www.endcorporalpunishment.org/pages/pdfs/reports/GlobalReport.pdf

UN. 2016. *Sustainable Development Goals.* Viewed 5 October 2018, from https://www.un.org/sustainabledevelopment/sustainable-development-goals/.

UNICEF. 2014. *Ending violence against children: Six strategies for action.* New York.

UNICEF. 2017. *A familiar face: Violence in the lives of children & adolescents.* New York.

World Health Organization (WHO). 2016. *INSPIRE: Seven strategies for ending violence against children.* World Health Organization, Geneva.

CHAPTER 3

Afifi, T.O., Mota, N.P., Dasiewicz, P., MacMillan, H.L., & Sareen, J. 2012. Physical punishment and mental disorders: Results from a nationally representative US sample. *Pediatrics*, 130(2):184-192. Viewed 13 January 2020, from https://pediatrics.aappublications.org/content/pediatrics/130/2/184.full.pdf/.

Badenhorst, J., Steyn, M. & Beukes, L. 2007. Die dissipline dilemma in post-apartheid Suid-Afrikaanse hoërskole: 'n kwalitatiewe ontleding. (The dilemma of disciplinary problems within secondary schools in a post-apartheid South Africa: a qualitative analysis. *Tydskrif vir Geesteswetenskappe*, 47(3):301-319.

Brady, C. M. M. 2000. Rod, 1134. In: D. N. Freedman, A. C. Myers, & A. B. Beck (eds.). *Eerdmans Dictionary of the Bible.* William B. Eerdmans, Grand Rapids. Logos edn.

Branson, R. D. & Botterweck, G. J. 1990. *yāsar; mûsār*, 127-135. In: G. J. Botterweck & H. Ringgren (eds.). *Theological Dictionary of the Old Testament*, Volume VI, Transl. by D. E. Green. William B. Eerdmans, Grand Rapids.

Brendtro, L.K., Brokenleg, M. & Van Bockern, S. 1990. *Reclaiming youth at risk: Our hope for the future.* National Education Service, Bloomington.

Brown, W.P. 2008. To discipline without destruction: The multifaceted profile of the child in Proverbs, 63-81. In: M.J, Bunge, T. Fretheim & B.R. Gaventa (eds.). *The child in the Bible.* William B Eerdmans, Grand Rapids.

Brümmer, W. 2019. *Lyfstraf: 'Dit is hoekom geen raps onskuldig is nie'*. 3 Oktober 2019. Viewed 13 January 2020, from https://www.netwerk24.com/Stemme/Aktueel/lyfstraf-dit-is-hoekom-geen-raps-onskuldig-is-nie-20191002/.

Busienei, A.J. 2012. Alternative methods to corporal punishment and theirefficacy. *Journal of Emerging Trends in Educational Research and PolicyStudies,* 3(2):155-161.

Christian Education SA v Minister of Education 2000 (4) SA 757 (CC). Viewed 28 January 2020, from http://www.saflii.org/za/cases/ZACC/2000/11.pdf/.

Department of Education. 2000. *Alternatives to corporal punishment.* Government Printers, Pretoria.

Equal Education. 2016. *Of "Loose papers and vague allegations". A social audit report on the safety and sanitation crisis in Western Cape schools.* Equal Education, Cape Town.

Fox, M.V. 2008. *Proverbs 1-9: A New Translation with Introduction and Commentary.* The Anchor Bible, Vol. 18A. Yale University Press, New Haven/London. Logos edn.

Fish, M.J. 2008. An eye for an eye: Proportionality as a Moral principle of punishment. *Oxford Journal of Legal Studies* 28(1):57-71. doi:10.1093/ojls/gqm027.

Global initiative to end all corporal punishment of children. 2019a. *Corporal punishment of children in South Africa.* Viewed 14 January 2020, from https://endcorporalpunishment.org/wp-content/uploads/country-reports/SouthAfrica.pdf/.

REFERENCES

Global initiative to end all corporal punishment of children. 2019b. *Global Progress*, 106(12):1160-1163.

Howard, B.J. 1996. Advising parents on discipline: what works. *Pediatrics*, 98:809-815. Viewed 14 February 2020, from https://csds.qld.edu.au/sdc/Provectus/GAPP/Understanding%20behaviours/files/Howard%20Advising%20parents%201996.pdf

Jansen, G. & Matla, R. n.d. Restorative approaches. Fundamentals for wellbeing. Viewed 16 February 2020, from http://docplayer.net/140488069-Greg-jansen-rich-matla-restorative-approaches-fundamentals-for-wellbeing.html

Jones, C. 2019. Sterker morele toewyding kort: Misbruik is endemies. *Die Burger*, 19 Desember 2019, 14.

Joubert, J. 2019. Honderde onderwysers skuldig oor lyfstraf. Viewed 13 January 2020, from https://maroelamedia.co.za/nuus/sa-nuus/honderde-onderwysers-skuldig-oor-lyfstraf/

Joubert, R. & Serakwane, J. 2009. Establishing discipline in the contemporary classroom. *Journal of Educational Studies*, 8 (Special volume):125-137.

Ipsos, 2017. Importance of religion or faith. *Ipsos Global Trends*. Viewed 14 January 2020, from https://www.ipsosglobaltrends.com/importance-of-religion-or-faith/

Laskey, L. 2015. What are the best ways to discipline kids? *The Conversation*. Viewed 14 January 2020, from https://theconversation.com/what-are-the-best-ways-to-discipline-kids-34966/

Lessing, A.C. & de Witt, M.W. 2011. Stemme uit die Suid-Afrikaanse Onderwysuniegeledere oor dissipline (Voices from the ranks of the South African Teachers Union on discipline). *Tydskrif vir Geesteswetenskappe*, 51(3):403-418.

Maphosa, C. & Shumba, A. 2010. Educators' disciplinary capabilities after the banning of corporal punishment in South African schools. *South African Journal of Education*, 30:387-399. Viewed 17 February 2020, from http://www.scielo.org.za/pdf/saje/v30n3/v30n3a04.pdf

Marais, P. & Meier, C. 2010. Disruptive behaviour in the foundation phase of schooling. *South African Journal of Education*, 30(1):41–57.

Marumo, M.L. & Zulu, C.B. 2019. Teachers' and learners' perceptions of alternatives to corporal punishment: A human rights perspective, 45-66. In: C.B. Zulu, I.J. Oosthuizen & C.C. Wolhuter (eds.). *A scholarly inquiry into disciplinary practices in educational institutions* (NWU Education and Human Rights in Diversity Series Volume 2). AOSIS, Cape Town. https://doi.org/10.4102/aosis.2019.BK157.03.

Mathews, S. & Martin, L. 2016. Developing an understanding of fatal child abuse and neglect: Results from the South African child death review pilot. *South African Medical Journal*, 106(12):1160-1163.

Mathews, S. 2018. *Violence in the lives of children – what have we learnt from the Birth to 20+ Study*. Viewed 14 January 2020, from http://www.ci.uct.ac.za/overview-violence/media-summaries/violence-in-the-lives-of-children-what-have-we-learnt-from-the-birth-to-20-plus-study/.

Merriam-Webster, (n.d.). Discipline. In: *Merriam-Webster.com dictionary*. Viewed 14 February 2020, from https://www.merriam-webster.com/dictionary/discipline.

Morrell, R. 2001. Corporal punishment in South African schools: a neglected explanation for its persistence. *South African Journal of Education*, 21(4): 282-299.

Moyo, G., Khewu, N.P.D. & Bayaga, A. 2014. Disciplinary practices in schools and principles of alternatives to corporal punishment strategies. *South African Journal of Education*, 34(1):1-14. https://doi.org/10.15700/201412120952.

Mulaudzi, L.M.P. & Mudzielwana, N.P. 2016. Assessment of gender understanding of classroom discipline in South Africa: The case of Thohoyandou Community. *Gender and Behaviour*, 14(2):7519-7524.

Ntuli, T.L. & Machaisa, P.R. 2014. Effects of banning corporal punishment on discipline in South African schools: A case study of secondary schools in Sekhukhune District, Limpopo Province. *Mediterranean Journal of Social Sciences*, 5(23):1781-1790. https://doi.org/10.5901/mjss.2014.v5n23p1781.

Oosthuizen, I.J., Roux J.M. & van der Walt J.L. 2003. A classical approach to the restoration of discipline in South African schools. *Koers*, 68(4): 373-390.

Republic of South Africa. 1996a. *Constitution of the Republic of South Africa 1996*. Government Printer, Pretoria.

Republic of South Africa. 1996b. *South African Schools Act 84 of 1996*. Government Printer, Pretoria.

Republic of South Africa. 1996c. National Education Policy Act 1996. *Government Gazette*, 370(17118):1-18. Cape Town, President's Office.

Republic of South Africa. 1997. *Abolition of corporal punishment Act 33 of 1997*. Government Printer, Pretoria.

Reyneke, J.M. 2012. Creating a safe educational environment through restorative justice and the promotion of human rights in school discipline. *International Journal for Education Law and Policy*, 8(2):1-22. Viewed 5 Feburary 2020, from https://www.academia.edu/8428366/Creating_a_Safe_Environment_through_restorative_justice_and_the_promotion_of_human_rights_in_school_discipline/.

Reyneke, J.M. 2013. 'The best interests of the child in school discipline in South Africa'. PhD thesis, Tilburg University, Tilburg.

Reyneke, J. M. 2014. The development of the best-interests-of-the-child concept by the South African constitutional court – implications for school discipline. *International Journal for Education Law and Policy*, special issue, 133-158.

Reyneke, J. M. 2016. Realising the child's best interests: Lessons from the Child Justice Act to improve the South African Schools Act. *Potchefstroom Electronic Law Journal*, 19:1-29. DOI http://dx.doi.org/10.17159/1727- 3781/2016/v19n0a1228.

Reyneke, J. M. & Pretorius, J. L. 2017. Aligning school discipline with the best interests of the child: Some deficits in the legislative framework. *Perspectives in Education*, 35(1):112-128.

Reyneke, J.M. and Reyneke, R. 2020. *Restorative school discipline. The law and practice.* Juta, Cape Town.

Richter, L., Mathews, S., Kagura, J. & Nonterah, E. 2018. A longitudinal perspective on violence in the lives of South African children from the Birth to Twenty Plus cohort study in Johannesburg-Soweto. *South African Medical Journal*, 108(3):181-186.

Sæbø, M. 1997. "ysr" to chastise, 714-717. In: E. Jenni, & C. Westermann (eds.). *Theological lexicon of the Old Testament*, 3 Volume set, Transl. by M. E. Biddle. Hendrickson, Peabody.

Sandoval, T. J. 2013. Proverbs, 100-103. In: J. B. Green & J. E. Lapsley (eds.). *The Old Testament and Ethics. A book-by-book survey.* Baker Academic, Grand Rapids.

Saunders, B., & Naylor, B. 2012. Parents, it's never okay to hit your kids. *The Conversation.* Viewed 16 January 2020, from https://theconversation.com/parents-its-never-okay-to-hit-your-kids-8049/.

Sonke Gender Justice. 2018. *Landmark moment for child rights in South Africa.* Viewed 15 January, from https://genderjustice.org.za/news-item/landmark-moment-for-child-rights-in-south-africa/.

United Nations, Economic and Social Council. 2019. *Special edition: progress towards the Sustainable Development Goals,* Goal 16. Promote peaceful and inclusive societies for sustainable development, provide access to justice for all and build effective, accountable and inclusive institutions at all levels: 21-22. United Nations Department of Public Information, United Nations, New York, NY. Viewed 14 January 2020 from https://undocs.org/E/2019/68/.

UNICEF. *Children's rights to an adequate standard of living.* 2015. Viewed 15 January, from https://www.unicef.org/southafrica/SAF_resources_factschildrens22.pdf/.

Von Rad, G. 1972. *Wisdom in Israel*, Study edn. SCM Press, London.

Youngblood, R.F. (ed.). 2014. *Nelson's Illustrated Bible Dictionary*. New and Enhanced edn. Thomas Nelson, Nashville. Kindle edn.

CHAPTER 4

Althaus-Reid M. 2000. *Indecent Theology: Theological perversions in sex, gender and politics.* Routledge, Taylor & Francis Group, London.

Althaus-Reid, M. 2003. *The queer God.* Routledge, New York.

Boonzaaier, M. & van der Walt, C. 2019. Co-creating transformative space through dialogue: Inclusive and affirming ministries partnership with the Faculty of Theology, Stellenbosch University, 79-111. In: L.J. Claassens, C. van der Walt, & F.O. Olojede (eds.). *Teaching for change: Essays on Pedagogy, Gender and Theology in Africa.* African Sun Media, Stellenbosch.

Breshears, D. & Le Roux, A. 2013. Outsider discourse surrounding children's experiences of familial identity in same-sex-parented families, 1-20. In: C. Lubbe-De Beer & J. Marnell (eds.). *Home affairs: Rethinking lesbian, gay, bisexual and transgender families in contemporary South Africa.* Fanele in association with Gay and Lesbian Memory in Action (GALA), Auckland Park.

Breshears, D. & Lubbe-De Beer, C. 2016. Creating supportive learning environments: experiences of lesbian and gay-parented families in South African schools. *Education as Change*, 20(2):86-105.

Bunge, M.J. 2001. Introduction, 1-28. In: M.J. Bunge (ed.). *The child in Christian thought*. Eerdmans, Grand Rapids.

Bunge, M. 2006 The child, religion, and the academy: Developing robust theological and religious understandings of children and childhood. The *Journal of Religion*, 86(4):549-579.

Butler, J. 1990. *Gender Trouble: Feminism and the subversion of identity*. Routledge, New York.

Coakley, S. 2013. *God, sexuality, and the self: An essay on the Trinity*. Cambridge University Press, Cambridge, United Kingdom.

Cornwall, S. (ed.). 2015. *Intersex, theology, and the Bible: troubling bodies in church, text, and society*. Palgrave MacMillan, New York.

Cheng, P.S. 2011. *Radical love: An introduction to queer theology*. Seabury Books, New York.

Cranny-Francis, A., Waring, A., Stavropoulos, P. & Kirby, J. 2003. *Gender studies: Terms and debates*. Palgrave Macmillan, London.

Davids, H.R. & Jones, C. 2018. Theological-ethical contours for the full inclusion of LGBTIQ+ bodies in the church, 89-117. In: C. Jones (ed.), *Justice-based ethics: Challenging South African perspectives*. AOSIS, Cape Town. https://doi.org/10.4102/ AOSIS. 2018. BK77.04.

DeFranza, M.K. 2015. *Sex difference in Christian theology: male, female, and intersex in the image of God*. Eerdmans, Grand Rapids.

Department of Basic Education. 2019. Comprehensive sexuality education. Viewed 14 November 2019, from https://www.education.gov.za/Home/ComprehensiveSexualityEducation.aspx/.

Department of Basic Education. Basic Education clarifies comprehensive sexuality education to Portfolio Committee. Viewed 14 November

2019, from https://www.gov.za/speeches/sexuality-education-portfolio-17-sep-2019-0000.

Foucault, M. 1980. Truth and power, 107-13. In: C. Gordon (ed.). *Power/Knowledge*, Harvester, Brighton.

Foucault, M. 1990. *The history of sexuality volume I: An introduction*. Transl. by R. Hurley. Vintage, New York.

Francis, D.A., Brown, A., Mcallister, J., Mosime, S.T., Thani, G.T.Q., Reygan, F., Dlamini, Nogela, L. & Muller, M. 2019. A five country study of gender and sexuality diversity and schooling in Southern Africa. *Africa Education Review*, 16(1):19-39.

Global Interfaith Network. Johannesburg Declaration. Viewed 10 October 2019, from http://www.gin-ssogie.org/johannesburg-declaration/.

Grobbelaar, J. 2016a. The grammar of combining the vocabulary of theology, children and Africa, 51-91. In: J. Grobbelaar & G. Breed (eds.). *Theologies of childhood and the children of Africa*. AOSIS, Cape Town. http://dx.doi.org/10.4102/aosis.2016.tcca02.02/.

Grobbelaar, J. 2016b. Doing Child Theology: History and methodology, 42-87. In: J. Grobbelaar & G. Breed (eds.). *Welcoming Africa's children – Theological and ministry perspectives*. AOSIS, Cape Town. http://www.dx.doi. org/10.4102/aosis.2016.waccs13.02.

Grobbelaar, J. & Breed, G. (eds.). 2016a. *Welcoming Africa's children – Theological and ministry perspectives*. AOSIS, Cape Town.

Grobbelaar, J. & Breed, G. (eds.). 2016b. *Theologies of childhood and the children of Africa*. AOSIS, Cape Town.

Isherwood, L. & Stuart, E. 1998. *Introducing body theology: Introductions in feminist theology*. Sheffield Academic Press, Sheffield.

Isherwood, L. & Althaus-Reid, M. 2004. *The sexual theologian: Essays on sex, God and politics*. T&T Clark, London.

Jordan, M.D. 2002. *The Ethics of Sex*. Blackwell Publishing, Malden.

Kumalo, S. 2018. *You have to be Gay to know God*. Kwela Books, Cape Town.

Kretzschmar, L. 2013. Human Sexuality and ethics, 51-70. In: L. Kretzschmar & L. Hulley (eds.). *Questions about life and morality: Christian ethics in South Africa today*. JL van Schaik Religious Books, Pretoria.

Loughlin, G. (ed.). 2007. *Queer Theology: Rethinking the Western Body*. Blackwell Publishing, Malden.

Lubbe-De Beer, C., & Marnell, J. (eds.). 2013. *Home affairs: Rethinking lesbian, gay, bisexual and transgender families in contemporary South Africa*. Fanele in association with Gay and Lesbian Memory in Action (GALA), Auckland Park.

Mabenge, L. 2018. *Becoming Him: A trans memoir of triumph*. MF Books Joburg, Johannesburg.

McEwen, H. 2018. Weaponising rhetorics of "family": the mobilisation of pro-family politics in Africa. *African Journal of Rhetoric*, 10(1):142-178.

Migliore, D.L. 2014. *Faith seeking understanding: An introduction to Christian Theology*. Eerdmans, Grand Rapids.

Morison, T., Lynch, I. & Reddy, V. (eds.). 2018. *Queer kinship: South African perspectives on the sexual politics of family-making and belonging*. Unisa Press, Johannesburg.

Mutua, M. 2011. Sexual orientation and human rights: Putting homophobia on trial, 452-462. In: S. Tamale (ed.). *African sexualities. A reader*. Pambazuka Press, Cape Town.

Nelson, J.B. 1978. *Embodiment: an approach to sexuality and Christian theology*. SPCK, London.

Sanger, N. & Sanger, C. 2013. "The best interests of the child": Reflecting on the family and the law as sites of oppressive hetero-socialisation, 50-67. In: C. Lubbe-De Beer & J. Marnell (eds.). *Home affairs: Rethinking lesbian, gay, bisexual and transgender families in contemporary South Africa*. Fanele in Association with Gay and Lesbian Memory in Action (GALA), Auckland Park.

Sigurdson, O. 2016. *Heavenly bodies: Incarnation, the gaze, and embodiment in Christian theology.* William B. Eerdmans, Grand Rapids.

Stuart, E. 2002. *Gay and lesbian theologies: Repetitions with critical difference.* Ashgate, Aldershot.

Stuart, E. 2007. Sacramental flesh, 65-75. In: G. Loughlin (ed.). *Queer theology: Rethinking the western body.* Blackwell Publishing, Malden.

Tamale, S. 2011. *African sexualities: A reader.* Pambazuka Press, Cape Town.

Thatcher, A. 2007. *Theology and families.* Blackwell Publishing, Malden.

Thatcher, A. 2011. *God, sex, and gender. An introduction.* Blackwell Publishing, Malden.

Volf, M. 2003. The Trinity and gender identity, 155-178. In: D.A. Campbell (ed.). *Gospel and gender: A trinitarian engagement with being male and female in Christ.* T & T Clark International, London.

West, G. O. 2015. Reading the Bible with the marginalised: The value/s of contextual Bible reading. *Stellenbosch Theological Journal,* 1(2):235-261. DOI: http://dx.doi.org/10.17570/stj.2015.v1n2.a11.

West, G., Van der Walt, C. & Kaoma, J.K. 2016. When faith does violence: Reimagining engagement between churches and LGBTI groups on homophobia in Africa. *HTS Teologiese Studies/Theological Studies,* 72(1):a3511. http://dx.doi. org/10.4102/hts.v72i1.3511.

West, G.O. 2019. Deploying indecent literary and socio-historical detail for change: Genesis 2:18- 24 as a resource for choice of sexual partner, 57-77. In: L.J. Claassens, C. van der Walt & F.O. Olojede (eds.). *Teaching for change: Essays on Pedagogy, Gender and Theology in Africa.* African Sun Media, Stellenbosch.

Windvogel, K. & Koopman, K. (eds.). 2019. *They called me Queer.* Kwela Books, Cape Town.

Williams, R.D. 2002. The body's grace, 309-321. In: E.F. Rogers (ed.). *Theology and sexuality: Classic and contemporary readings*. Blackwell Publishing, Oxford.

White, K.J. & Wilmer, H. 2006. *An introduction to child theology*. Child Theology Movement, London.

CHAPTER 5

Bell, E., Andrew, G., Di Pietro, N., Chudley, A.E.N., Reynolds, J. & Racine, E. 2016. It's a shame! Stigma against Fetal Alcohol Spectrum Disorder: Examining the ethical implications for Public Health practices and policies. *Public Health Ethics*, 9(1):65-77. doi: 10.1093/phe/phv012.

Bos, A.E.R., Pryor, J.B., Reeder, G.D. & Stutterheim, S.E. 2013. Stigma: Advances in theory and research. *Basic and Applied Social Psychology*, 35(1):1-9. doi: 10.1080/01973533.2012.746147.

Bourke-Taylor, H., Howie, L. & Law, M. 2010. Impact of caring for a school-aged child with a disability: understanding mothers' perspectives. *Australian Occupational Therapy Journal*, 57(2):127-136. doi: 10.1111/j.1440-1630.2009.00817.x.

Brown, J., Trnka, A., Harr, D., Dodson, K.D., Wartnik, H.A.P. & Donaldson, K. 2018. Fetal alcohol spectrum disorder (FASD): A beginner's guide for mental health professionals. *Journal of Neurology and Clinical Neuroscience*, 2(1):13-19.

Choate, P. & Badry, D. 2019. Stigma as a dominant discourse in fetal alcohol spectrum disorder. *Advances in Dual Diagnosis*, 36-52. doi: 10.1108/ADD-05-2018-0005.

Cockroft, J.D., Adams, S.M., Bonnet, K., Matlock, D., McMillan, J. & Schlundt, D. 2019. "A scarlet letter": Stigma and other factors affecting trust in the health care system for women seeking substance abuse

REFERENCES

treatment in a community setting. *Substance Abuse*, 40(2):170-177. doi: 10.1080/08897077.2018.1544184.

Corrigan, P.W., Lara, J.L., Shah, B.B., Mitchell, K.T., Simmes, D., & Jones, K.L. 2017. The public stigma of birth mothers of children with Fetal Alcohol Spectrum Disorders. *Alcoholism: Clinical and Experimental Research*, 41(6):1166-1173. doi: 10.1111/acer.13381.

Corrigan, P.W., Watson, A.C. & Miller, F.E. 2006. Blame, shame, and contamination: The impact of mental illness and drug dependence stigma on family members. *Journal of Family Psychology*, 20(2):239-246. doi: 10.1037/0893-3200.20.2.239.

Croxford, J. & Viljoen, D. 1999. Alcohol consumption by pregnant women in the Western Cape. *South African Medical Journal*, 89(9):962-965.

Davies, L., Dunn, M., Chersich, M., Urban, M., Chetty, C., Olivier, L. & Viljoen, D. 2011. Developmental delay of infants and young children with and without fetal alcohol spectrum disorder in the Northern Cape Province, South Africa. *African Journal of Psychiatry*, 14(4):298-305. doi: 10.4314/ajpsy.v14i4.7.

Day, J.H., Miyamura, K., Grant, A.D., Leeuw, A., Munsamy, J., Baggaley, R. & Churchyard, G.J. 2003. Attitudes to HIV voluntary counselling and testing among mineworkers in South Africa: Will availability of antiretroviral therapy encourage testing? *AIDS Care*, 15(5):665-672. doi: 10.1080/0954012030001595140.

Drotsky, L. 2019. Mothers' facilitation of the occupational engagement of their children with FASD: A qualitative descriptive study in an under-resourced district in South Africa. MSc thesis, Department of Health and Rehabilitation Sciences, University of Cape Town.

FASfacts, n.d., *FAS and crime*. Viewed 06 January 2020, from http://www.fasfacts.org.za/Resources/Article-View/ArticleId/9/FAS-and-crime.

Gibbard, W.B., Wass, P. & Clarke, M.E. 2003. The neuropsychological implications of prenatal alcohol exposure. *The Canadian Child and Adolescent Psychiatry Review*, 12(3):72-76.

Grinfeld, H. 2009. Alcohol abuse in pregnancy, 179-200. In: A.G. de Andrade, J.C. Anthony & C.M. Silveira (eds.). *Alcohol and its consequences: dealing with multiple concepts*. Tamboré, Editora Manole Ltda.

Hammarlund, R.A., Crapanzano, K.A., Luce, L. Mulligan, L.A. & Ward, K.M. 2018. Review of the effects of self-stigma and perceived social stigma on the treatment-seeking decisions of individuals with drug- and alcohol-use disorders. *Substance Abuse and Rehabilitation*, 9:115-136. doi: 10.2147/sar.s183256.

Harris, J.C. 2014. New classification for neurodevelopmental disorders in DSM-5. *Current Opinion in Psychiatry*, 27(2):95-97. doi: 10.1097/YCO.0000000000000042.

Hoyme, H.E., Kalberg, W.O., Elliott, A.J., Blankenship, J., Buckley, D., Marais, A.S., Manning, M.A., Robinson, L.K., Adam, M.P., Abdul-Rahman, O., Jewett, T., Coles, C.D., Chambers, C., Jones, K.L., Adnams, C.M., Shah, P.E, Riley, E.P., Charness, M.E., Warren, K.R. & May, P.A. 2016. Updated clinical guidelines for diagnosing Fetal Alcohol Spectrum Disorders. *PEDIATRICS*, 138(2). doi: 10.1542/peds. 2015-4256.

Jones, K.L.L. & Smith, D.W. 1973. Recognition of the Fetal Alcohol Syndrome in early infancy. *The Lancet*, 302(7836):999-1001. doi: 10.1016/S0140-6736(73)91092-1.

Jones, K.L.L., Smith, D.W., Ulleland, C.N., Streissguth, P. & Streissguth, A.P. 1973. Pattern of malformation in offspring of chronic alcoholic mothers. *The Lancet*, 1(7815):1267-1271. doi: 10.1097/00006254-197401000-00013.

Kalichman, S.C. & Simbayi, L.C. 2003. HIV testing attitudes, AIDS stigma, and voluntary HIV counselling and testing in a black township in

Cape Town, South Africa. *Sexually Transmitted Infections*, 79(6):44-447. doi: 10.1136/sti.79.6.442.

Larson, E. 1998. Reframing the meaning of disability to families: The embrace of paradox. *Social Science and Medicine*, 47(7):865-875. doi: 10.1016/S0277-9536(98)00113-0.

Louw, J.G., Tomlinson, M., & Olivier, L. 2017. Unrealistic optimism with regard to drinking during pregnancy among women of childbearing age in a South African community. *South African Journal of Psychology*, 48(2):219-229. doi: 10.1177/0081246317717105.

May, P.A., Baete, A., Russo, J., Elliott, A.J., Blankenship, J., Kalberg, W.O., Buckley, D., Brooks, M., Hasken, J., Abdul-Rahman, O., Adam, M.P., Robinson, L.K., Manning, M. & Hoyme, H.E. 2014. Prevalence and characteristics of fetal alcohol spectrum disorders. *Pediatrics*, 134(5): 855-66, doi: 10.1542/peds.2013-3319.

May, P.A., Brooke, L., Gossage, J.P., Croxford, J., Adnams, C., Jones, K.L., Robinson, L. & Viljoen, D. 2000. Epidemiology of fetal alcohol syndrome in a South African community in the Western Cape Province. *American Journal of Public Health*, 90(12):1905-1912. doi: 10.2105/ajph.90.12.1905.

Meiberg, A.E., Bos, A.E.R., Onya, H.E. & Schaalma, H.P. 2008. Fear of stigmatization as barrier to voluntary HIV counselling and testing in South Africa. *East African Journal of Public Health*, 5(2):49-54.

Odendaal, H.J., Steyn, D.W., Elliott, A. & Burd, L. 2009. Combined effects of cigarette smoking and alcohol consumption on perinatal outcome. *Gynecologic and Obstetric Investigation*, 67(1):1-8. doi: 10.1159/000150597.

Olivier, L. 2017. Fetal Alcohol Spectrum Disorders in South Africa, PhD thesis, Dept. of Psychology, Maastricht University. doi:/10.26481/dis.20171212lo.

Olivier, L., Curfs, L.M.G. & Viljoen, D.L. 2016. Fetal Alcohol Spectrum Disorders: Prevalence rates in South Africa. *South African Medical Journal*, 106(6) Suppl. 1, S103-S106. doi: 10.7196/SAMJ.2016.v106i6.11009.

Orji, R., Vassileva, J. & Mandryk, R. 2012. Towards an effective health interventions design: An extension of the health belief model. *Online Journal of Public Health Informatics*, 4(3):40-41. doi: 10.5210/ojphi.v4i3.4321.

Ornoy, A. & Ergaz, Z. 2010. Alcohol abuse in pregnant women: effects on the fetus and newborn, mode of action and maternal treatment. *International Journal of Environmental Research and Public Health*, 7(2): 364-379.doi: 10.3390/ijerph7020364.

Peadon, E., Rhys-Jones, B., Bower, C. & Elliott, E.J. 2009. Systematic review of interventions for children with Fetal Alcohol Spectrum Disorders. *BMC Pediatrics*, 9(1):1-9. doi: 10.1186/1471-2431-9-35.

Pei, J. & Kerns, K. 2012. Using games to improve functioning in children with Fetal Alcohol Spectrum Disorders. *Games for Health Journal*, 1(4): 308-311. doi: 10.1089/g4h.2012.0036.

Pietro, N.D.I., Vries, J.D.E., Paolozza, A., Reid, D., Reynolds, J.N., Salmon, A.M.Y., Wilson, M. & Stein, D.A.N.J. 2016. Ethical challenges in contemporary FASD research and practice. *Cambridge Quarterly of Healthcare Ethics*, 726-732. doi: 10.1017/S096318011600044X.

Popova, S., Lange, S., Probst, C., Gmel, G. & Rehm, J. 2017. Estimation of national, regional, and global prevalence of alcohol use during pregnancy and fetal alcohol syndrome: a systematic review and meta-analysis. *The Lancet Global Health*, 5(3):e290-e299. doi: 10.1016/S2214-109X(17)30021-9.

Reporter, A. 2018. Bogopane-Zulu: Arrest women who drink alcohol while pregnant. Viewed 13 November 2019, from https://www.iol.co.za/news/south-africa/bogopane-zulu-arrest-women-who-drink-alcohol-while-pregnant-16942576 1/2.

Riley, E.P., Court, A., Diego, S., Warren, K.R., Infante, M.A. & Warren, K.R. 2011. Fetal Alcohol Spectrum Disorders: An overview. *Neuropsychology Review*, 21(2):73-80, doi: 10.1007/s11065-011-9166-x.Fetal.

Roozen, S., Peters, G-J.Y., Kok, G., Townend, D., Nijhuis, J. & Curfs, L. 2016. Worldwide prevalence of Fetal Alcohol Spectrum Disorders: A systematic literature review including meta-analysis. *Alcoholism: Clinical and Experimental Research*, 40(1):18-32. doi: 10.1111/acer.12939.

Sanders, J.L. & Buck, G. 2010. A long journey: Biological and non-biological parents' experiences raising children with FASD. *Journal of Population Therapeutics and Clinical Pharmacology*, 17(2):e308-e322.

Santos, P., Luisa, A., Casela, M., Monteiro, É.P., Correia, G., Ferreira, L., Verônica, J., Freitas, T. De, Machado, N.M., Regina, A. & Noto, A.R. 2016. Stigma and health psychosocial understanding of self-stigma among people who seek treatment for drug addiction. *Stigma and Health*, 3(1):42-52. doi: 10.1037/sah0000069.

Stassen, W. 2012. Headway in the fight against FAS. Viewed 23 July 2012, from http://www.health-e.org.za/news/article.php?uid=20033646.

Urban, M., Chersich, M.F., Fourie, L.A., Chetty, C., Olivier, L. & Viljoen, D. 2008. Fetal alcohol syndrome among grade 1 schoolchildren in Northern Cape Province: prevalence and risk factors. *South African Medical Journal*, 98(11):877-882.

Van der Sanden, R.L.M., Bos, A.E.R., Stutterheim, S.E., Pryor, J.B. & Kok, G. 2013. Experiences of stigma by association among family members of people with mental illness. *Rehabilitation Psychology*, 58(1):73-80. doi: 10.1037/a0031752.

Watson, S., Hayes, S., Radford-Paz, E. & Coons, K. 2013. "I'm hoping, I'm hoping...": Thoughts about the future from families of children with Autism or Fetal Alcohol Spectrum Disorder in Ontario. *Journal on Developmental Disabilities*, 19(3):76-93.

World Health Organization. 2018. Global status report on alcohol and health 2018, 65. World Health Organization, Geneva. doi: 10.1037/cou0000248.

Yang, L.H., Wong, L.Y., Grivel, M.M. & Hasin, D.S. 2017. Stigma and substance use disorders: An international phenomenon. *Current Opinion in Psychiatry*, 30(5):378-388. doi: 10.1097/YCO.0000000000000351.

CHAPTER 6

Anon. 2011. Desolation on the road to manhood. *City Press*, 5 February, n.p.

Barker, G. 2005. *Dying to be men: Youth and masculinity and social exclusion*. Routledge Taylor & Francis Group, Oxford.

Barker, G. & Ricardo, C. 2005. *Young men and the construction of masculinity in Sub-Saharan Africa: Implications for HIV/AIDS, conflict and violence*. Social development papers no. 26. Conflict prevention and reconstruction series. The World Bank. Washington, DC.

Besent, M. 2018. Parliament passes Customary Initiation Bill. *SABC News Online*, 5 December. Viewed 23 October 2019, from http://www.sabcnews.com/sabcnews/parliament-passes-customary-initiation-bill/.

Bogopa, D. 2007. Challenges facing the initiation schools: The case of Nelson Mandela Metropole in the Eastern Cape. *Acta Criminologica*, 20(4): 55-60.

Bogopa, D. 2010. Health and Ancestors: The Case of South Africa and Beyond. *Indo-Pacific Journal of Phenomenology* 10(1):1-7. Viewed 13 February 2020, from http://www.scielo.org.za/pdf/ipjp/v10n1/08.pdf/.

Broude, G. 2005. Initiation and rites of passage. In: W.H. McNeill, J.H. Bentley, D. Christian, D. Levinson, H. Roupp & J.P. Zinsser (eds.). *Encyclopedia of World History*. Berkshire Publishing Group LLC, Great Barrington, Vol. 1(9):1339-1345.

REFERENCES

Brunsdon, A. 2016. Hurting children and the dangerous rite of ritual male circumcision. 246-273. In: J. Grobbelaar & G. Breed (eds.). *Theologies of childhood and the children of Africa.* AOSIS, Cape Town.

Campbell, C. 2001. Going underground and going after women: Masculinity and HIV transmission amongst black workers on the gold mines, 275-286. In: R. Morell (ed.). *Changing men in Southern Africa.* University of Natal Press/Zed Books, Pietermaritzburg.

Commission for the Promotion and Protection of the Rights of Cultural, Religious and Linguistic Communities. 2010. Report on public hearings on initiation schools in South Africa. The Commission for the Promotion and Protection of the Rights of Cultural, Religious and Linguistic Communities, Research and Policy Development Unit, Johannesburg.

Commission for the Promotion and Protection of the Rights of Cultural, Religious and Linguistic Communities. 2014. Executive summary of the report on public hearings on initiation schools in South Africa. The Commission for the Promotion and Protection of the Rights of Cultural, Religious and Linguistic Communities, Research and Policy Development Unit, Johannesburg.

Connell, R.W. 2003. Masculinities, change, and conflict in global society: Thinking about the future of Men's Studies. *Journal of Men's Studies,* 11(3):249.

Dora, T.T. 2018. The role of the church in ending female genital mutilation / cutting in order to promote the flourishing of women: a case study of the Wolaita Kale Heywet Church, Southern Ethiopia. Viewed 21 January 2020, from http://hdl.handle.net/10019.1/103621/.

Du Toit, L. 2014. Drie wyses: Besnyding. *Rapport, Weekliks,* 19 Julie, p. 29.

Ellis, S. 1997. Young soldiers and the significance of initiation: Some notes from Liberia. Afrika-Studiecentrum, Leiden. Viewed 18 October 2019, from http:/www.asc.leidenuniv.nl/pdf/.

Gilmore, D. 1990. *Manhood in the making: Cultural concepts of masculinity.* Yale University Press, New Haven, CT.

Githiga, J.G. 2009. *Initiation and pastoral psychology: Toward African personality theory.* 2nd edn. Evangel, Nairobi.

Hammond-Tooke, D. 1994. Creed and confession in South African ancestor religion: Indigenous healing in South Africa (Margaret Shaw Lecture 4). South African Museum, Cape Town, SA.

Jones, C. 2018. Statistics are telling a not-so-good story about South Africa. *Cape Argus,* 28 November, p. 12.

Jones, C. 2019. Do more to eradicate initiation schools. *Cape Argus,* 28 January. Viewed 9 October 2019, from https://www.iol.co.za/capeargus/opinion/do-more-to-eradicate-illegal-initiation-schools-18992025/.

Jones, C. 2019. Child killings in the Western Cape. *HTS Teologiese Studies/Theological Studies,* 75(1):a5455. https://doi.org/10.4102/hts.v75i1.5455/.

Mabuza, W. 2010. Foreword. In: Report on public hearings on initiation schools in South Africa. The Commission for the Promotion and Protection of the Rights of Cultural, Religious and Linguistic Communities, Research and Policy Development Unit, Johannesburg.

Malisha, L., Mahara, P. & Rogan, M. 2008. Rites of passage to adulthood: Traditional initiation schools in the context of HIV/AIDS in the Limpopo Province, South Africa. *Health, Risk & Society,* 10(6):585-598.

Marsiglio, W. 1998. Adolescent male sexuality and heterosexual masculinity: A conceptual model and review. *Journal of Adolescent Research,* 3(3-4): 285-303.

Mbaya, H. 2020. Personal communication dated 13 February 2020.

Mead, M. 1973. *Coming of age in Samoa: A psychological study of primitive youth for western civilization.* American Museum of Natural History, New York University Press, New York.

REFERENCES

Meissner, O., & Buso, D.L. 2007. Traditional male circumcision in the Eastern Cape – Scourge or blessing? *South African Medical Journal,* 97(5): 371-373.

Ngcukana, L. 2018. Losing their manhood in becoming men. *City Press,* 24 June. Viewed 9 October 2019, from https://www.news24.com/SouthAfrica/News/losing-their-manhood-in-becoming-men-20180623/.

Pollack, W.S. 1998. *Real boys: Rescuing our sons from the myths of boyhood.* Henry Holt and Company, New York.

Rijken, D.J. & Dakwa, P. 2013. Ulwaluko: problem analysis of the situation in Pondoland,1-12. Viewed 24 October 2019, from https://ulwaluko.co.za/Downloads_files/Analysis.pdf/.

Sindelo, S. 2019. Personal communication dated 9 November 2019.

Turner, V. 1982. Liminal to limuloid, in play, flow, ritual: An essay in comparative symbology, 20-60. In: V. Turner (ed.). *From ritual to theatre: The human seriousness of play.* Performing Arts Journal Publications, New York.

Turner, V.W. 1969. *The ritual processes.* Aldine Publishing Company, Chicago.

Van den Heever, J. 2014. Drie wyses: Besnyding. *Rapport, Weekliks.* 19 Julie, p. 29.

Van Gennep, A. 1960. *The rites of passage.* University of Chicago Press, Chicago.

Vincent, L. 2008a. Cutting tradition: The political regulation of traditional circumcision rites in South Africa's liberal democratic order. *Journal of Southern African Studies,* 34(1):77-91.

Vincent, L. 2008b. Boys will be boys: Traditional male circumcision, HIV and sexual socialization in contemporary South Africa. *Culture, Health & Sexuality,* 10(5):431-446.

Westercamp, N. & Bailey, R.C. 2007. Acceptability of male circumcision for prevention of HIV/AIDS in Sub-Saharan Africa: A review. *Aids and Behavior*, 11:341-355.

White, S. 1997. Men, masculinities and the politics of development. *Gender and Development*, 5(2):16.

WHO/UNAIDS. 2001. *The health and development of African male adolescents and young men*. World Health Organization, Geneva.

WHO. 2003. *Integrating gender into HIV/AIDS programmes*. World Health Organization, Geneva.

CHAPTER 7

Brouard, P. & Crewe, M. 2012. Sweetening the deal? Sugar daddies, sugar mummies, sugar babies and HIV in contemporary South Africa. *Agenda*, 26(4):48-56.

Centre for Human Rights. 2018. A report on child marriage in Africa. Research report. Centre for Human Rights, South Africa. Viewed 13 January 2020, from https://www.chr.up.ac.za/images/publications/centrepublications/documents/child_marriage_report.pdf/.

Department of Health, Medical Research Council & OrcMacro. 2007. *South Africa Demographic and Health Survey 2003*. Department of Health. Viewed 2 July 2020, from https://dhsprogram.com/pubs/pdf/FR206/FR206.pdf.

Devenish, G.E. 1999. *A commentary on the South African Bill of Rights*. Butterworth, Durban.

Forced child marriages. 2019. Video recording, *Carte Blanche*, South Africa. Viewed on 13 December 2019, from https://m-net.dstv.com/show/carte-blanche/videos/forced-child-marriages/video/.

REFERENCES

ICASEES. 2010. *Enquête par grappes à indicateurs multiples MICS, RCA 2010 Rapport final*. RCA ICASEES. Viewed 2 July 2020, from https://mics-surveys-prod.s3.amazonaws.com/MICS4/West%20and%20Central%20Africa/Central%20African%20Republic/2010/Final/Central%20African%20Republic%202010%20MICS_French.pdf/.

Institut National de la Statistique et ICF International. 2013. *Enquête Démographique et de Santé et à Indicateurs Multiples du Niger 2012*. INS et ICF International. Viewed 2 July 2020, from https://dhsprogram.com/pubs/pdf/FR277/FR277.pdf.

Maswikwa, B., Richter, L., Kaufman, J. & Nandi, A. 2015. Minimum Marriage Age Laws and the Prevalence of Child Marriage and Adolescent Birth: Evidence from Sub-Saharan Africa. *International Perspectives on Sexual and Reproductive Health*, 41(2):58-68.

Mwambene, L. & Sloth-Nielsen, J. 2011. Benign accommodation? Ukuthwala, 'forced marriage' and the South African Children's Act. *African Human Rights Law Journal*, Volume 11(1):1-22.

Mudarikwa, M., Roos, E. & Mathibela, N. 2018. *Girls must not be brides: An evaluation of South Africa's compliance with international, regional and national obligations towards protecting children from child and forced marriages, in its current legal framework of civil and customary marriages*. Legal Resource Centre. Viewed 14 January 2020, from http://lrc.org.za/art_external/pdf/2018%20GIRLS%20MUST%20NOT%20BE%20BRIDES.pdf/.

Potgieter, C., Strebel, A., Shefer, T. & Wagner, C. 2012. Taxi "sugar daddies" and taxi queens: Male taxi driver attitudes regarding transactional relationships in the Western Cape, South Africa. *Journal of Social Aspects of HIV/AIDS*, 9(4):192-199.

Shefer, T. & Strebel, A. 2012. Deconstructing the "sugar daddy": A critical review of the constructions of men in intergenerational sexual relationships in South Africa. *Agenda*, 26(4):57-63.

Svanemyr, J., Scolaro, E., Blondeel, K., Chandra-Mouli, V. & Temmerman, M. 2013. The contribution of laws to change the practice of child marriage in Africa. Research report. Inter-Parliamentarian Union. Viewed on 14 January 2020, from https://www.girlsnotbrides.org/wp-content/uploads/2018/04/IPU-WHO-Child-marriage_study-October-2013.pdf/.

United Nations Human Rights Council. 2014. *Preventing and eliminating child, early and forced marriage.* Human Rights Council. Twenty-sixth session. Viewed on 14 January 2020, from https://www.ohchr.org/EN/HRBodies/HRC/RegularSessions/Session26/Documents/A-HRC-26-22_en.doc/.

Wodon, Q., Male, C., Nayihouba, A., Onagoruwa, A., Savadogo, A., Yedan, A., Edmeades, J., Kes, A., John, N., Murithi, L., Steinhaus, M. & Petroni, S. 2017. Economic Impacts of Child Marriage: Global Synthesis Report. The World Bank and International Center for Research on Women: Washington, DC. Viewed on 14 January 2020, from http://documents.worldbank.org/curated/en/530891498511398503/Economic-impacts-of-child-marriage-global-synthesis-report/.

CHAPTER 8

Africa Media online. 2016. A History of Apartheid in South Africa. *South African History Online.* Viewed 26 November 2019, from https://www.sahistory.org.za/article/history-apartheid-south-africa/.

Anderson, A. & Dougé, J. 2019. Talking to children about racial bias. Viewed 24 November 2019, from https://www.healthychildren.org/English/healthy-living/emotional-wellness/Building/.

Burt, C.H., Kit Lei, M. & Simons, R.L. 2017. Racial discrimination, racial socialization, social problems. *Social Problems*, 64(3):414-438.

REFERENCES

Clark, K.B. & Clark, M.P. 1947. Racial identification and preference in Negro children. Viewed 1 December 2019, from https://i2.cdn.turner.com/cnn/2010/images/05/13/doll.study.1947.pdf.

Davis, J.L. & Gandy, O.H. 1999. Racial identity and media orientation: Exploring the nature of constraint. *Journal of Black Studies*, 29(3): 367-397.

Feldman, H., 2018. What white people didn't learn from Bantu Education. Viewed 5 December 2019, from https://www.news24.com/Columnists/HowardFeldman/what-white-people-didnt-learn-from-bantu-education-20180418/.

Eye-Witness News. 2018. H & M pulls ad after social media outcry over racism. Viewed 10 January 2020, from https://ewn.co.za/2018/01/09/h-and-m-pulls-ad-after-social-media-outcry-over-racism.

Gumede, W. 2016. The media and systemic racism. Viewed 12 January 2020, from https://democracyworks.org.za/the-media-and-systemic-racism/.

Harris, M.S. (ed.). 2013. *African American perspectives: Family dynamics, health care issues and the role of ethnic identity.* NOVA Science Publishers, Tacoma.

Hewitt, A.A. 2018. 'Black Panther' and the importance of racial socialization. How the film can help parents talk to their kids about race. Viewed 28 November 2019, from https://www.psychologytoday.com/za/blog/you-empowered/201802/black-panther-and-the-importance-racial-socialization/.

Joorst, J. 2019. Racism is still rife in South African schools. What can be done about it? Viewed 25 November 2019, from https://www.skillsportal.co.za/content/racism-still-rife-south-africas-schools-what-can-be-done-about-it.

Kang, S. 2017. Talking to your children about racism prejudice can affect kids' mental health. Viewed 20 December 2019, from https://health.

usnews.com/wellness/for-parents/articles/2017-02-02/talking-to-your-children-about-racism/.

Katz, P.A. (ed.). 1976. Document resume: Development of children's racial awareness and intergroup-attitudes. Viewed 27 November 2019, from https://eric.ed.gov/?id=ED207675/.

Kelly, T. 2018. The influence of social context on perceptions of racism. MA thesis, Dept. of Community Psychology, Concordia University, Portland.

Klein, G. 1985. *Reading racism into children's literature and learning materials. Bias in children's literature and learning materials.* Routledge and Kegan Paul, London.

Lee, K. 2019. Talking to kids about race and cultural diversity. Viewed 3 December 2019, from https://www.verywellfamily.com/teaching-kids-about-race-and-cultural-diversity-621099/.

Levy, N. 2015. Bantu Education or the street?' *South African History online.* Viewed 2 December 2019, from https://www.sahistory.org.za/article/bantu-education-or-street-norman-levy/.

Massey, D. 2009. Concepts of space and power in theory and in political practice. *d'Anàlisi Geogràfica, [en línia],* 2009, 55:15-26. Viewed 26 November 2019, from https://ddd.uab.cat/pub/dag/02121573n55/02121573n55p15.pdf.

Mbobo, K. 2019. Why is it important for black parents to talk about racism? Viewed November 2019, from https://www.parent24.com/Family/Parenting/why-is-it-important-for-black-parents-to-talk-about-racism-20190710.

McAdoo, H.P. 1999. Families Color: Strengths that come from diversity, 3-14. In: McAdoo, H.P. (ed.). *Family Ethnicity: Strength in Diversity,* Second edition. Sage Publications, Thousand Oaks.

MacCann, D. & Maddy, Y.A. 2001. *Apartheid and racism in South African children's literature, 1985-1995.* Routledge, New York and London.

REFERENCES

McCarthy, C. 2019. How racism harms children. Viewed 20 November 2019, from https://www.health.harvard.edu/blog/how-racism-harms-children-2019091417788.

Meier, C. & Hartell, C. 2009. Handling cultural diversity in education in South Africa. *SA-eDuc Journal*, 6(2):180-192. Viewed 29 November 2019, from https://www.nwu.ac.za/files/files/p-saeduc/All_articles/handling.pdf

Mtwana, N. & Bird, W. 2006. Revealing race: An analysis of covering race and xenophobia in the South African print media. *Media Report Project*. Viewed 5 December 2019, from https://www.mediamonitoringafrica.org/images/uploads/Final_report_v5_Print_final.pdf.

National Academies of Sciences, Engineering, and Medicine. 2016. Parenting Matters: Supporting Parents of Children Ages 0-8. The National Academies Press Washington, DC. doi: 10.17226/21868. Viewed 2 December 2019, from https://www.ncbi.nlm.nih.gov/books/NBK402024/pdf/Bookshelf_NBK402024.pdf

Oelofsen, R. 2015. Decolonisation of the African mind and intellectual landscape. Viewed 28 November 2019, from http://www.scielo.org.za/scielo.php?script=sci_arttext&pid=S1561-40182015000200008/.

Pachter, L.M., Bernstein, B.A., Szalacha, L.A. & Coll, C.G. 2010. Perceived racism and discrimination in children and youth: An exploratory study. *Health and Social Work*, 35(1):61-9. https://doi.org/10.1093/hsw/35.1.61 .

Qureshi, A., Collazos, F., Revollo, HW. & Ramos, M. 2008. Racism is an ethical issue. *European Psychiatry*, 23(Supplement 2):S4-S5. https://doi.org/10.1016/j.eurpsy.2008.01.017

Russell, K. 2017. Are we born racist? The talk you must have with your children. Viewed 20 November 2019, from https://www.parentmap.com/article/are-we-born-racist-the-talk-you-must-have-with-your-children.

Smalls-Glover, C., Williams, J.L., Zuckerman, A. & Thomas, D. 2013. Parental socialization in response to racism: Implications for family health. *Psychology Faculty Publications* 137. Viewed 23 November 2019, from https://scholarworks.gsu.edu/psych_facpub/137.

South African Human Rights Commission Report. 2000. Faultlines: An Inquiry into Racism in the Media: South African government. Viewed 2 December 2019, https://www.sahrc.org.za/home/21/files/Reports/Racismin%20the%20media.pdf2000.pdf.

Swart, H., Hewstone, M., Christ, O. & Voci, A. 2010. The impact of crossgroup friendships in South Africa: Affective mediators and multigroup comparisons. *Journal of Social Issues*, 66 (2):309-333. Viewed 9 January 2019, from http://www.hermannswart.com/wp-content/uploads/2014/09/2010_Swart-Hewstone-Christ-Voci_JSI.pdf/.

Thompson, K. 2017. Diversity is nature's greatest strength-it should be ours, too. *The Funders Network*. Viewed 2 December 2019, from https://www.fundersnetwork.org/diversity-is-natures-greatest-strength-it-should-be-ours-too/.

Van Zuydam, L. 2014. Diversity good for SA racial tolerance. viewed 4 December 2019, from https://www.iol.co.za/news/south-africa/gauteng/diversity-good-for-sa-racial-tolerance-1680591.

Wipfler, P. 2019. *Inoculating our children against racism*. Viewed 6 December 2019, from https://www.handinhandparenting.org/article/inoculating-our-children-against-racism/.

Zungu, W-E. 2017. Our schools are the breeding ground of racism in South Africa. Viewed 28 November 2019, from https://www.huffingtonpost.co.uk/entry/our-schools-are-the-breeding-ground-of-racism-in-south-africa_uk_5c7e961ee4b078abc6c10e25/.

REFERENCES

CHAPTER 9

Agüero, J.M., Carter, M. & Woolard, I. 2007. The impact of unconditional cash transfers on nutrition: The South African child support grant. *IPC Working Paper No 39*, International Poverty Centre, Brasilia.

Bengtsson, N. 2012. The marginal propensity to earn and consume out of unearned income: Evidence using an unusually large cash grant reform. *Scandinavian Journal of Economics*, 114(4):1393-1413.

Blaauw, P.F. 2017. Informal employment in South Africa: Still missing pieces in the vulnerability puzzle. *Southern African Business Review*, 21(1): 339-361.

Branson, N., Ardington, C. & Leibbrandt, M. 2013. Trends in teenage childbearing and schooling outcomes for children born to teens in South Africa. *SALDRU Working Paper No 98*. University of Cape Town (Southern African Labour and Development Research Unit), Cape Town.

Budlender, D. 2018. Income support for children in the context of poverty and inequality, 93-100. In: K. Hall, L. Richter, Z. Mokomane & L. Lake. (eds.). *South African Child Gauge 2018*. Children's Institute, University of Cape Town, Cape Town.

Burger, P. & Calitz, E. 2019. Sustainable fiscal policy and economic growth in South Africa. *Stellenbosch Working Paper Series No WP15/2019*. Stellenbosch University (Department of Economics), Stellenbosch.

Case, A. & Deaton, A. 1998. Large cash transfers to the elderly in South Africa. *Economic Journal*, 108(450):1330-1363.

Cluver L.D., Boyes, M., Orkin, F.M., Patelic, M., Molwena, T. & Sherr, L. 2013. Child-focused state cash transfers and adolescent risk of HIV infection in South Africa: A propensity-score-matched case-control study. *The Lancet Global Health*, 1(6):362-370.

Cluver, L.D., Orkin, F.M., Boyes, M. & Sherr, L. 2014. Cash plus care: Social protection cumulatively mitigates HIV-risk behaviour among adolescents in South Africa. *AIDS*, 28(3):S389-S397.

Cluver, L.D., Orkin, F.M., Yakubovich, A.R. & Sherr, L. 2016. Combination social protection or reducing HIV-risk behavior among adolescents in South Africa. *Journal of Acquired Immune Deficiency Syndromes*, 72(1): 96-104.

Coetzee, M. 2013. Finding the benefits: Estimating the effects of the South African child support grant. *South African Journal of Economics*, 81(3): 427-450.

d'Agostino, G., Scarlato, M. & Napolitano, S. 2017. Do cash transfers promote food security? The case of the South African child support grant. *Journal of African Economies*, 27(4):430-456.

Delany, A., Ismail, Z., Graham, L. & Ramkissoon, Y. 2008. *Review of the child support grant: Uses, implementation and obstacles.* Community Agency for Social Enquiry (CASE), Johannesburg.

Duflo, E. 2003. Grandmothers and granddaughters: Old-age pensions and intra-household allocation in South Africa. *World Bank Economic Review*, 17(1):1-25.

Evans, D.K. & Popova, A. 2017. Cash transfers and temptation goods. *Economic Development and Cultural Change*, 65(2):189-221.

Eyal, K. & Woolard, I. 2013. School enrolment and the child support grant: Evidence from South Africa. *SALDRU Working Paper No 125*. University of Cape Town (Southern African Labour and Development Research Unit), Cape Town.

Fanta, A.B., Berkowitz, B., Khumalo, J., Mutsonziwa, K., Maposa, O. & Ramsamy, P. 2017. Digitisation of social grant payments and financial inclusion of grant recipients in South Africa – Evidence from FinScope surveys. FinMark Trust, Johannesburg.

Festus, L., Kasongo, A., Moses, M. & Yu, D. 2016. The South African labour market, 1995-2015. *Development Southern Africa*, 33(5):579-599.

Goldblatt, B. 2006. Gender and social assistance in the first decade of democracy: A case study of South Africa's child support grant. *Politikon*, 32(2):239-257.

Granlund, S. & Hochfeld, T. 2020. 'That child support grant gives me powers' – Exploring social and relational aspects of cash transfers in South Africa in times of livelihood change. *Journal of Development Studies*. 56(6):1230-1244.

Grinspun, A. 2016. No small change: The multiple impacts of the child support grant on child and adolescent well-being, 44-54. In: A. Delany, S. Jehoma & L. Lake (eds.). *South African Child Gauge 2016*. Children's Institute, University of Cape Town, Cape Town.

Hall, K., 2019. Demography of South Africa's children, 216-220. In: M. Shung-King, L. Lake, D. Sanders & M. Hendricks (eds.). *South African Child Gauge 2019*. Children's Institute, University of Cape Town, Cape Town.

Hall, K. & Richter, L. 2018. Introduction: Children, families and the state, 22-31. In: K. Hall, L. Richter, Z. Mokomane & L. Lake (eds.). *South African Child Gauge 2018*. Children's Institute, University of Cape Town, Cape Town.

Harvey, P., Slater, R. & Farrington, J. 2005. Cash transfers – mere "Gadaffi Syndrome", or serious potential for rural rehabilitation and development? *Natural Resource Perspectives Number 97*. Overseas Development Institute, London.

Heinrich, C., Hoddinott, J., Samson, M., MacQuene, K., Van Niekerk, I. & Renaud, B. 2012. The South African child support grant impact assessment: Evidence from a survey of children, adolescents and their households. Department of Social Development, South African Social Security Agency & UNICEF, Pretoria.

Hochfeld, T. & Plagerson, S. 2011. Dignity and stigma among South African female cash transfer recipients. *IDS Bulletin,* 42(6):53-59.

James, D. 2014. "Deeper into a Hole?" Borrowing and lending in South Africa. *Current Anthropology,* 55(Supplement 9):S17-S29.

Khosa, P. & E. Kaseke. 2017. The utilisation of the child support grant by caregivers: The case of Ba-Phalaborwa Municipality in Limpopo Province. *Social Work,* 53(3):356-367.

Leibbrandt, M. & Woolard, I. 2010. The evolution and impact of unconditional cash transfers in South Africa. *SALDRU Working Paper No 51.* Children's Institute, University of Cape Town, Cape Town.

Lund, F. 2007. *Changing social policy in South Africa: The child support grant in South Africa.* Human Sciences Research Council, Pretoria.

Maboshe, M. & Woolard, I. 2018. Revisiting the impact of direct taxes and transfers on poverty and inequality in South Africa. *WIDER Working Paper 2018/79.* United Nations University World Institute for Development Economics Research, Helsinki.

Makiwane, M. 2010.The child support grant and teenage childbearing in South Africa. *Development Southern Africa,* 27(2):193-204.

National Treasury. 2001. *Intergovernmental fiscal review 2001.* National Treasury, Pretoria.

National Treasury. 2004. *Intergovernmental fiscal review 2004.* National Treasury, Pretoria.

National Treasury. 2005. *Intergovernmental fiscal review 2005.* National Treasury, Pretoria.

National Treasury. 2007. *Estimates of national expenditure 2007.* National Treasury, Pretoria.

National Treasury. 2008. *Estimates of national expenditure 2008.* National Treasury, Pretoria.

National Treasury. 2009. *Estimates of national expenditure 2009*. National Treasury, Pretoria.

National Treasury. 2010. *Estimates of national expenditure 2010*. National Treasury, Pretoria.

National Treasury. 2011. *Estimates of national expenditure 2011*. National Treasury, Pretoria.

National Treasury. 2012. *Estimates of national expenditure 2012*. National Treasury, Pretoria.

National Treasury. 2013. *Estimates of national expenditure 2013*. National Treasury, Pretoria.

National Treasury. 2014. *Estimates of national expenditure 2014*. National Treasury, Pretoria.

National Treasury. 2015. *Estimates of national expenditure 2015*. National Treasury, Pretoria.

National Treasury. 2016. *Estimates of national expenditure 2016*. National Treasury, Pretoria.

National Treasury. 2017. *Estimates of national expenditure 2017*. National Treasury, Pretoria.

National Treasury. 2018. *Estimates of national expenditure 2018*. National Treasury, Pretoria.

National Treasury. 2019. *Estimates of national expenditure 2019*. National Treasury, Pretoria.

Patel, L. 2012. Poverty, gender and social protection: Child support grants in Soweto, South Africa. *Journal of Policy Practice*, 11(1-2):106-120.

Patel, L. & Hochfeld, T. 2011. It buys food but does it change gender relations? Child support grants in Soweto, South Africa. *Gender and Development*, 19(2):229-240.

Patel, L., Hochfeld, T., Ajefu, J. & Bryer, M. 2018. Measuring the impact of the child support grant: Tracking educational and health wellbeing outcomes for child recipients from 2008 to 2014. Unpublished research report. University of Johannesburg (Centre for Social Development in Africa), Johannesburg.

Patel, L., Hochfeld, T., Moodley, J. & Mulwali, R. 2011. The gender dynamics and impact of the child support grant in Doornkop, Soweto. Unpublished research report. University of Johannesburg (Centre for Social Development in Africa), Johannesburg.

Patel, L., Hochfeld, T., Ross, E., Chiba, J. & Luck, K. 2019. Connecting cash with care for better child well-being. Unpublished research report. University of Johannesburg (Centre for Social Development in Africa), Johannesburg.

Patel, L., Knijn, T. & Van Wel, F. 2015. Child support grants in South Africa: A pathway to women's empowerment and child well-being? *Journal of Social Policy*, 44(2):377-397.

Patel, L. & Plagerson, S. 2016. The evolution of the child support grant, 39-43. In: A. Delany, S. Jehoma and L. Lake (eds.). *South African Child Gauge 2016*. Children's Institute, University of Cape Town, Cape Town.

Rosenberg M., Pettifor, A., Nguyen, N., Westreich, D., Bor, J. & Bärnighausen, T. 2015. Relationship between receipt of a social protection grant for a child and second pregnancy rates among South African women: A cohort study. *PLoS ONE*, 10(9):1-12.

Samson, M., Lee, U., Ndlebe, A., MacQuene, K., Van Niekerk, I., Gandhi, V., Harigaya, T. & Abrahams, C. 2004. The social and economic impact of South Africa's social security system. Unpublished report commissioned by the Economics and Finance Directorate of the Department of Social Development. Economic Policy Research Institute, Cape Town.

REFERENCES

Siebrits, F.K. 2019. Social insurance and social assistance, 16-191. In: E. Calitz, F.K. Siebrits & T.J. Steenekamp (eds.). *Public economics*. 7th edn. Oxford University Press, Cape Town.

South African Reserve Bank. n.d. Online statistical query (historical macroeconomic timeseries information). Viewed 22 August 2019, from https://www.resbank.co.za/Research/Statistics/Pages/OnlineDownloadFacility.aspx/.

South Africa. 2019. Towards a 25-year review. The Presidency, Pretoria.

South African Social Security Agency. 2009. *SASSA annual report 2008/09*. South African Social Security Agency, Pretoria.

South African Social Security Agency. 2018. *SASSA annual report 2017/18*. South African Social Security Agency, Pretoria.

South African Social Security Agency. 2019. Annual performance plan and budget 2019/20. Presentation to the Portfolio Committee on Social Development, Parliament of South Africa, Cape Town, 3 July 2019.

Spaull, N. 2015. Schooling in South Africa: How low-quality education becomes a poverty trap, 34-41. In: A. de Lannoy, S. Swartz, L. Lake & C. Smith (eds.). *South African Child Gauge 2015*. Children's Institute, University of Cape Town, Cape Town.

Statistics South Africa. 2017a. Poverty trends in South Africa: An examination of absolute poverty from 2006 to 2015. *Report No. 03-10-06*. Statistics South Africa, Pretoria.

Statistics South Africa. 2017b. Living Conditions Survey 2014/15. *Statistical Release P0310*. Statistics South Africa, Pretoria.

Statistics South Africa. 2018. Men, women and children: Findings of the Living Conditions Survey 2014/15. *Report No. 03-10-02*. Statistics South Africa, Pretoria.

Statistics South Africa. 2019a. Inequality trends in South Africa: A multidimensional diagnostic of inequality. *Report No. 03-10-19*. Statistics South Africa, Pretoria.

Statistics South Africa. 2019b. Consumer price index November 2019. *Statistical Release P0141*. Statistics South Africa, Pretoria.

Statistics South Africa. 2019c. Quarterly labour force survey Q3/2019. *Statistical Release P0211*. Statistics South Africa, Pretoria.

Torkelson, E. 2020. Collateral damages: Cash transfer and debt transfer in South Africa. *World Development,* 126:1-11.

Van der Berg, S. & Siebrits, F.K. 2010. Social assistance reform during a period of fiscal stress. *Stellenbosch Working Papers No. 17/10*. Stellenbosch University (Department of Economics and Bureau for Economic Research), Stellenbosch.

Von Fintel, D., Von Fintel, M. & Buthelezi, T. 2019. The complementarity between cash transfers and financial literacy for child growth. *SALDRU Working Paper No 241*. University of Cape Town (Southern African Labour and Development Research Unit), Cape Town.

Vorster, J. & De Waal, L. 2008. Beneficiaries of the child support grant: Findings from a national survey. *The Social Work Practitioner-Researcher,* 20(2):233-248.

Williams, M.J. 2007. The social and economic impacts of South Africa's child support grant. *EPRI Working Paper No. 39*. Economic Policy Research Institute, Cape Town.

Woolard, I., Harttgen, K. & Klasen, S. 2011. The history and impact of social security in South Africa: Experiences and lessons. *Canadian Journal of Development Studies,* 32(4):357-380.

World Bank. 2018. *Overcoming poverty and inequality in South Africa: An assessment of drivers, constraints and opportunities*. The World Bank, Washington, D.C.

Wright, G., Neves, D., Ntshongwana, P. & Noble, M. 2015. Social assistance and dignity: South African women's experiences of the child support grant. *Development Southern Africa,* 32(4):443-457.

Zembe-Mkabilea, W., Surrender, B., Sanders, D., Jackson, D. & Doherty, T. 2015. The experience of cash transfers in alleviating childhood poverty in South Africa: Mothers' experiences of the child support grant. *Global Public Health*, 10(7):834-851.

CHAPTER 10

Adams, K., Encarnação, P., Rios-Rincón, A.M. & Cook, A.M. 2018. Will artificial intelligence be a blessing or concern in assistive robots for play? *Journal Human Growth Development*, 28(2):213-218. DOI: http://dx.doi.org/10.7322/jhgd.147242.

Aslani, G., Senobari, M., Rostaminejad, M.A. & Jafari, E.M. 2013. Identification and management of ethical challenge in e-learning systems. *Procedia – Social and Behavioural Sciences*, 83:214-218. DOI: http://doi.org/10.1016/j.sbspro.2013.06.042.

Barbovschi, M. & Dreier, M. 2013. Vulnerable groups of children, 60-63. In: M. Barbovschi, L. Green & S. Vandoninck (eds.). *Innovative approaches for investigating how children understand the risk of new media. Dealing with methodological and ethical challenges*. EU Kids Online & London School of Economics and Political Science, London.

Bergen, M. 2017. Inside Google's struggle to filter lies from breaking news. *Bloomberg Businessweek*, 16 November. Viewed 10 February 2020, from https://www.bloomberg.com/news/articles/2017-11-16/inside-google-s-struggle-to-filter-lies-from-breaking-news.

Bulger, M., Burton, P., O'Neill, B. & Staksrud, E. 2017. Where policy and practice collide: Comparing United States, South African and European Union approaches to protecting children online. *New Media and Society*, 19(5):750-764. https://doi.org/10.1177/1461444816686325/.

Byrne, J. & Burton, P. 2017. Children as internet users: how can evidence better inform policy debate? *Journal of Cyber Policy*, 2(1):39-42.

Byrne, J., Albright, K. & Kardefelt-Winther, D. 2016. *Using research findings for policy-making*. Global Kids Online, London. Viewed 20 November 2019, from http://globalkidsonline.net/wp-content/uploads/2016/05/Guide-11-Policy-making-Byrne-Albright-Kardefelt-Winther.pdf/.

Clement, J. 2020. Worldwide digital population as of January 2020. Viewed 16 February 2020, from https://www.statista.com/statistics/617136/digital-population-worldwide/.

Cranmer, S., Selwyn, N. & Potter, J. 2009. "Exploring primary pupils" experiences and understandings of "e-safety". *Educational Information Technology*, 14:127-142. DOI: http://doi.org/10.1007/s10639-008-9083-7.

Dreyfus, H. 2001. *On the internet*. Routledge, London and New York.

DQ Institute. 2018. Outsmart the cyber-pandemic: 2018 DQ Impact Report. DQ Institute. Viewed 8 January 2020, from https://www.dqinstitute.org/2018DQ_Impact_Report/#Cyber-Pandemic.

Ephraim, P.E. 2013. African youths and the dangers of social networking: a culture-centered approach to using social media. *Ethics and Information Technology*, 15:275-284.

Epstein, R. & Robertson, R. 2015. The search engine manipulation effect (SEME) and its possible impact on the outcomes of elections. In: *Proceedings of the National Academy of Sciences of the United States of America*, 112(33):E4512-E4521. Viewed 6 January 2020, from https://www.pnas.org/content/suppl/2015/08/03/1419828112.DCSupplemental.

European Commission (EC). 2012. Communication from the Commission to the European Parliament, the Council, the European Economic and Social Committee and the Committee of the Regions: European strategy for a better internet for children. COM/2012/0196 final. European Commission, Brussels. Viewed 28 December 2019, from https://eur-lex.europa.eu/legal-content/EN/ALL/?uri=CELEX%3A52012DC0196.

REFERENCES

Fourie, L.C.H. 2020. End of privacy as an afterthought. *Business Report*, 7 February. Viewed 17 February 2020, from https://www.iol.co.za/business-report/technology/end-of-privacy-as-an-afterthought-42261230.

Fourie, L.C.H., Heath, W. & Fourie, J.L. 2011. Cyber-jurisprudence and social networking. Paper presented at the Defence, Science and Research Conference (DSR 2011), Singapore, 3-5 August.

Graafland, J.H. 2018. New technologies and 21st century children: Recent trends and outcomes. *OECD Education Working Papers*, 179, EDU/WKP 15. OECD Publishing, Paris. Viewed 20 January 2020, from https://one.oecd.org/document/EDU/WKP(2018)15/en/pdf.

Grant, C.T. 2010. Successful engagement of undergraduate Information Technology Management students in a compulsory course in ethical issues in IT in a large class environment. *Information Systems Education Journal*, 8(66):3-16.

Hachiya, R.F. 2017. Dangers for principals and students when conducting investigations of sexting in schools. *The Clearing House: A Journal of Educational Strategies, Issues and Ideas*, 90(5-6): 177-183.

Human Rights Council. 2016. The promotion, protection and enjoyment of human rights on the Internet: draft resolution. In: *United Nations General Assembly Human Rights Council 32nd Session, Promotion and protection of all human rights, civil, political, economic, social and cultural rights, including the right to development: A/HRC/32/L.20*. Viewed 16 January 2020, from http://www.ohchr.org/documents/HRBodies/UPR/A_HRC_32_2_EN.docx.

IBM. 2019. Everyday ethics for artificial intelligence. IBM Corp. Viewed 10 February 2020, from https://www.ibm.com/watson/assets/duo/pdf/everydayethics.pdf.

ITU & UNICEF. 2015. Guidelines for industry on child online protection. ITU & UNICEF, Geneva. Viewed 11 Feb 2020, from https://www.unicef.org/csr/files/COP_Guidelines_English.pdf.

Keeley, B. & Little, C. (eds.). 2017. *The state of the world's children 2017: Children in a digital world.* UNICEF, New York. Viewed 3 January 2020, from https://www.unicef.org/publications/files/SOWC_2017_ENG_WEB.pdf.

Kendall, L. 1999. Recontextualizing cyberspace: Methodological considerations for on-line research, 57-75. In: S. Jones (ed.). *Doing internet research.* Sage, Thousand Oaks & London.

Krasodomski-Jones, A. 2016. Talking to ourselves? Political debate online and the echo chamber effect. Demos. Viewed 15 December 2019, from https://www.demos.co.uk/wp-content/uploads/2017/02/Echo-Chambers-final-version.pdf.

Kosenko, K., Luurs G. & Binder, A. 2017. Sexting and sexual behavior, 2011-2015: A critical review and meta-analysis of a growing literature. *Journal of Computer-Mediated Communication,* 22(3):141-160. DOI: http://dx.doi.org/10.1111/jcc4.12187.

Lennie, S. 2013. Ethical complexities in the virtual world: Teacher perspectives of ICT based issues and conflicts. D.Phil. thesis, University of Toronto, Toronto.

Lin, Y. 2019. 10 Internet statistics every marketer should know in 2020. Viewed 16 January 2020, from https://www.oberlo.co.za/blog/internet-statistics.

Livingstone, S. 2013. "Knowledge enhancement": The risks and opportunities of evidence-based policy, 93-109. In: B. O'Neill, E. Staksrud & S. McLaughlin (eds.). *Towards a better internet for children? – Policy pillars, players and paradoxes.* Nordicom, Göteborg. Viewed on 18 November 2019, from https://www.nordicom.gu.se/sites/default/files/publikationer-hela-pdf/toward_a_better_internet.pdf

Livingstone, S. & Haddon, L. 2009. Introduction, 1-15. In: S. Livingstone & L. Haddon (eds.). *Kids online: opportunities and risks for children*. The Policy Press, Bristol. Viewed on 27 November 2019, from https://www.researchgate.net/publication/265491994_Conclusion_kids_online_opportunities_and_risks_for_children/.

Livingstone, S., Carr, J. & Byrne, J. 2015. One in three: Internet governance and children's rights. *Paper Series* 22. Centre for International Governance Innovation and The Royal Institute of International Affairs, Waterloo, Ontario & London.

Livingstone, S., Haddon, L., Görzig, A. & Ólafsson, K. 2011. Risks and safety on the internet: The perspective of European children: Full findings and policy implications from the EU Kids Online survey of 9-16 year olds and their parents in 25 countries. EU Kids Online Network, London.

Livingstone, S., Kirwil, L., Ponte, C. & Staksrud, E. 2014. In their own words: what bothers children online? *European Journal of Communication*, 29(3):271-288. DOI: http://doi.org/10.1177/0267323114521045.

Livingstone, S., Ólafsson, K., Helsper, E.J., Lupiáñez-Villanueva, F., Veltri, G.A. & Folkvord, F. 2017. Maximizing opportunities and minimizing risks for children online: The role of digital skills in emerging strategies of parental mediation. *Journal of Communication*, 67(1):82-105. DOI: http://doi.org/10.1111/jcom.12277.

Löfberg, C. 2003. Ethical and methodical dilemmas in research with/on children and youths on the net. In: M. Thorseth (ed.). *Applied ethics in internet research*. Norwegian University of Science and Technology, Trondheim. Viewed on 28 November 2019, from http://www.hf.ntnu.no/fil/anvendt_etikk/eng/.

Lupton, D. & Williamson, B. 2017. The datafied child: The dataveillance of children and implications for their rights. *New Media & Society*, 19(5): 780-794. DOI: http://dx.doi.org/10.1177/1461444816686328.

Mack, E. 2011. Facebook's "like" button illegal in German state. *Cnet*. Viewed 15 February 2020, from https://www.cnet.com/news/facebooks-like-button-illegal-in-german-state/.

Mascheroni, G. & Ólafsson, K. 2018. *Accesso, usi, rischi e opportunità di internet per i ragazzi italiani. I risultati di EU Kids Online 2017*. EU Kids Online & OssCom. Viewed on 12 December 2019, from http://www.lse.ac.uk/media-and-communications/assets/documents/research/eu-kids-online/reports/EU-Kids-Online-Italy-report-06-2018.pdf/.

Mascheroni, G., Murru, M.F., Aristodemou, E. & Laouris, Y. 2013. Parents: Mediation, self-regulation and co-regulation, 211-225. In: B. O'Neill, E. Staksrud & S. McLaughlin (eds.). *Towards a better internet for children? – Policy pillars, players and paradoxes*. Nordicom, Göteborg. Viewed on 25 November 2019, from https://www.nordicom.gu.se/sites/default/files/publikationer-hela-pdf/toward_a_better_internet.pdf/.

Matyjas, B. 2008. Cyberculture: Dangers for childhood. *The New Educational Review*, 16(3):195-208.

Middaugh, E., Clark, L.S. & Ballard, P.J. 2017. Digital media, participatory politics, and Positive Youth Development. *Pediatrics*, 140(2):127-131. DOI: http://dx.doi.org/10.1542/peds.2016-1758Q.

Minić, S.G. & Spalević, Z. 2014. Abuse of computer networks in cyberspace: The role of the family in the modern information age. *Teme: Časopis za društvene nauke*, 38(1):417-431.

Mishna, F., McLuckie, A. & Saini, M. 2009. Real-world dangers in an online reality: A qualitative study examining online relationships and cyber abuse. *Social Work Research*, 33(2):107-118.

Newall, M. 2018. Cyberbullying: A global advisor survey, 1-12. Ipsos Public Affairs. Viewed on 5 February 2020, from https://www.ipsos.com/sites/default/files/ct/news/documents/2018-06/cyberbullying_june2018.pdf/.

REFERENCES

OECD. 2016. *Trends shaping education 2016*. OECD Publishing, Paris. Viewed on 6 November 2019, from http://dx.doi.org/10.1787/trends_edu-2016-en.

O'Neil, C. 2016. *Weapons of math destruction*. Crown, New York.

O'Neill, B. 2013a. Who cares? Practical ethics and the problem of underage users on social networking sites. *Ethics and Information Technology*, 15: 253-262. DOI http://doi.org/10.1007/s10676-013-9331-4.

O'Neill, B. 2013b. Internet hotlines: A reporting solution for Internet safety?, 39-56. In: B. O'Neill, E. Staksrud & S. McLaughlin (eds.). *Towards a better internet for children? – Policy pillars, players and paradoxes*. Nordicom, Göteborg. Viewed on 14 December 2019, from https://www.nordicom.gu.se/sites/default/files/publikationer-hela-pdf/toward_a_better_internet.pdf/.

Paniagua, A. & Istance D. 2018. *Teachers as designers of learning environments: The importance of innovative pedagogies*. OECD Publishing, Paris. Viewed on 10 January 2020, from http://dx.doi.org/10.1787/9789264085374-en.

Phyfer, J., Burton, P. & Leoschut, L. 2016. Global Kids Online South Africa: barriers, opportunities and risks. A glimpse into South African children's internet use and online activities. Technical Report. Centre for Justice and Crime Prevention, Cape Town. Viewed on 20 January 2020, from http://eprints.lse.ac.uk/71267/2/GKO_Country-Report_South-Africa_CJCP_upload.pdf/.

Popovac, M. & Leoschut, L. 2012. Cyber bullying in South Africa: Impact and responses. *Centre for Justice and Crime Prevention Issue Paper*, 13:1-16.

Regan, P.M. & Jesse, J. 2019. Ethical challenges of edtech, big data and personalized learning: twenty-first century student sorting and tracking. *Ethics and Information Technology*, 21(3):167-179.

Republic of South Africa (RSA). 1996. *Films and Publications Act*, Act No. 65 of 1996. Viewed on 29 January 2020, from http://pmg-assets.s3-website-eu-west-1.amazonaws.com/161115ACT.pdf/.

Republic of South Africa (RSA). 2005. *The Children's Act*, Act No. 38 of 2005. Viewed on 2 February 2020, from https://www.justice.gov.za/legislation/acts/2005-038%20childrensact.pdf/.

Republic of South Africa (RSA). 2013. *Protection of Personal Information Act*, Act No. 4 of 2013. Viewed on 2 February 2020, from https://www.gov.za/documents/protection-personal-information-act/.

Republic of South Africa (RSA). 2015. *Criminal Law (Sexual Offences and Related Matters) Amendment Act*, Act No. 5 of 2015. Viewed on 10 January 2020, from https://www.justice.gov.za/legislation/acts/2015-005.pdf/.

Republic of South Africa (RSA). 2019a. *Films and Publications Amendment Act*, Act No. 11 of 2019. Viewed on 12 February 2020, from https://www.gov.za/sites/default/files/gcis_document/201910/42743gon1292.pdf/.

Republic of South Africa (RSA). 2019b. *The Children's Amendment Bill*. Viewed on 3 January 2020, from https://www.gov.za/sites/default/files/gcis_document/201810/42005gon1185.pdf/.

Rideout, V. 2015. The common sense census: Media use by tweens and teens. Common Sense Media, San Francisco. Viewed on 6 January 2020, from https://www.commonsensemedia.org/sites/default/files/uploads/research/census_researchreport.pdf/.

Rizza, C. & Pereira, A. 2013. Social networks and cyber-bullying among teenagers. European Union, Luxembourg. Viewed on 8 January 2020, from https://ec.europa.eu/jrc/en/publication/eur-scientific-and-technical-research-reports/social-networks-and-cyber-bullying-among-teenagers.

Ságvári, B. & Máder, M.P. 2013. Industry: Towards the socially responsible internet: Industry CSR practices across Europe, 93-109. In: B. O'Neill, E. Staksrud & S. McLaughlin (eds.). *Towards a better internet for children?*

REFERENCES

– *Policy pillars, players and paradoxes*. Nordicom, Göteborg. Viewed on 14 December 2019, from https://www.nordicom.gu.se/sites/default/files/publikationer-hela-pdf/toward_a_better_internet.pdf.

Sando, S. 2003. Vulnerable bodies as ethical sensors. In: M. Thorseth (ed.), *Applied ethics in internet research*. Norwegian University of Science and Technology, Trondheim. Viewed on 18 December 2019, from https://www.academia.edu/2110306/Vulnerable_bodies_as_ethical_sensors.

South African Law Reform Commission. 2015. Sexual offences: pornography and children. Issue Paper no. 30, Project 107, 5 August. Viewed on 12 February 2020, from https://www.justice.gov.za/salrc/ipapers/ip30_prj107_SexualOffences-PC-2015.pdf.

Staksrud, E. & Kirksæther, J. 2013. Filtering & content classification, 23-37. In: B. O'Neill, E. Staksrud & S. McLaughlin (eds.). *Towards a better internet for children? – Policy pillars, players and paradoxes*. Nordicom, Göteborg. Viewed on 14 December 2019, from https://www.nordicom.gu.se/sites/default/files/publikationer-hela-pdf/toward_a_better_internet.pdf.

Stückelberger, C. 2014. Globethics.net principles on ethics in the information society, 19-25. In: A.V. Preisig, H. Rösch & C. Stückelberger (eds.). *Ethical dilemmas in the information society: How codes of ethics help to find ethical solutions*. Globethics.net, Geneva. Viewed on 8 November 2019, from https://www.ifla.org/files/assets/faife/publications/misc/ethical-dilemmas-in-the-information-society.pdf.

The Guardian, n.d. The Cambridge Analytica files. *The Guardian*. Viewed on 13 February 2020, from https://www.theguardian.com/news/series/cambridge-analytica-files.

Third, A., Bellerose, D., De Oliviera, J.D., Lala, G. & Theakstone, G. 2017. Young and online: Children's perspectives on life in the digital age (The state of the world's children 2017 companion report). Western Sydney University, Sydney. Viewed 18 January 2020, from http://doi.org/10.4225/35/5a1b885f6d4db.

UNICEF Innocenti Research Centre. 2012. Child safety online: Global challenges and strategies. Technical Report. UNICEF, Florence. Viewed 7 January 2020, from https://www.unicef-irc.org/publications/pdf/ict_techreport3_eng.pdf.

United Nations (UN). 1989. Convention on the Rights of the Child (Adopted and opened for signature, ratification and accession by General Assembly resolution 44/25 of 20 November 1989, entry into force 2 September 1990, in accordance with article 49). United Nations, New York. Viewed on 16 January 2020, from https://www.ohchr.org/en/professionalinterest/pages/crc.aspx.

United States (US) Department of Justice. 2015. *18 USC Ch. 110: Sexual exploitation and other abuse of children (From Title 18 – crimes and criminal procedure: Part I – crimes)*. Viewed on 12 January 2020, from https://uscode.house.gov/view.xhtml?path=/prelim@title18/part1/chapter110&edition=prelim.

Valentine, G. & Holloway, S. 2001. On-line dangers?: Geographies of parents' fears for children's safety in cyberspace. *Professional Geographer*, 53(1): 71-83.

Vesnaj, L. & Niveditha, D. 2012. Ethics in cyberspace – a philosophical approach. *International Journal of Advancements in Research & Technology*, 1(3):1-5.

Whittlestone, J., Nyrup, R., Alexandrova, A., Dihal, K. & Cave, S. 2019. *Ethical and societal implications of algorithms, data, and artificial intelligence: a roadmap for research*. Nuffield Foundation, London.

Wojniak, J. & Majorek, M. 2016. Children and ICT European initiatives and policies on protecting children online. *Universal Journal of Educational Research*, 4(1):131-136.

Yang, Y. 2019. Nudge or puppet? Decision-making, ethics, and leadership in the information age. M.A. in Leadership Studies: Capstone Project Papers 55. University of San Diego, San Diego.

www.ingramcontent.com/pod-product-compliance
Lightning Source LLC
Chambersburg PA
CBHW080222170426
43192CB00015B/2718